T0354812

ECHOES OF THE MIND

A Book for Finnan and Cormac

RICHARD KELLY

ECHOES OF THE MIND
A BOOK FOR FINNAN AND CORMAC

iUniverse books may be ordered through booksellers or by contacting:

iUniverse
1663 Liberty Drive
Bloomington, IN 47403
www.iuniverse.com
1-800-Authors (1-800-288-4677)

ISBN: 978-1-5320-6252-0 (sc)
ISBN: 978-1-5320-6253-7 (e)

Library of Congress Control Number: 2018913428

Print information available on the last page.

iUniverse rev. date: 12/03/2018

To Joan, who has shared the path for a half century,
and to Brendan, Darrin, and Deirdre
who soon joined the conversation

Welcome to this journey, this odyssey of self-discovery.

PART I

Over the River and Through the Woods

Finnan, the image of a day can represent generations, even epochs in biblical terms: the sunset of my life compared with your dawn. I want to talk to you about what comes in between, about memories and events that promote ideas for you to consider and become an accumulation of influences.

In our life off these pages, I look forward to our talks and cherish listening to you, but we cannot do that here, so we will imagine that we are speaking back and forth. Our conversation will have flashbacks, as if in a novel or a movie. While we move from subject to subject, and back again, *"Don't forget to remember I might be wrong,"* as one country singer has put it.

You may not fully understand many of the ideas threaded through our talk, but if you understand some of them, even in part, as *"insights of this hour,"* I think you'll find it helpful. You can look at my ideas as seeds, some of which will later grow. If you contemplate them again, even years later, they may inspire you and the actions you take in this world, thoughts becoming dreams achieved. But for the moment, let's imagine leaving this room to go to where our adventure begins, outside at the edge of wildness. It will be fun, but try to remember we have another purpose, which we will talk about as we go.

CHAPTER 1

A Walk in the Woods

We begin with a question that I think we should always be asking, Finnan: where are we? Our walk is down the hill, behind the barn in back of our home. We are only a thousand yards east of the West Branch of the Ausable River, yet it is like another world. And we are only a half-dozen miles west of Marcy Dam, a gateway to the High Peaks of the eastern Adirondacks. We start our short journey knowing we are in a hollow on our land, surrounded by ancient mountains of the Northeast.

These mountains rise out of valleys where winter snows and Adirondack rain flow in 30,000 miles of streams and rivers into 3,000 lakes and ponds. The rivers flow in three directions, north into the western St. Lawrence River, east into Lake Champlain then again into the St. Lawrence River and ultimately to the North Atlantic Ocean, or south into the Hudson River, passing New York City as it enters the mid-Atlantic. These mountains, rivers, and lakes hold life together in a connected story. They were formed about 12,000 years ago by glaciers of the last Ice Age. We are fortunate that we can still see so much evidence of the dramatic results.

The word Adirondack is said to have been an insult, a name given to the eastern Algonquin Indians by their traditional enemy tribe, the Iroquois. The word means *"bark-eater"*: people who cannot hunt, grow, or gather enough so they must eat the bark of trees to survive. Someday we should talk about why people think they have to be traditional enemies, hating the people their ancestors hated. A description of early times in these mountains, during the French and Indian War of 1757–1763, is provided by James Fenimore Cooper in his 1826 novel *The Last of the Mohicans*. The panoramic scenes in the 1992 movie, with Irish actor Daniel Day-Lewis, were one inspiration for your grandmother's and my move to these mountains.

I hope you sense that the Adirondacks are a wonderfully dramatic place to live. We are a two-hour drive north of Albany, the capital of New York State; two hours west of Burlington, the largest city in Vermont; two hours south of Montreal, Canada; and six hours from New York City and Lattingtown Harbor, on Long Island Sound, where my children, including your father, grew up. Here in Lake Placid, we are 700 miles southwest of St. John, New Brunswick, Canada, where you were born, Finnan. We are over 400 miles west of Gouldsboro and 250 miles from Bates College in Lewiston, both in Maine. You lived the first two years of your life in these last three places. It is over 3,500 miles northwest from here to Sitka, Alaska, where you then moved.

These are all places that are worth studying, and it is best to start with a map if you want to know where anything is; but there is a second point to be made. The question for you is: Why does it matter where you are? I love the Adirondacks, and Lattingtown Harbor, dearly, and I hope you will learn to love and understand these places as well. But why should you? I think the answer lies in understanding the importance of a sense of place. What is this sense? It is an attraction. First, our astonishment at beauty appreciated and developed over the millennia of our evolving experience as humans. Second, is the more immediate shared experience we have with a particular place. What we are looking at is a local connection to the environment, its food and resources, its way of life, and a sense of belonging to a community. Where we are at a given time has a number of facets and consequences.

People live with nature and need to recognize our connectedness. Regardless of the place we focus upon, *"Where we are,"* as the joke goes, *"is here."* We notice elements of whatever environment we live in, and when we go away and come back, we see them with new eyes, notice anew the smell and texture, the hurried or measured pace of this locale. Our sense of place can be a rural village as we have been discussing, but we should also be open to daily moments of life even when we are in the dense and diverse environment of a city: *"Eyes open – teetering staccato burst of birdsong, resplendence of creamsicle – light creeping up white walls, St. Louis dawn or streetlights, in the alley,"* in the words of Darrin Kelly in *"Street Lights in the Alley"* (2008).

Indeed urban living is the only reality to many people, and has been for a long time. A common thought of this classical time was that *"All roads lead to Rome."* A great many people, including me while growing up, could not readily envision not living in a city with its vibrant diversity, daily novelty, and fertile chaos—an exciting place to live that encouraged connections with like-minded people available for all sorts of creative activity, able to work with anyone who will listen and respond. Urban living provides exposure to so many of life's experiences: culture and entertainment, politics and economic interests.

Economic advantage is a most important one. We need activity, issues to address, things to build, analyze, or count, and particular problems to learn from and solve. The ability to test our endeavors and readily abandon ideas that will not work is crucial as we become more successful at what we are doing. There are people to accept us and to reject us; we learn the other half of life, living with many others. Competition breeds ambition, motivates us to get ahead, and provides discipline, which is how competent people can best live their lives. Competition is a large part of our social and commercial interactions in the process of earning enough to serve our purposes in life. It requires skill as well as will to achieve economic self-sufficiency. You need to become proficient at something and then to have the opportunity to practice what you have learned. Let me stress that this economic success requires you to compete, yet astonishingly so many people do not even enter the race, which so often starts in a place like a city. And earning money is a worthy activity; it is both achieved by and allows you to focus upon what you do best. So you may often feel compelled to choose that path, to trade a green, brown, and blue world for a concrete, brick, glass, and steel one, and live in a city for a while. All the people of differing talents and ideas, thinking and working at a fast pace, feeding off of each others' energy, advancing commerce, technology, and the arts produce wonders and riches far greater than the magic carpets of the Arabian nights, for those who create them and control them. At least this is one view of the world. There is another opposing truth that forever chasing more things, and growth itself, can be pursued to excess, but I am suggesting to you that I am ultimately a Westerner who has concluded that great and directed effort early in life provides dividends for more tranquil rewards later. In any event, where you live is a decision, with numerous consequences to appreciate.

Such geographic location and connection to economic opportunity greatly differs from broader intellectual concepts and emotional feelings for a place, such as love of one's nation. This second sense of value is well expressed in the poem about collective home: *"Breathe there a man with soul so dead, who never to himself hath said, this is mine own, my native land"* from <u>Innominatus</u>, by Sir Walter Scott, referring to Caledonia (Scotland). Folk singer Woody Guthrie put it as: *"This land is your land, this land is my land, this land was made for you and me."* There are other more immediate ways to look at the land.

I will arise and go now, and go to Innisfree,

and a small cabin build there of clay and wattles made...

— *"The Lake Isle of Innisfree,"*
William Butler Yeats

Walking our own land, as we are now doing, is not too different from the yearning of the Irish poet Yeats. It is also close to our evolved reaction to a pleasing geography, like

Henry David Thoreau's *Life in the Woods* near Walden Pond. While living only three miles from civilization, he tells us about a very personal experience of the power of place in the natural world as he sought to confront essential facts in nature, *"to suck out all the marrow of life."* And, as he put it, *"If you know where you are you know who you are."*

To get back to our walk, it is only a few years from now when a grandfather and grandson step into the Adirondack woods in search of what might be there, which will depend upon what they are able to see. At the bottom of the hill behind our barn there is a running brook, where we sit down on a log and look at a red fox moving through still wet ferns. There is a great deal to discover in our adventure, and if you recall where we had our talk you are more likely to remember it.

To Make Our Imagination Dance

We care about the time of day for our exploration. Every hour is a moment for something, and just now, we are on a hunt. The time is early in the morning. This is important because most animals are more likely to be seen at the beginning and end of the day, looking for a first meal or a last before night sets in. As we move through the shadow of trees this morning, we are looking for patterns more than anything, recurring ideas prompted by what we experience and so imply a repetition in nature, and thus further suggest some model or possible guide to the habits of animals, or some cyclic process or truth about life that we can use. The hope is these thoughts will provide intuition and someday become *"the furniture of our minds"*, to use a phrase of British writer G.K. Chesterton.

Our search depends upon what we can see, but it also depends upon what the animals can see, hear, and feel. If we are still, they will come near. We can see the light coming through the treetops to our left as we begin to hear the soft songs of birds. There is a trill. It is a junco, I think. Finnan, your Dad knows birdsongs well. We'll have to ask him. Then, some small thing skittles away from our steps, as a red squirrel in a tree announces we have joined her among these remarkable subtle colors of green moss and vegetation all along the floor. Decomposing matter is feeding the shiny green world around us, as shadows in the early light beneath the shade of the leaves imitate the rows of long trees. Some trees lie on the ground, while others are hinged off the ground at thirty-degree angles. This is the result of a recent storm, which lined them up; we note this is mostly by threes. Tree roots ordinarily reach deep into the earth, seeking moisture and nutrients. Yet in the Adirondacks, blowdown leaves an appearance of chaos, whole root balls of larger trees exposed because the glaciers scoured away the land, and even after ten thousand years of plant decomposition, the soil is still a thin mix of gray clay which is ground-up mountain that has become sand. When strong winds blow, this thin dirt gives up the roots of larger trees that have grown together, and so they bowl over like pins. Smaller trees that are not whipped out of the earth often snap, leaving jagged-headed sentinels guarding the floor. This appearance is in such stark contrast to the meadow on the other side of our land where a red fox prances and chases voles.

We have stepped into the natural world, and after a while the fox comes along, springing briskly through the forest floor toward home. Because we are still, we see it, tail traveling a narrow line, taking close steps in light snow, toward a glacial hill holding a carpet of long turned brown leaves. There is something in its mouth: a vole from that meadow a fifth of a mile away. The fox approaches her den and begins to feed small yellow eyes that we will not see until the mother leaves. For now, she sits on top of the hole in the sand of gray clay and ground rock, guarding the kits. Then she travels a few feet down to the brook to drink and prances off, probably back to the meadow to find lunch. Seeing this is special Finn, a treasure. When we walk up the steep hill past the barn to home, we will look up foxholes and learn that five or six dens are built at a time, with food stored in each. The vixen is ready to move at any sense of danger, having given herself multiple alternatives. Now that is an idea to learn, Finnan: giving yourself alternatives if things do not work out as you first planned.

We go back later to see if the mother and kits have sensed our presence, and they have left. We sit on the log by the brook, looking at the pile of sand that the glacial ice pushed here. Sliding a branch diagonally down into the shaft of the fox den, we find it is narrow, about six feet deep. We don't know what ideas will come to us sitting here in this hollow, but no need to rush.

In some ways, seeing is like hunting for meaning in the stories we will be exploring: we find what we seek. If we walked deeper into the hollow, a few hundred feet east, we would reach deeper depressions in the earth where black bears sometimes make their winter dens. I see in your eyes that this is of some interest, yes, Finn? It is natural to crave some excitement. As you grow, you will see that there is an evolutionary biological side to this. As we think about it, we will see a developing sense of it all. As hunter-gatherers, people were attuned to the alerts of danger and the resulting adrenaline rush, a state where the body is capable of fast, focused movement, needed to catch the prize or avoid being it. Then, as now, we subsequently required reassuring rest and growth. Contemplating an attraction to a possible near encounter with a bear yet feeling apprehension at the same time reminds me of a story in *Orthodoxy* by G.K. Chesterton, an English author of a century ago. He suggests that what we so often really want out of life is the adventure of high risk, like sailing off to sea, followed by security, of soon finding that we have landed, and on the other side of the same island.

An imagined encounter with a bear has that tingle of anxiety and calm. I know that you have already discovered bear dens in winter with your father in Maine. Now, the bears would be finished hibernating and out and about, so the risk seems to outweigh the reward; let's let the bear be.

My grandson, when your father, Darrin, was about nine years of age he read numerous books and interviewed people living nearby and wrote a natural history of Locust Valley, Long Island, where we lived. These kinds of studies are very useful but not exactly what we are doing today. We have focused on looking directly at nature.

There are different ways of looking at things. Some college professors studied how we see by asking foreign students at the University to look at a scene and then to look away.

They found a sharp difference of habit between the American students and students from Asia. The Western students first focused on the center of the picture, the point of it all you might say, and then noticed some details. The Asian students first looked at the broad scene and only later moved to the center. As we might expect, each group had diverse views of what they saw based on the perspective they first chose. Now if we pursued this idea we might, indeed would, determine that the difference is related to culture. Traditionally, Chinese and Japanese emphasize the collective perspective of society, which is important to function in their complex communal network. The American and European emphasis on the self-reliant individual makes social context apparently less important.

The broad view of things—looking at the macrocosm—allows comprehensive consideration. When we take a wide view, we expand our horizon to see many diverse things; we are able to consider their meanings and have far greater chance to find interconnections. The focused view—looking at the microcosm—takes a more careful interest in the individual details. When we dig down deep and pursue one subject wherever it leads, we have greater chance of deeper discovery. I want you to appreciate the idea that observation gives us insights in unexpected places and times, yet the more you know before you start, the more you may see. Being prepared makes us far more able to differentiate as we explore.

A renowned scientist once said we only really know a subject when we understand the adjacent fields of study, say physics, chemistry, and biology; or quantum physics, biochemistry and biology; or biological immunization and engineering; or sociology, history, economics, and law. For example, the study of snow and ice encompasses physics, chemistry, and meteorology in examining the interactions and transfers of temperature and pressure between gradients of atmosphere, water, and land; and the formation of crystals and latticework of molecules. Obviously, understanding the material makeup of snow is a far different objective from smelling or painting snow; we will put off implications of these thoughts about different ways of approaching a subject.

For now, we open our eyes and we look. To actually see what we look at is important. In Spring several years past I was walking this path we are on today with Alex, the son of a long-time friend, and with his young Chinese bride. They were here on a visit from Beijing. It was a slow walk as they stopped and observed the texture of the land and details of tree buds, moss, and mushrooms. They spent most of the time looking down at the mossy carpet to see what could be found. This is dramatically different than most visitors to the Adirondacks who look up at trees, sky, and mountains. Looking at the world around us, wondering about our surroundings and adopting these images and adapting to them, we see *"what we are becoming,"* to use the phrase of the novelist Cormac McCarthy.

Alex, had here once before and had texted Yan, then still his fiancée, that he was calling this the Mushroom House because of the growths he saw on the ground and trees. What we might first gather from this scene is that, again, what we see depends on where we look and what we choose to see. There are many different choices we can make. Why not see as much as we can, Finnan, and notice barriers to seeing as well?

What we think depends upon the choices we make in framing our selections until they become habits, a predisposition.

Rudyard Kipling, the late nineteenth-century poetic apostle of British imperialism, once wrote, *"East is East and West is West and never the twain shall meet, until earth and sky stand presently by at God's great judgment seat."* Why not? There is much to be learned in comparing differing life approaches. This is certainly true of East and West, yet we are getting closer to meeting the twain today, even if there is still much to be learned. One recent lesson that comes to mind is the story of a Japanese teacher asking his students to draw a three-dimensional figure, then selecting the student having the most trouble to draw it on the blackboard. This is the exact opposite of what would happen in an American classroom. The Japanese process of learning takes advantage of mistakes as central to learning. This provides a great clue for those who wish to learn well. From my experience in college, I never learned a subject as well as when explaining to someone else why a thing was what it was, and was not something else. I found multiple misunderstandings I had not noticed before.

Let's expand this idea some more, and see where it might lead. There are many ways to find our way in nature; and in life. To be *"oriented"* in the right direction literally means "to face the east." To ignore *"the East"* would mean choosing to see half the world.

We could state this concept of revisiting the subject in a poetic sense with a metaphor of a moon that every evening follows the sun as it rises in the east, but arises from a differing direction. Or we might construct a tale of the immortality of ideas which circle around the earth while being reshaped and retold, ever closer to the truth in the retelling. If this is not actually what happens, it at least sounds like the best alternative. Would you want to write a poem about this idea, maybe swimming with this thought like a river through time? Well, why not then?

A different experiment with college students focused on *"the blindness of inattention."* The students were asked to watch a video and count how many times the players with white shirts passed a basketball. After a half-minute a woman in a gorilla suit walked into the crowd and walked away. Half the viewers missed her. In another experiment, radiologists were asked to focus upon slides of cancer cells, and in one control group a small silhouette of a gorilla was set on the corner of the slide. The scientists all missed it. In similar experiments with joggers assigned a mental task of counting steps or predesignated object, many missed a pre-arranged fight along the way. Concentration can be a great virtue, but we are also prone to seeing what we expect to see and nothing more. Indeed, a perceptive realist modern painter of motion in dancers and horses, Edgar Degas, emphasized in his painting and words the truth that: *"One sees only what one wishes to see."*

Contrast this with the recognition that new information often comes from unexpected places and that big leaps in understanding can come from unanticipated discovery. It is useful to remember this when searching for information: where and how we look can alter our perception and how, with newly focused attention, we may now be able to see things for the first time.

There are numerous other ways of seeing, too. Your Uncle

Brendan would tell you that in the view of Chinese medicine, there is a very close connection between people and the natural world and a holistic vantage of the nature of things is found in the details. Natural forces of life can be referred to as the Tao (*"dao"*), or *"the way."* From a Chinese view of health, both personal and global, there is an appreciation that not only is it important to look below the surface, but that the small picture is a reflection or echo of the larger picture or sound, and that there is too much of an interconnection to ignore either. You will have to ask Brendan to explain all of that, and I know he would welcome the opportunity.

We might think about this little tale as well. Arthur Conan Doyle's characters the British detective Sherlock Holmes and his sidekick Dr. Watson went camping, let us say, in the Adirondack Mountains. At night, as they crawled into sleeping bags, Watson said to Holmes that he saw that the stars were brilliant and an inspiring reminder of the insignificance of man in the universe. Holmes was silent. *"What do you see?"* Watson asked him. Holmes responde: *"I see that someone has apparently stolen our tent."* We might also want to consider what we do not see.

Dan Berggren, a Professor, an Adirondack folk song writer, and environmentalist, among other things, wrote the following lyrics which expands the point. *"It's the tip of the iceberg. We don't see what doesn't show. Our granddaughters and grandsons will be the ones who will know what lies below, if the iceberg melts away."*

What if we shift our vision to the edge of a scene? There is such variation in nature that artists can spend most of their time studying just the light at the fringes of the picture with blending of the differing colors. Some profitably expend a lifetime at such edges, yet it would be a waste not to also see the entire picture. Many go further and say that what we see is closer to meaningless than its opposite if we do not see the whole. The widely used description is *"not seeing the forest for the trees."* We can commit to both the center and the whole, the particular and the general, the trees and the forest if our vision is both expanded and focused. We then have *"double vision,"* adopting the advantages of two views of the world, which gives us the more sophisticated viewpoint.

Let's get back to our walk. Strolling the other way, to the west from the foxhole, is the brook that was barely audible yesterday because it had not rained. We then heard the quiet absence of sound. As we approach it now, we hear the brook gurgle as it passes under fallen trees and then drops northwest a half mile toward the river. We follow the hoots of an owl as we go.

The outside is about seeing, listening, feeling, and jumping. The chill feels good, but let's go home, Finnan. We'll come back, maybe tomorrow.

Back inside, we can learn about courtesy, charm, character, and cuisine. Hot cocoa with nutmeg is just right in front of the fire. As a log burns, the fire whips through its little ridges like a swift brook cutting through a soft bank. Are these burning ridges exposed soft spots and weaknesses in the log? I don't know, Finn, but it seems so. That's a project you could pursue.

CHAPTER 2

Listen to the Peepers on a Spring Night

Be kind and tender to the Frog, and do not call him names,

as "Slimy skin" or "Polly-wog," or likewise "Ugly James."

— Hilaire Belloc

We are delighted to have your little brother join us tonight, Finnan, and you are most welcome, Cormac. As we leave the house, a snowshoe hare is hiding in the brush by the trees. She looks hilarious, doesn't she, sitting so still, hiding with her fur half white from the snow camouflage she is shedding and with still only half the brown coat she will have in summer. Her newborns should be coming soon.

It is time for a night visit. Ferns are green everywhere this spring as we are being called by the evening chorus of peepers rising in the air. We pause in the dark, wondering if their singing means anything. But of course it does. Let's take a look at the magic of this night music we are hearing.

At the bottom of the hill there is a pond of peepers. They usually are less than a half-inch and yet can jump fifty times their length. Gentlemen, your mother was studying frogs, tadpoles, and such in New Brunswick and then Maine at the time you were born, and you can both learn much more about them from her. We are here by the bog to learn slightly different lessons. For now, we are studying this pond, which empties out on the other side of River Road into the West Branch of the Ausable River. Yesterday we went out to see the forest floor. Now we are here to listen to the vibrations of night sound and its absence, silence, to find ways to learn. Tomorrow we'll climb to feel a breeze of mountaintop air. To see, listen, and feel life are all part of the lesson of understanding.

What can you learn from what you experience? An idea that you can say: - to be able to *"articulate a notion"* - and then we can see if we can come to a sense of whether or not this inspiration is a path that can lead us somewhere. Truly knowing requires an open mind to as many questions as we can find. You are still very young, my beautiful grandchildren, and I no longer have the patience for all the possible and paralyzing options. So rather than going through the entire dizzying array, we are just picking thoughts and are having fun with them.

But let's remember the question we started out with: Why do the peepers sing? And does it lead to a more important lesson? Well, it turns out that with the lengthening, warming days, male peepers sing on early Spring nights to attract mates, a most basic reason. They do this in enormous numbers for a few days after the ground thaws. When you study all kinds of other animals you will find that males of just about all species try to impress the females—with bright tail feathers, large antler racks, and just about any showy thing they have evolved to do.

And what about people? Well, F. Scott Fitzgerald began his celebrated novel *The Great Gatsby* exploring the lifestyle of Americans during the Roaring Twenties He began the book with this French poem: *"Then wear the gold hat, if that will move her; If you can bounce high, bounce for her too. Till she cry 'Lover, gold-hatted, high-bouncing lover, I must have you!'"*

As you go through life, there will be opportunities to wear gold and jump high. This is one of the first of many lessons: it is often best to jump. There are many ways of doing this, and now that you are aware, you will find them— learning more with each way you see and hear. One important way is listening, to look into someone's eyes as they speak, capturing each word. Listening is a big secret in life, and this is a good season to dwell on it.

This awakening of life in Spring is exciting, but now it's late, we're tired. Let's leave our muddy boots here on the porch. We'll clean them first thing tomorrow. It's time for hot chocolate and then bed.

CHAPTER 3

Hike the Mountain

*"Shadow," said he, where can it be, this land of
Eldorado?"*

*Over the mountains of the moon, down the valley
of the shadow,*

*Ride boldly, ride," the shade replied, —if you seek
for Eldorado."*

— *"Eldorado"*, Edgar Allen Poe

The trees we see here at Boulderwood are the result of a long
process. The mix is white birch and evergreen trees. The birch
were the pioneers as their lighter seeds blew in when there was
a disturbance of the canopy. Sometimes this was caused by
fire. Construction of bridle trails and earlier farming on this
land by the Lake Placid Club created space for seedlings on
our land. The birch seeds germinated and grew, later joined
by the evergreens, whose higher spruce and pine trees are
casting dark shadows over, and ultimately superseding the
white birch. Below, by our meadow, hardwoods also grow.

I think the most noticeable of the trees on our land are the tamaracks with their yellow needles in autumn; they are the only conifer that is not evergreen. By now, you are have probably learned the drill, children: What are conifers? They are pines, hemlocks, spruces, cedars, and all the trees that have needles rather than leaves, as do the hardwood deciduous trees. One way to pay attention to trees is to a hike up a mountain and let the wind say what it has to say to them, as we will do today.

It is early and still misty as we start off down the hill toward the trailhead.

As we pass the meadow, we notice the beginning of painted brush, a wide carpet of orange, blooming together with other yellow wildflowers. They begin small and delicate in the spring but paint a broad dramatic landscape that takes your breath away. They remind us that it is not enough simply to walk the land, but that we must do our best to seek astonishment as we do so. Today it is glory in wild mountains, which goad us toward *"the fierce imagination of the muses."*

> *"I wandered lonely as a cloud that floats on high o'er vales and hills,*
>
> *When all at once I saw a crowd, a host, of golden daffodils…"*
>
> --- William Wordsworth

They say that the movement of animals is measured by geography while the movement of forests is gauged by time, with each usually going where it is most comfortable. Here in the High Peaks of the Adirondack Mountains, the animal of most distinction is the black bear, discovered mostly by campers who fail to hoist their food high enough on the branches of trees. There was even one famous local bear, Yellow-Yellow, who could open the "*bear-proof*" food canisters required here in the High Peaks. But we will not likely see animals during the day, so that is a story for another time.

Our pace is restrained as we climb. This is not soft grass or moss like yesterday. It's a mountain trail with lots of rocks and root after root as the trail goes higher, forward, toward the sun. The sand on the trail as we climb is once again evidence of how thin is post-glacier soil in the Adirondack Mountains. The air is scented with pine. We see plants with three red leaves, trillium, along the side; they bloom in early Spring, "*before the robins wake,*" they say. We see them among the hardwood, birch, and pines, and then spruce on the way up. Further along we come to white bunchberry flowers. It is the beginning of the red berry season, but as we move up the mountain, there will be no berries and then no white flowers on these plants. It is said that each hundred feet of climb is equal to a day earlier in the season. There is a wonderful book called *North With the Spring*, written by a man named Edwin Teale who, three-quarters of a century ago, drove north from the southern tip of Florida on the first day of Spring, arriving at Mt. Katadhin, Maine on the first day of summer. He recorded an experience in the Smoky Mountains of North Carolina, on the same day seeing rhododendrons fully flowering at the bottom of a mountain and just starting to bud at the top. It is a wonderful book to experience, and I recommend it to you.

As we continue up Algonquin Mountain today, we might keep in mind the way of the Buddha, that is to seek what is there, not what we want to be there, for it is more than enough; it is ideal for this moment and place. Close to the tree line, we come upon a mysterious backdrop: "*krumholtz*", stunted tangled black spruce and balsam fir that have become dwarfed by the harsh conditions on the mountaintop. Above this timberline, at about 4,000 feet, we move into an alpine meadow of delicate, blue-violet aster flowers, emphasizing the enchantment of this special place. On this climb toward the summit, we have moved into a harsh environment, yet you can still see the same little bluet flowers we found on the mossy trails of our property. This is because they like the acidic soil of both places. As we scamper up the bald rock to the summit, we see it is a world of moss and lichens and small tundra vegetation, a heritage of a post-glacial time you usually find in Arctic environments well north of us. You are already familiar with such terrain, Finnan and Cormac, but we are here to see if we can learn something new.

It is a grand scene, sitting on a mountaintop exposed to elemental and audacious forces of nature. Sitting here on top, we are once more reminded of glacial soil as we gaze out at slides of boulders and the wiped out descending path of trees that were created by heavy rain washouts on the mountainside. They slope and rapidly descend, openly inviting the daring to try to ski them, at least once. Maybe in a few years you will, my grandsons.

While we sit on the rock, a wind blows from behind and then, all at once, it is still. If we could look down from the tops of trees, we could see the water that came from rainclouds flowing down rivulets and streams to brooks beneath, and then on to rivers wandering and tumbling along to lakes, and finally to the ocean. This flow brings together earth, rock, root, mountain stream, and a sense of geological and ecological time as one unfolding story of the ages that is too seldom seen. Feel how aware you can be when you know you are in a place like this; speculation in our own temple, you value life and yourself.

Another way to get this sense of detachment from mundane, everyday life is to look at your life from the outside, as if in a novel. It is possible to see yourself from a distance and hear the heartbeat of life as a force moving you along, passing the day and using it to be happy, being of use. Paying homage to the beauty and wonder around us could become a spiritual practice.

Let me jump from the single to the collective to suggest that you may one day find that there are ways that even whole tribes can respect the idea of a beautiful life for everyone, even overcome past wounds, and to use this same way of seeing the beauty in all life to move continually toward life healthy for all.

Well, it has been a good day. Let's eat a peach before we begin the easier descent off this mountain and talk along the way home.

What else might be a lesson today? We have been talking about trees and mountains, rivers and lakes, and although we did not use these words I hope you are beginning to sense, the magic of life's changes, its evolution. We will soon enough be moving into subjects like confidence, cooperation, and civilizations. Until this moment we have been concentrating upon the outdoors.

Now we'll make some fun. See Lake Champlain and its

farmland, thirty miles east? That lake, easily seen from here, is "*big water,*" as you boys sometimes described it. On the other side of the lake are the Green Mountains of Vermont, the state bordering New York. A few years ago, the senior United States Senator from Vermont changed the definition of "*the Great Lakes*" in a federal funding law that year to include Lake Champlain, and since no one apparently reads the details of these bills, it easily passed. The effect was that Lake Champlain became a smaller "*Great Lake*," eligible to receive $40 million for federal water study research. The fourteen United States Senators and Congressional representatives from the seven states bordering the contiguous (until then) five Great Lakes had always thought that these were and should be the only "Great Lakes" and wanted to change this negative image. Comedians had a wonderful time explaining this to their audiences. Mark Russell from Buffalo, New York was the most gleeful, explaining that it turns out Lake Champlain is not to be a Great Lake; it can be "*a very nice lake*", just not a "*Great Lake*". The obliging Vermont senator had only one request in return for agreeing to correct the definition in the legislation. Vermont kept the money.

Vermont and New York could well need a lot more if the thousands of freight cars now rolling daily from the northwestern tar sands fields to within inches of Lake Champlain were to tip into the lake on their way south. That's an important story, but for another day.

See what did I just did, children? I changed the subject. I did this for merriment and diversion today, but watch for this trick by those who want to escape from an inconvenient fact or discussion.

CHAPTER 4

Think About It, Once and Twice

There is always one moment in childhood when the door opens and lets the future in.

— *The Power and the Glory*, Graham Greene

The day after the hike we need rest, so we walk the mossy path from the house to the lean-to and sit. Notice that I have begun suggesting that we live both in nature and in history. Silence can serve us in contemplating our place in the natural world; communication with others serves us best when we seek shared experience. This duality allows us to find life through examining our practices of the mind, which tune you in to both the worlds of nature and culture.

Let us reflect upon on what we have done so far, Finn and Cormac. Down in a hollow we saw a fox who had built a series of dens as options for herself. In a bog we heard peepers highly motivated to find a mate and continue the cycle of life. Up a mountain (without any bears) we talked about our experiences, and turned to talking about water and the sea.

These ideas we are pursuing are meant to echo throughout this book and thereafter.

> *The waves have a story to tell me, as I lie on the lonely beach;*
>
> *Chanting aloft in the pine-tops, the wind has a lesson to teach…*
>
> — *"The Three Voices,"* Robert Service

Next we will choose a fine point, one detail, to evoke a larger point—let's say the earthy quality of a place, where the edge of the sea meets land—and plunge into it. One such place is the marsh behind the home where your Dad grew up in Lattingtown Harbor. Not only was there a great blue heron living in the marsh behind our home, there was a collection of other *"outdoor pets"* for your father, including pheasants that had escaped from an estate up the road. If you walk up to them hiding behind the rushes, those stems of marsh plants with purple leaves, the birds would startle you with a burst of noise in their escape, flying low like bomber planes trying to clear the ground. Along the canal lived muskrats that swam underwater into their homes on the muddy embankment. When your Dad was not much older than you are now, we went out holding a net with a long handle and ran along the canal to swoop up a muskrat to get a good look. There were raccoons; three of these babies who had lost their mother lived in our garage one summer. When one climbed a tree and was afraid to come down, Darrin, your Dad, took a ladder and went up to fetch it. Darrin then gently returned it to where it belonged.

The backwaters of this marsh went in and out of Frost Creek, which emptied a thousand feet away into Long Island Sound. The water was brackish, about equal parts fresh and salt water, I would guess. Species that swim upstream to spawn or live in this mix of fresh and salt water are called *"anadromous."* That's a word you can use, to be both accurate and to sound sophisticated.

But notice two things. One, you did not learn any new fact about nature by using a word to describe what you already knew, but you now have a shorthand means of thinking about and classifying animals with a similar characteristic. Two, this ability to live in brackish water does not necessarily mean it is the only place they live; it is only one of the places they live. Salmon and trout, two of your favorite fish, both of which live in Maine, Vermont, New York, and Alaska, are other examples of anadromous life. So are alligators in the tidal coast and salt marshes of Callawassie Island in South Carolina, where we now have a vacation home. They live mostly in ponds and streams because quick full tides bring in more salt water than they are ordinarily accustomed. If you are aware specific facts you can quickly find broader application.

Getting back to our life on Long Island, we later had a cooperative apartment on the sands of Long Beach on the Atlantic Ocean. Long Island was created by the same retreating glacier of *"twelve millennia"* ago that we spoke of earlier. Were those two words in quotes a good way to put it, children? Does it sound better than twelve thousand years ago?

And this glacial concept might also remind us of the flowing stream of time. Poetry is made of such comparisons of space and time. I know the next natural question is: What really is poetry? Is it thought-provoking sounds and images? Or an expression crafted with rhymes and meters, as it was defined in Classical times? Why are these comparisons poetic, because they dramatize events or ideas? Sometimes it is a new insight, minute or grand, a possibility or transcendence from the mundane moment to the philosophical question, which appeals to the collective imagination. *"What oft was thought, but ne'er so well expressed"* as one great poet, John Donne, said of another, Alexander Pope. Well, I gave you a couple of hints, but let's leave the rest of the definition of the power of poetry for another time, perhaps on *"a pleasant walk, a pleasant talk, along the briny beach,"* as the Walrus put it in Lewis Carroll's *Through the Looking Glass.*

Notice that there are a lot of diverse and fascinating places here in New York State that can focus us upon the history of life. You already have had incredible outdoor experiences, Finnan. You were born in St. John, New Brunswick on the Atlantic Ocean, and lived in Acadia National Park in Maine and then Sitka, Alaska, all before three years of age. Cormac, you were born in Sitka and soon moved a bit up the Pacific coast to Juneau. So while young, you have lived in magical places with expansive landscapes and horizons to explore. The fact is that you will both certainly learn much more about the fundamentals of natural history and science from your parents than I could teach you. It helps to ask them about and to think of what actually is happening as you have the experience. The habit is likely to be fruitful as your talks expand your thoughts from the specific facts to the general proposition it suggests.

The main purpose of our journey, yours and mine, all of what we are doing, is to think about thinking and awaken our feelings as a part of the natural processes and rhythms of this earth. We talked about avoiding distractions in order to see and hear, and feel, better in our earlier adventures. Well, what is seeing? A scene sends passages of light like a dream to the mind. We then sense or decide what pattern we see, then what emotion we feel, or what thought is likely or unlikely. We think about what our minds have learned and where it fits in our life experiences. We begin to know where we are, which helps us sense who we are. The twentieth-century philosopher Alfred North Whitehead recommended getting out into nature often to gather facts but, more to the point, to find a sense of reality. When we do this, we are more attuned to what we will call here intuitive or instinctive truth, our often used default response.

In *Thinking Fast and Slow*, the Nobel Prize-winning economist Daniel Kahnemann writes about two systems of thought: the first is quick decision, contrasted with the concentrated effort to think it through. A glance gives us an instant thought, an instinct that something is right or wrong. From another perspective, *"thinking fast"* is an immediate interpretation of what is going on around us at a given moment, a habitual thought reaction we learn from our prior experience, which we might compare to the instantaneous motor memory reaction of a finely tuned athlete. One example the author gives is of a fire captain immediately ordering his men out of a burning building upon seeing a burst of flame coming from behind a wall and recognizing only after the evacuation that his prior experience warned him of the blowout.

Let's dally a little longer on this important work, *Thinking Fast and Slow*. Complex interactions, associations, and their responses mean that far more than we recognize, it is the intuition built upon our prior experiences that shape our assumptions, with an ultimate effect on our decisions and thus our actions.

Indeed, we can be *"primed"* toward a particular reaction, and we can so influence others. An example is that those who speak first at a meeting are likely to have far greater influence. This is amplified because of another tendency of people: to avoid disagreement or appearing foolish. As always, there is a reverse lesson to be learned as well. I had a client in my practice of law, whose Executive Director always spoke last at the meeting of its Board of Directors, summarizing all the points made and leaving the impression that he was leading the organization, not acknowledging that he was following what had been said before. This is not a bad tactic if you do not know which way to go, or if your primary objective is to avoid offending those who control your fate.

Kahenmann also notes the powerful *"familiarity effect"*, in which something repeated often enough takes on an appearance of being right. He points out the biological evolutionary basis for this: the world has always been a dangerous place, and cautious approach to what is new increased the likelihood of surviving to pass on to our descendants a proclivity to suspect fresh circumstances.

"Thinking slow" is the judgment process, logical but still resting upon the apparent rightness of our conclusion from the reality of prior experience. Even as we build anew, we use familiar elements from our past. The *"likelihood"* suggested by the past guides our decisions. But as we do this we should be cautious about certitude that this assumption of *"likely"* gives us. Questions of probability and doubt will frame our discussion of assumptions throughout this book. But in thinking about deciding in a *"blink,"* let's remember that much of the better instinct for the truth comes from previously getting into reality, which begins with the natural. Right now we are taking it all personally, trying to find out what we are all about. Bridging the gap between instinct and logic, early scientists called themselves natural philosophers, and we learn best when we consider these ancients as well as modern speculation and experiment.

Another aspect of the mind we touched upon earlier is the propensity to see what we want to see. When we are making decisions it is can be a *"confirmational bias,"* where we notice only the evidence that supports our prior conclusions, validating our prior judgment, confirming it by selecting and interpreting those facts that substantiate our existing belief.

Is That All There Is to It?

When we think about using our talents, it is useful to recognize that there are many kinds of talent. Albert Einstein is supposed to have said, *"Everybody is a genius, but if you judge a fish by its ability to climb a tree, it will live its whole life believing that it is stupid."* We only mention it here, but studies over the past three decades have shown that people have at least eight different types of intelligence. In many books such as *Frames of Mind* and *Changing Minds*, Howard Gardner, a Harvard psychologist and educational theorist, explains that what we in the West use to assess intelligence quotient, or IQ, is more the analytical, logical, mathematical, and linguistic faculties and forms of thought. There are other kinds of intelligence, other sides of human talent that are directed toward different facets of life. The varied abilities to process specific forms of information in certain kinds of ways are all to be valued. They include spatial capacity and bodily kinetics that you might observe in a young man or woman cutting off an antelope in the plains or a ball heading toward second base, or in an architect conceiving how a building should be shaped. This ability to discriminate in the natural world was so important to our early ancestors. There is also the capacity to create music or art, deal with personal relationships, and the intrapersonal capacity to meditate and fathom existence itself. In this conversation, we will not dissect these separate intelligences, but we can recognize that our trips into the natural world and our journeys following thoughts where they lead enhance these talents. As we will later explore, behavior combines aspects of both the mind and emotion. There are multiple ways we can proceed, process, and succeed.

One of the important multiple intelligences, which we will talk about later, is the ability to discern and respond appropriately to the moods, temperament, motivations, and desires of other people.

So we start life with an inborn capacity, but we learn much from our experiences and efforts in watching.

We quickly notice that not everyone hears the same music or moves to the same drummer. Your potential friend, adversary, or neutral party may each act and react differently, and you need judge how they may or may not be moved, by self-interest, emotion, or rational appeal. In doing so the surroundings also matter. Throughout this book, my grandsons, we refer to recent behavioral research. Psychologists and neuroscientists are now working in a branch of this study called *"embedded cognition."* Looking at why people do what they do can be important to understanding why so much happens. One simple yet dramatic study has shown that a change in temperature from hot to cold can have a direct impact on our reaction. We may literally feel emotionally warmer towards others, or cooler, because of our body temperature. How has this mood reaction been measured? In a study, professors handed people in an elevator a cup that was sometimes hot and sometimes cold and rated their subsequent response. They found a remarkable correlation between the outside influence of physical temperature and the reaction of the mind, as people warmed up or cooled off in assessing another. Surroundings do matter, and it has long been known in a more general sense that if you want to convince someone it is probably best to set them in a cozy room. Lawyers especially try to arrange for business negotiations or trial depositions in their office to gain the psychological advantage of apparent control *"on the home field."*

While talking about these different ways of thinking we might also take a different perspective, to consider the mathematical faculty in decision making. We people have had language as our way of thinking for a long time in our evolution. Yet until much more recently in our development, our ability to sort and count has been far more limited. In more modern times, Arabic numerals, the ability to add, subtract, and multiply, and mathematical notations transformed us, leading to the Scientific Revolution. More recently, the binary system of organizing information as just 0s and 1s, essentially yes or no, has allowed us to make ever better machines that gave rise to the Information Age. We have in our homes and in our pockets computers to record, store, and process mass amounts of information, with greater and greater efficiency, while translating data in ways that allow us to measure our ideas and to influence the decisions made by people and institutions. Many "just want the facts," and the information provided by data or statistical analysis is what convinces them.

Even here, the way issues are presented makes a big difference. We will talk of this later, but one quick example is that behavioral researchers have found that when you ask people if they want to save twenty percent of their earnings, they focus upon what they have to give up and there is a low affirmative response. But when you ask people if they can live on eighty percent of their income the focus is shifted to what they need, and there is a higher acceptance of this choice, to save. Yet, of course, it is the same choice.

Whatever the influence, interpreting our world is a creative act with decisions to be made, and differences between us will result in conflicts. There are many alternatives in dealing with disagreement, largely dependent upon how serious the issue.

How we frame the choice can make the difference in how we decide. Often it is the impassioned appeal that moves us most.

During the vital debate on whether to declare independence during the American Revolutionary struggle, Patrick Henry famously responded to cries of *"treason"* (or is supposed to have responded) with: *"If this be treason, make the most of it."* While grounded in his view of reality, it was an appeal to emotion. He also acknowledged two sides of decision making when he said: *"I know not what course others may take; but as for me, give me liberty or give me death."* This might first remind us that acts have their consequences, and courage is more than rashness. At its best, the reasoned decision to take risk is not the mechanical act of a computer but the consequence of a person who has built character for such moments. In any event, the framing in Patrick Henry's speech proved inspirational for those assembled at the Virginia Convention in 1775, even with that sobering reminder to all present of the consequences of their collective action... liberty or death.

This is a good time to visit the realization imbedded above, that we can accomplish little without the cooperation of others. Asserting courage is one means of appeal. Being *"laid back"* in times of such disturbance may also yield the result. What may matter most is a soft or sly observation thought out in advance, or a gallows humor as found in the response of Benjamin Franklin at this time of the American Revolution: *"We must, indeed, all hang together, or most assuredly we shall all hang separately."* The broad psychological point might be compared with a folk saying such as *"Laugh and the world laughs with you, cry and you cry alone."* Calm determination lessens tensions, breeds courage, and often wins the day. As

Rudyard Kipling put it in the poem *"If"*: *"If you can keep your head when all about you are losing theirs and blaming it on you … you'll be a Man, my son!"* A famous and interesting, if slightly off-point survey, found that people who watched funny movies after surgery required twenty-five percent less medication. A similar survey found that people who watched funny videos before taking a cognitive test did better on them. What's the point, my grandsons? A relaxed attitude helps, especially in times of trouble.

> *Some believe in heaven, some in rest …*
>
> *until everyone we love is safe, is what you said.*

> — Ellen Bryant Voigt, *Practice*

I am interpreting the world and how we live in it, suggesting that habits laboriously built up, like an Olympic athlete training daily, provide confident efficiency that serve us well in inevitable times of stress.

Continuing effort, not extraordinary talent, is the key to unlocking our potential. Actions, at first intentional, become instinctive. This adds to our previous talk about accumulation of inclinations and practices that become part of our routine, our personality, become our lives. Memories begin early, and these leanings go back to when we were very young; as we make our way in the world, we can expand or repress the tendencies that are shaped by our experiences. The eminent psychiatrist Carl Jung called the repressions of the negative *"the shadow that is hidden within us"*.

My advice is that as we embrace our experiences. If they

are negative, deal with them now, since they will otherwise not go away. In a future discussion, we'll see that history teaches that the same is true for our communities, which also must deal with our past to better build our future.

As with the growth of these habits, in the same manner, education becomes our store of knowledge and the process of our thinking. Information and training form an investment, the capital to fund your future, to adopt a concept from economics that we will return to much later.

Our accumulation of assets provides the inventory, the currency of exchange, to give us the ability to feed, house, transport, and educate ourselves and to enjoy our lives. We need both personal and material resources and should be conscious of building them both, but it begins with an accumulation of habits, practices, education, and then money. You should not put these in reverse priority. Indeed, I urge you both as strongly as possible, Finnan and Cormac, to build and value character, education, and prosperity in that order, but I also want you to recognize that all of these contribute to a full life.

In this discussion of the habits guiding our lives, it is useful also to recognize that balance is an important part of living well. *"Moderation in all things"* (even moderation) was an ancient Greek idea shared by many other civilizations. It's essence to me, Coramc and Finnan, can be compared to the ancient Chinese belief that the world is made of two opposing forces, yin and yang, which still resonates as an Eastern foundational concept today. In his book *Salt: A World History*, Mark Kurlansky tells a fascinating tale of the world's only and essential edible rock. He stresses that the balancing of hot and cold has been basic to cooking throughout the world; cooks experiment in finding the right combination of spicy, salty, sweet, sour, and bitter, a search for balance and counterbalance that applies to all of life. Of course, this balancing of life's ingredients depends upon the environment in which we live and the culture of our times. For example, in *Salt* we read that since the Middle Ages, schoolchildren in China have been learning a jingle of the seven daily necessities: *"firewood, rice, oil, salt, soy sauce, vinegar, and tea"*. Many children today might be surprised that cell phones, televisions, and computer games are not on the list. No, they are not.

As is becoming more and more our custom in our wandering, we ask: Is there any more that can be mined from this concept of *"practice"*? The answer as usual is in the affirmative. Instincts come from our experiences. When we work hard at a skill we get better and may eventually master it. Yet progress is not a steady linear slope. Sometimes there are breakthroughs and sometimes stuttering progress. As we learn another language or practice a hand-eye coordination sport, we may start fast but then we hit a plateau and find it harder to improve. Sometimes just taking a pause and reconsidering makes the difference, and we again move forward. As we pass from adequate to good and then toward greater proficiency, we often have to go back and break earlier habits and routines that now hold us back as we internalize the nature of what we are doing to achieve a natural gracefulness to our thinking or acting. We play with the task, let loose to see it poetically anew.

And if we do not? We are not likely to improve. The

distinct point I would like you to internalize, my grandsons, is that habits lead to acts that have consequences, which can leave scars in the best of times, and far worse when we keep repeating mistakes.

We might also remember that, like everything else in this world, it is often the last of the effort that matters enough to win the prize. Hanging tough when we and others are exhausted makes us winners.

There is another useful way to view this continual experience of practice. Recent studies of the repetitive practices of ball players and chess players have shown that they gain great advantage in this doing and redoing, as it allows them to *"chunk"* information together as they are then able to immediately see the full field and are ready to react in an instant. This ability to *"see it all at once"* is likely to apply beyond a ball field or a chessboard, fully across the spectrum of human activity whether it is a battlefield, an active trading room floor, a courtroom, or an impromptu musical score. We have been there before, and we now have intellectual muscle memory for the scene unfolding before us. While we do not always fully understand, we cultivate the process of instinctive total reaction.

Round, we go round, in the same sweet circle,

it's a dizzy, dreamy dance we do.

Adirondack Blue— Adirondack songwriter
Roy Hurd,

Keeping with this general theme, people, like all living

things, become accustomed to the natural world around them. We live more effectively when we are aware that the broad flow of our lives includes time as well as the space around us. There is a consistency to the rhythms of life that are worth our focus.

The sun rises each morning and we wake; it sets each evening and we go to sleep. It gets cold half the year in the middle latitudes of the earth and we add on clothes and chop wood for fires; we stay inside more often. There is rebirth after the winter Solstice as the sun and the slow magic of life return as Winter turns into Spring. The sun shines for more than half the day, the snows melt, and the rivers run swiftly. The sky is a beautiful blue everywhere yet seems special in our place. On the summer Equinox, June 21, the sun shines about two-thirds of the day where we now are, somewhere around the 45th parallel, hallway between the Equator and the North Pole; and that is when we are literally most awake. The seconds and the centuries fly by as the sunlight provides the energy for the food we eat, the fuel that moves our vehicles, and the heat that warms us. Forests, farms, orchards, lakes, streams and oceans provide for and nourish our bodies and spirits.

The place we choose to live, on a hill or in a valley, along a river or on an ocean, in a city or on a campus as well as how we build our houses of mud and straw, or wood and stone, or glass and metal, reflects our climate, which also dictates much of the design and whether we let in light and heat or keep them out. This becomes a part of our cultural identity.

We directly connect to the world through our habitat, food and drink. There is a natural harmony that develops between the edible plants, the vegetables and fruits, and the animals of a place, that is the food that fits its climate and soil. When we pay close attention, we notice that the cuisine of a place is shaped by those who raise its ingredients as well as we who eat it. Imagination in the cultivation and in the preparation of both matter. Beer and wine are perfect examples of how attention to the fruit of particular geography brings zest to life. Variety and abundance provides great advantage in achieving prosperity and a life well lived.

The habitat that people choose affects their outlook on life and on the world, as these conditions shape thoughts and behaviors. This sense of the place helps define us all, arouses our senses, provides powerful encouragement for the level of our emotions and actions.

These first decisions, of the place our ancestors or we chose to live, have an effect on all that comes after for us all, as we literally reap what we sow.

As we do now, our ancestors went out each day to provide for the daily needs of life. They walked in search of plants to gather. They mirrored the movements of animals they hunted. If water was close, they watched for fish to catch and looked for shells to forage. People moved with purpose as they followed the perceived patterns of their surroundings and adopted strategies to adapt to them. It is likely they would have been drawn to moving in wider and wider circles before they drifted back home as they struck out further into new territory, motivated by necessity or a sense of opportunity or adventure. Every now and then in this exploration people became attuned to a new and keen sense of a question that suddenly arose: *Can I eat it or can it eat me?* As they dared to try the new, they discovered how to catch, gather, or grow newly favored foods, and the patterns changed again, governed by where they had placed themselves. Fields were sown where plants could grow toward sunlight. They planted, reaped, and gathered. They sat around meals in the evening and shared the day, as their lives were structured by events important to them in the cycle of birth, rites of passage, marriage, and death. People joined together in recalling and becoming engaged in their history. The cooking and conversation developed *"a culture of the table."* The special moments of life were celebrated with feasts and stories, rituals became important to bind people closer, encourage a sense of togetherness, and provide implications of a sacred concern for the extraordinary, beyond their individual selves. Hunting parties led to cooperation, greater success and growing commitment to communities as more food meant more time for making better tools, clothes, art, culture, leisure, and innovation as everyone became better off. From the natural rhythms of this environment, new ways of life evolved. Step after step, the repetition of living created habits that became ways, traditions, which eventually became a culture. As societies evolved they ventured to new places, over mountains and lakes which, particularly if seafaring, greatly impacted what people did in shaping different environments, which became their history.

> *Why, just show you God's menu? Hell, we are all starving — let's eat.*
>
> — Hafiz, Sufi poet

The personal part of the continuing story is you and me, as we do the same today. What we do each day is not trivial. I emphasize this basic point because it is folly to be diverted from the fundamental fact that this traditional living each day is the essence of our lives, which we may modify but do not abandon because it has become us.

Indeed, I have just read about an archeological site in a Siberian town called Soloneshnoye, where a small cave of about 3,000 square feet was found with evidence of habitation for over a quarter of a million years. The New York Times reported that on a recent warm Spring day, the scent of pine on nearby rock outcroppings and a stream bubbling a hundred yards away show the appeal for this place, the only known site on earth with evidence of the bones and interbreeding of three types of early humans: Neanderthals, Denisovans, and Homo Sapiens. In the remains of early living, they have found a 50,000-year-old needle and ancient decorative beads, showing that ingenuity and quest for beauty goes way back in our ancestry.

The story always continues, and advances. Eventually, men felled forests, damned rivers, drained marshes, cultivated fields, and built granaries, roads, canals, and docks. In due time, the natural habitat became a land of cities with railroads and airports between them, and metropolises with factories and manufactured goods; and the people living in them came to possess an advanced ability to communicate and to control the ecosystem.

Peoples experiences, their history ricocheted a long way through time and place affecting far away worlds. When Napoleon won his wars in Europe, one result was the lifting of the Portuguese embargo on the export of their merino sheep, prized for thick fleece. This, in turn, provided Vermont farmers of the early Eighteenth Century a new opportunity to raise these sheep and make textiles to sell, which in turn changed the New England landscape during the early days of Industrial Revolution. One consequence was that trees were cut and replaced by rock fences, and the evidence is still found in fields and forests throughout the state.

To stay with our general story, we humans have a collective evolving narrative, our history described with language created from our consciousness to give a coherent structure for people who develop values and personalities through these shared experiences. Everything matters. We imagine ourselves in the stories that are told, become conscious that we define ourselves as a group, and the story becomes a collective story we still tell ourselves about ourselves. This matters a great deal since the explanations we profess frame what we do.

The whole is often greater than the sum of its parts, and in groups, people have greater resources to meet the demands of life. So, people are motivated to live together, which means they need learn to place value on social interaction. This experience, whose repetition is part of human history, is often the result of geography. For example, logging in the Adirondacks in the Nineteenth Century required water that flowed south down to the Hudson River in order to move logs to markets further south in New York State. Early settlements were found in these logging camps that had access to lakes and rivers. The motivation may change from economic survival to a pursuit of the advantages of prosperity such as at the turn of the Twentieth Century, when wealthy travelers from the cities sought to escape the heat of summers and to seek the beauty of nature. This still happens to be in the same places today, where the lands meet the waters. That has not changed a century later, as more people move up here for the life-enhancing surroundings. Our history is the result of our consequent habits, our reactions and responses to exigencies and circumstances. Their repetition in daily lives was our past, and becomes our future. Do notice how the advantages of a particular geography, or the paucity of them, can determine where and how we live.

We are linked to these ancient parts of ourselves which began with observation and labeling what we learned, then repeating and expanding these lessons. The biological fact is the neurons in our brain fire together, wire together; we become what we say as we repeat words, which become commitment to thoughts, which lead to actions and then habits, which becomes character, strength, and temperament, which predicts destiny.

Let's say that one more time. I think we do what we think and we become what we do, poet or priest, fearful or courageous; habitual acts become how you are and define you. The story becomes the man or woman. As we continue to learn, we will change. Sometimes the change can be sudden.

And so, Finnan and Cormac, if we would change our fate we change our habits, which might suggest a change in location.

> *The situation changes from a great upheaval to a
> great peace once every seven or eight years. Ghosts
> and monsters jump out by themselves...*

> — Mao Zedong

Earlier we spoke of Western cultures stressing individual reliance, while East Asian civilizations such as China and Japan have adopted a collective outlook. We have been getting into another habit of asking, "Why?" so why not here, Cormac?

It is likely that most in society have a natural predisposition to accept their culture as best, and to see no reason to do otherwise. It remains an interesting question whether there was a reason why a dominant predisposition toward common action prevails in Asian societies.

There are studies now being conducted at the University of Virginia, reported in *Science* magazine, suggesting an answer. As we might suspect, it is grounded in living in a particular environment, and it turns out that the crucial factor unsurprisingly seems to be agriculture. The staple food of the West is wheat, and the East is rice. One researcher proposed that before mechanization, a farmer growing rice had to work twice as many hours as he would growing wheat. The theory was that the need for greater labor led to developing cooperative labor exchanges and staggered farm schedules to get the job done. Since almost everyone in the society was a farmer, this collective attitude came to dominate society. As it turns out, this theory proved readily testable. Parts of north China grow wheat, not rice. A large series of interviews showed a propensity toward solidarity and collectivism in the rice-growing areas. It was found that these attitudes and opinions did not depend upon individual wealth or where the person was born. In interviews in the wheat-growing northern region, however, self-reliance emerged as the dominant trait of the culture.

We have been developing the theme that habits are vital, but now we might confirm that they are also changeable in changing circumstances. We might follow the thought and trend and ask: Is this increase in wheat production a small point or does this make a big difference to us today? *The Economist* magazine's *2014 World Statistics* publication reports that China is currently growing more wheat than the United States. Wheat is now about forty-five percent of China's total grain (rice and wheat) harvest. Furthermore, as the economics of making a living has changed in formerly *"group think Asian societies,"* such as Korea, Taiwan, Hong Kong, and Singapore, the attitudes of self-reliance usually seen in more capitalistic societies clearly have been adopted as well.

We have been looking for patterns, and it is worthwhile to see the long-term importance of changing facts on the underlying model of economic behavior and indeed apparently consequent social behavior over time as well. With this change in outlook there is a change in the culture, then a change in policy and ways of governing. There are historical exceptions to this theory, and China braces against the full-blown democracy of the West as well, but greater individualism in modern China may, nevertheless, not be far behind. It likely will not become the fully rugged individualism of the West, but personal economic ambition will push it in that direction, in my opinion, my grandsons.

Social cohesion is critical for any society to survive and prosper. Even more primitively organized peoples, such as the Native Americans at the time that the Europeans came, recognized the importance of social balance since without established norms within the tribe, and without allies in the geographic neighborhood, disorder and continual bloodshed was inevitable. Beyond that elemental unity, in daily lives and transactions, whether a society's emphasis is on the interests of the individual or the group makes a big difference in how each life is lived.

No government can ignore this fact that the unity found in consensus, and trust, is needed to hold a functioning society together. Beyond that, basic assumptions tend to weigh on how other choices are made. In collective Asian societies, deciding what is best for everyone is a weighty matter. As former United States Secretary of State Henry Kissinger notes in *On China*, rarely did Chinese statesmen risk the outcome of a conflict on simple *"all or nothing"* wars. Elaborate multi-year maneuvers were closer to their style. Too great an emphasis on achieving total mastery over specific events could upset *"the harmony of the universe"*. Excellence in the Eastern tradition is not achieved by winning every battle; psychological advantage is prized: *"Appear not to be. When near, appear far; when far, appear near."* The Chinese collective ideal stressed subtlety, indirection, and the patient accumulation of relative advantage in a protracted campaign. The greatest victory is defeating the enemy's strategy and winning without ever fighting at all.

This principle affects how people think and thus how they act. The Western tradition prized the decisive clash of forces while emphasizing feats of individual heroism, as we first observe in detail in looking at the ancient Greeks.

The games played in the East and West emphasize their different approaches to implementing strategic plans, and controlling board in games as well, it turns out. The West favors the game of chess and its aim at total victory while East Asia plays Chinese *wei qi*, or *"Go"* in Japan, the goal is much more long term, which is won by encirclement, building up positions of strength while all the while contemplating to deny an opponent necessary reinforcements.

As has become our custom in these conversations, Finnan and Cormac, we look to see if there is another point to pursue. In this case: Can we see an independent point of view in our daily choices of living as well?

Well, it seems there is. When we are thinking independently as *"rugged individuals"* in the Western world, we often want to call attention to ourselves, will volunteer to go forward, readily participate in class discussion, and gain advantage by putting ourselves at the fore, which can serve our ambition well. When we are thinking of ourselves as a part of the interdependent web of a cooperating community, as in the Eastern civilizations, we tend not to go directly to the front of the class or group but to hold back, part of a group. There are, of course sub-cultures with contrary values, such as the concept of saintly selflessness and humility preached in Christian sects but these seem more talking points than actuality in reflecting our civilization.

Two historical anecdotes may help us see a *"social*

pull" on the self-centered assertive personality in Western culture. Napoleon was said to have commented that he was consistently amazed how much European men would dare personal feats of bravery for a small metal medal of praise, emphasizing *"the opinion of others"* as powerful motivation even in an individualistic society. Conversely, President Ronald Regan, a man of recognized charm but certainly not seen as a withdrawing personality, noted that it is amazing how much can be accomplished if you are willing to give the credit to someone else. The larger point to grasp from these counterintuitive uses of persuasion, of course, is that in any culture we are still social in our essence, so recognition of others is a way for achieving what you are trying to do in any group.

> *"To see the world in a grain of sand, and heaven in a wild flower, hold infinity in the palm of your hand, and eternity in an hour."*

> — William Blake, *"Auguries of Innocence"*

As societies in the East have embraced free markets and advanced industrialization over the past sixty years (more recently in the case of China), their cultures have also seen greater emphasis upon Western economic ways of doing things. Yet for a contrary suggestion of a reverse side to this cultural blending, that the traditional Eastern medical perspective can be an important lessons for the West, I recommend you read Uncle Brendan's *The Yin and Yang of Climate Crisis: Healing*

Personal, Cultural and Ecological Imbalance with Chinese Medicine.

Brendan's book compares what is happening on two entirely different scales, to the individual body and to the planet. The Western way of galloping growth, frantic production, and consequent waste has resulted in much too much devastation of the environment and consequent ill health. He emphasizes we are best served by the traditional Eastern way of awareness of the ill effects of excesses in the world, as well as in our bodies. When we consider an agricultural perspective that takes on a philosophical tone. I think you will notice that the book's style parallels some of our conversation about examining the assumptions that underlie the way we live our lives.

There is much that can be gained from comparison which may be most evident when we examine differing cultures. I urge you to read this book many times, once just before you go off to a University for another reason as well. It uses one model, in this case, the observation of the personal and the natural world in the development of traditional Chinese medicine, as a lens to see what superficially seems an entirely different subject, our changing world climate. The book aims to reveal parallels and connections to underlying cultural assumptions of our way of life and our economy in order to understand the repeating cycles of all life. We can read the book to observe one model, one mode of thought, in order to inform our understanding of all the circumstances of our existence; a deep teaching lesson indeed.

We might next contemplate another habit of mind as well, an unwelcome one.

Your Uncle Brendan and Aunt Liz tell a story about a Taoist priest of long lineage, Dr. Jeffrey Yuen, with whom they studied medicinal herbs, acupuncture, and the philosophy of life from an Eastern perspective. He often reminds his students that we are also what we cannot let go of, tired habits, reactions, weaknesses, and fears that do not serve us but which we will not give up. Eventually it is time to move on and to let things go when they become stagnate. Unlearning what has us stuck in the past can be as important as the opposite. There come moments, as Sigmund Freud explained in the West, when we have to say to ourselves: This is crazy. If some large loss has you trapped, then revisit and escape; move, flee, change, re-conquer, whatever it takes. When we spend all our time ruminating about the past good life we are no longer living, or stew over what we are missing, life is passing us by. When a story is over, it will not take us in the direction we now need to go.

Instead, you need to embrace the life you are now working on. It is best to think about life as being lived now, yet to recognize that when we plan and prepare for the future, it is a different aspect of actively living. You use what you have. Imagine a general looking down at his army in battle, needing to decide where to deploy his troops or to find reserves and supplies at the critical moment. If you have fast cavalry you can attack the flank. If you have heavy artillery you may want some distance from you and the enemy as you bombard their lines. But before this and most importantly, you prepare. The advantage is obvious of having a plan that previously considers all various scenarios to compress the time needed when finally *"in the fog of war"* on the battlefield. You might think of this nursery rhyme to get a full flavor:

> *For want of a nail a shoe was lost, for want of a shoe a horse was lost,*
>
> *For want of a horse a rider was lost, for want of a rider a battle was lost,*
>
> *For want of a battle a kingdom was lost, and all for the want of a horseshoe nail.*

You can think through the possible second, third, fourth, and subsequent stages of a battle to anticipate how they help achieve the ultimate strategic objective. We can imagine that a general of rare genius might intuit a successful series of moves in the midst of battle, like some believe a chess player does. But in the heat of battle, it is madness and murder to risk troops without a plan thought through, step by step, with ready alternative courses of action. Even that rare general of intuitive genius is probably reacting to years of study akin to Napoleon rolling around on a large map of Italy and stretching his arms on different directions as he contemplates how many days his army would need in order to reassemble if he split his forces and deployed them in two directions, long considered a tactical error. Just as prior hard work developing habits leads to intuition of the moment, the likelihood of luck in a current endeavor comes to the prepared. The two concepts of having a plan to follow, yet still ready to make a necessary decision in the blink of an eye are mutually reinforcing. I would never want to give up either if I have a choice.

Plans do not have to be of a concrete time or place. Especially when facing a superior or formidable foe, disruption and mobility may be the plan, trading space for time in a war of attrition, committing depth of resources only at key moments and locations, slowly and permanently cutting off the enemy from its support. This was the strategy used by American forces in the Revolutionary War. General George Washington avoided a conclusive battle until the end. That time was only made ready when troops led by General Nathanael Green and local militias such as Francis Marion's fought against the British in South Carolina in 1780 and 1781. They exhausted British General Charles Cornwallis's Army in peripheral battles which eventually led Cornwallis, worn down chasing the rebels, retreated to rest in Virginia. Here Cornwallis was trapped at Yorktown by Washington as he finally saw a moment that, with the assistance of the French Army and Navy, he could win a final, decisive, battle of the American Revolution.

We might take an even broader view and bring this diplomatic and military campaign back to an earlier time when it then may have seemed far better to have a plan to avoid war altogether, to have prepared for peace. The longer our view, the greater the possibility for a plan with an ideal conclusion. And always, thinking it all the way through—"If they do this, we could do that"—is the task.

Another way to think of this process of planning is as looking at a map to determine where you want to go. As you walk along the path or browse through the story to consider what is important, you look for insights and obstacles along the way.

My grandsons, you will note that in our long conversation we repeat, or we expand upon, stories to emphasize lessons. One is the site of Lake Champlain, so close to the Adirondacks, which was a strategic place during three early wars critical to America. We also return to these stories for other lessons that can be gleaned from the experience, especially to come to appreciate how new lessons and deep understanding can be found upon re-examination.

The importance of opportunities and difficulties presented when looking at a map is wonderfully demonstrated by the position of Lake Champlain. It divides upper New York and Vermont, and provided a waterway to divide New England and New York from the Mid-Atlantic and Southern Colonies. The significance of its location led to major battles in three early wars in the America's history.

This map dictated where many struggles in the French and Indian War of 1757–1763 took place between the armies of France and their Canadian outposts against England and its colonies. The battles at upstate New York forts along Lake Champlain and Lake George could decide the fate of all the English colonies along the Atlantic Coast. After sailing across the Atlantic Ocean to the New World, English and European ships could take an inland route to their colonies. They could head to the north of what is now most of Canada into the St. Lawrence River, sail around the Gaspé Peninsula and west down past Quebec City to Montreal, make a left into the Richelieu River and sail into and down Lake Champlain, then portage into Lake George, and flow on down the Hudson River into New York Harbor. This route allowed a sea passage to cut off New York and New England from New Jersey from the South.

In the American Revolution, a few years later, the Colonists were not ready to oppose the great Army and Navy of England. Nevertheless, a relatively small number of patriots led by Benedict Arnold built and armed a fleet of not much more than sailing rowboats, which they hid behind Valcour Island near Plattsburgh on the Upper Lake, and then intercepted and damaged a British fleet, delaying its advance for a year. The year made a significant difference, and in 1777, a now-ready American army, including Benedict Arnold, intercepted and defeated the British army at Saratoga, New York. This victory proved we had a chance to win the war, which directly led to the French alliance with the Americans and, ultimately, victory and independence six years later at Yorktown.

In the War of 1812, the same route became crucial. The Americans knew the local terrain, and taking advantage of local waters, they once again hid behind Valcour Island. Geography, skillfully used, was destiny: local currents helped them to defeat the British Navy. This battle was one of a few that determined the outcome of our last war with England.

Three wars won within a half-century suggest that a good map can indeed help get you where you want to be. In all endeavors it is a useful process to examine the scene in advance. Contemplating future actions in this way, suggests that it is useful to think of it as a thought experiment, such as Einstein used in developing his theories.

There is a famous story of how the great scientist imagined a ray of light shining forward from the edge of an object already traveling at the speed of light. He asked: *Would the ray from the light travel faster than the object already traveling at the speed of light?* Einstein concluded, not at all, since the beam of light upon which he imagined he was riding was already traveling at the speed of light, which is as fast as anything can travel, according to Einstein's theory of relativity. But a conclusion based upon the maximum speed of light is not the point of our story. The process of thought, intellectually walking through the question, step by step, to its conclusion is the lesson we are looking at here.

I had a habit of sitting with clients in our law office and talking through their proposal, question by question, step by step, beginning to end: If you buy the business or produce the product or start the lawsuit, what happens next? What are the reasons and risks? How do you market and sell it? Who does what, and when, step-by-step? What is the exit strategy? What can you actually prove? What will a jury or judge really feel as well as think of your claim? It was wiser to know all this before drafting the merger agreement, the intellectual property contract, or the summons and complaint to start litigation. If our clients chose not to follow the course of action our review suggested, then we sent our opinion letter stating something to the effect that our office wanted a retainer paid up front if we were to go forward and represent the client. We did not depend upon the success of an assignment for payment when our assessment suggested it to be a rash venture.

Let's take note of another back story to add to our

understanding of a different *"thought walk"* through a venture. In Einstein's early twenties, he had a habit of walking with his scientist friends while talking about his ideas. This process provided opportunities for *"ah-ha moments"* at each step of his thoughts. We should remember that Einstein published his five seminal, earth-changing, papers including the theory of relativity, at age 26.

Similarly, while a student at Cambridge University a century earlier, Charles Darwin was known as *"the man who walks with Hinckley,"* one of Darwin's science professors. They spoke of the earth sciences. Darwin graduated soon after and was sailing around South America with these thoughts still resonating in his mind as he began to piece together how animal and vegetable species change.

These historical anecdotes vividly suggest that there is great value in the process of talking about, then circling around and through our ideas, as we follow them where they lead. Indeed, Socrates never even wrote his thoughts at all; he spoke them, often to Plato, who transcribed these reflections. The ideas they discussed became a bedrock of Western thought and civilization, as they were examined and explored at Plato's Academy, through a Socratic process of continual questioning. This inquiring and investigating is a habit I urge you to adopt. This will also mean you will need find those with whom you may do so.

A broader point of all this is that such preparation is a large part of the successful life. Planning is doing: it is preparing; wishing and fearing are not. Much depends upon the disposition your habits have given you. The training we've engaged in this book can be a beginning.

There is a Daoist approach of letting go, to seek spontaneity in what you do. Certainly, when you have honed your skills enough to be fully immersed in a task, you can then *"be in the zone"* or a *"state of flow"* as an opportunity to surpass your limit. Yet it is difficult to *"go on automatic"* and go anywhere worth going, until you have learned something about a subject, developed talents, and plotted a way to help you get there.

We have been talking about getting someplace you want to be. I think you will come to naturally understand that an attitude of emphasizing the positive will be fruitful in doing so, but first we will take a tangent, to look at some darker thoughts.

A Side Trip to Thinking, Conclusions, and Meaning

We are now going to quickly shift and focus your attention upon a very important lesson. Except for lawyers, statesmen, and others who prepare contracts and treaties, thinking is not about parsing sentences: it is about events, how we understand them, how we define them, and what we do about them.

Friedrich Nietzsche, the late nineteenth-century German philosopher, in an unkind but pointed way, stated that *"the tragedy of the common man is that he so often forgets what he is trying to do"*. This is a critically important point which we will return to throughout our conversations.

However, now we might carry this thought further and say that the common man may even forget to continue thinking. Even then, we lawyers might object that this *"assumes a fact not yet in evidence*": that he was ever doing more than moving on someone else's idea or initiative.

So again, to know what we are doing we must first recognize what we are thinking. We start by asking: What do we think we mean? First, we have a particular consideration in mind. As you noticed before, grandchildren, we start with a definition of the word itself, but then as we put words together, a logic is suggested by the series of words we choose. Put together the four words *"the meaning of life"*, and they take on other associations based on the values and ideas that people already have, such as leading a life in harmony with nature, or living fully through connection to family or tribe, or acting in the world according to a certain code in order to achieve eternity in heaven. One thing quickly leads to another as your mind runs along a mental track urging you forward, on a path previously trod. It is important to recognize whether it is your conclusion, or if you are merely unthinkingly repeating a common refrain without having consciously said to yourself: I have considered it and, yes, tentative as it may be, I have concluded it is true and, for now at least, I will act upon it.

We started this discussion asking *"What we were trying to do?"* Thinking about what we are trying to do without thinking through the options for ourselves is called *"notational thinking,"* the acceptance of commonly held thoughts or the unthinking use of familiar words and phrases. A cynic might say that this is an all-too-common occurrence, no more than agreeing with the last persons to whom we spoke, or whom we read. At its most painfully obvious, it can be reduced to tired analogies such as, *"You can catch more flies with honey than you can with vinegar"* to assert the advantage of good manners.

We might also recognize in this kind of sloppy thinking the tendency to find only what we seek, amounting to seeing what you believe rather than believing what you see. The outcome starts by recognizing what we are trying to do.

So, much belief can simply be very lazy acceptance of what one is told. These days it might be the tribal television news channel. Truly knowing something is far more subtle than relying on commonly accepted wisdom or easy analogies. A misplaced analogy, such as a falling row of dominoes as the spread of a political ideology, and the uncritical conclusions that result, can have grave consequences: a foreign policy decision that we should go to war in Vietnam.

The use of metaphors, comparing one thing to another, has its uses. So does the use of analogies, using one event, matter, or thing to point to or to explain a similar meaning for another event or thing. But there are grave difficulties doing so which begin when we assume that the examples are the same, indeed identical, without hard evidence. Are we looking at the relevant facts of this specific case or just relying upon a supposedly apt comparison? For example, the fact that Neville Chamberlain's negotiation with Adolf Hitler for Czechoslovakia in 1938 had terrible outcomes for Europe and the world does not necessarily offer any evidence whatsoever for how every political decision, negotiation, or war for which it has since been cited will play out in the same way. Every time you hear this overworked analogy, bells should ring that no one is thinking clearly, or even thinking.

This world could use more thought leadership, and let me state the obvious, this means calling out those who parrot a commonly cited past disaster as the rote answer to all future possibilities.

By the way, we are using that word *"metaphor"*, so we might begin by knowing what it means if we are to know what we intend to say by using it. Using a figurative comparison suggests another image and sets a particular tone. In poetry it suggests expanding our view of other possible meanings, purposes, or emotions. I think metaphor is important because well-phrased views capture our imagination and memory, and so become a part of us. So far, so good. When the comparison shifts to saying it is "like" another, then the poetic term is simile, such as, *"O my luve's like a red, red rose that's newly sprung in June."* Scottish poet Robbie Burns might be right that you may likely be in love in June, and it may be newly bloomed, yet human ardor and a plant are not the same. Still, the image of the red blood flowing through our impassioned body is apt enough, so it serves that flexible purpose, so long as we are clear that we are making comparisons and not describing actual reality, but merely a suggestion that one thing can be considered like another. But is it? Once more, we should remind ourselves that our ultimate quest is: What is true? What is real?

Reality is not just what can be scientifically verified in a laboratory. In considering what is real, we are not limited to what we can touch; we hear music in rhythms, see visions in poetry, and they raise our sights. Ambiguity in life offers multiple alternatives, which may provide purpose or meaningful symbols to persuade others to see what we see. Our understanding and our motivation often comes from the contest between emotion and intellect in which we often find ourselves.

Moreover, *"truth,"* especially a more difficult truth, is sometimes found in the inconsistencies of paradox. Affinity with the ambiguity of poetry that we have been emphasizing can sensitize you to subtle inference and unforeseen directions, joining expectation with reality, sometimes by the synthesis of opposites, or old and new. In looking at a proposition as *"fact,"* it is critical to be aware that our intuition, our suggesting a relationship of two things, also reflects this emotional side of ourselves. It may be a mere *"psychological prompting,"* or *"trick"* if you prefer that word.

An interesting aspect of a question or statement that we should pay attention to is how we frame the issue, and its consequent impact and power to convince. A famed thought experiment sometimes referred to as *"the trolley dilemma"* found that most people were willing to pull a lever to divert a train on a track with the result of killing one person in order to save five lives. Yet the same people were repulsed if they faced a variant of that decision, that they would need to push the one person into the way of the train in order to save the five.

Our political parties are becoming more and more studied in these ways of framed speaking: they do not propose *"more government programs"* but *"more jobs,"* or conversely, they speak not of *"investors seeking profits"* but *"job creators,"* or being in favor of *"cutting government spending"* but not offending by *"cutting peoples' services from government."* The subject of persuading through argument has been studied ever since the Ancient Greeks as rhetoric, and it is worth your time, Finnan and Cormac, to take such a course at the University; but that is a subject for another day.

For now let us recognize that stating something briefly and positively gets attention and lends credibility. The question remains: Is it true? A recent survey found that only about a third or so of Americans polled found the current President of the United States honest and trustworthy. A more dramatic way to state this would be that something close to two thirds of all citizens polled found the current President dishonest and untrustworthy, but this is not equally credible because there were those who had no opinion. This last point matters a great deal: to reverse a statement is a lie if the facts do not bear it out.

Whichever side you pick in these battles of political ideas, it seems that a rose by another name is not so sweet. Themes are developed as coded appeals, often launching personal attacks on opponents or proposals rather than criticizing the details of what the candidates or their proposals might actually say or do, which creates not only a partisan environment but a condition of lies.

Our society is better served by thinking about connections between us, fostering a culture of cooperation to overcome narrow, perceived short-term self-interest, if we are to solve the large problems in our society. If we can identify the differences that underlie opposing positions and then explore common ground for bridging them, we have already come a long way. But note that appealing to the *"better angels of our nature,"* as Abraham Lincoln put it in his first inaugural address, still involves self-interest: people working together because they now see that there is something in it for them, that cooperating in this common cause is to their long-term benefit, for self, family, nation, and any other good recognized as common to them all.

Persuasion and truth are not the same thing. Among the most important of the themes we are discussing are values. Mostly people do choose some moral view of the world, and we must consider values, theirs as well as ours, if we are to understand what others are thinking and doing, and what is happening in the world. People often form alliances for short-term goals, but in the longer term, collective efforts often grow out of shared values. Without beliefs and truths held in common by the group, goals achieved by the group will be, at best, over an intermediate period and based only on transactional interests.

This book covers many subjects, common themes that recur because life is interconnected, but I think you will find that people who have the insight and ambition to accomplish something of value will be those more likely to accomplish it if they also have the integrity of undertaking a task that affirms life.

Moving away from the concept of achieving, and getting back to thoughts about knowing, Socrates suggests that life itself, if unexamined, is not worth living. As always, we might ask: Why should we know what our life is about? Because our mind is the highest talent differentiating us from *"the dumb beasts,"* enhancing our advantage, polishing the soul with the ability to make considered moral decisions. And examining our own prospects in life? Well, we live in a world where we cannot escape acting, so it seems self-evident to me that we should act in a way that is not meaningless, but rather is relevant to who we think we are, and what we are trying to do as we learn the lessons of life. Awareness leading to self-awareness is what we are talking about. Alert to what we are seeing, hearing, thinking, and feeling is the point. OK, let's ask it again. What are we doing?

Our identities are defined by the stories we tell ourselves about ourselves—and are also altered by them. Our attitudes and preferences reflect values we choose, habits of the mind. Articulating what we believe and why is the way we begin to set our values. We can consider whether an idea makes sense, we decide if it is practicable before we adopt it. Such early understandings become pegs upon which we hang other and more subtle ideas and ideals which can ground us harmoniously with past, culture, and world. There is always power in stories that bridge the gaps between facts and events, reality and belief. In the end, for all that is our life, it is a matter of judgment. *"Probity"* is a good word for it, gentlemen. I'll let you look up that word on your own.

> *The people I love the best jump into work head first without dallying in the shallows and swim off with sure strokes almost out of sight.*

> — Margaret Piercey, *To Be of Use*

We do not start with a blank slate when we select the stories we tell ourselves about ourselves. To be legitimate, it must authenticate the life you have adapted to, and the values you have adopted in response to what you see as your need and the society of which you are a part.

Let's return to this subject of values by recognizing that the sacred in a temple of tall trees can be addictive and intoxicating enough to break through consciousness, to become grounded in the truth of reality, to find our identity, and to meet the demands and choices of this not always predictable world. I would call undertaking such a search *"the right thing,"* my gandsons. Much of this will be the consideration of our discussion of the evolution of civilization, politics, economics, law, literature, philosophy, cooperation, spirituality, and religion, and I hope that you will notice later in this book a sense of the sacred influencing all of these. And how will you notice it? Observance, then thought.

These are enormous questions in life. Reacting and connecting to all the information encountered takes a lot of energy and choice. Fortunately, decisions usually need be made only one by one. A major theme of our discussions is that by thinking about them you develop patterns of connections, themes, habits of mind that provide a consistency with the values you have chosen, and in turn we find further meaning in the patterns themselves in a way that is mutually supporting. Indeed, habitual questioning can lead to a sense of understanding that suggests authority and a nobility in the task in pursuing what others may at first ridicule, then oppose, and finally come to recognize as evident. It becomes a matter of judgement.

Another theme is that we can only do our best at the moment, and it is most fruitful to avoid brutal self-criticism and the melancholic paralysis it can breed. I find it useful to remember that every choice provides other tantalizing options, so it is not so much that we miss or do not do, as experience other alternatives. We select from abundant choices; when you are at the end of something you are at the beginning of something else.

Well, Finnan and Cormac, let's take our talk a little further and look at what we might as well understand early: that we have no choice in this life but to deal with our basic instincts—flight or fight, the love of competition, thrill of winning, sadness in failure. We people have an evolutionary history as both predator and prey, and a love of winning is a part of our biological heritage: it provides a spark to test ourselves and to achieve. We might even learn to appreciate the tensions of the times that test the integrity of these moments. From what I have seen of the sheer energy of your play, always in motion, I do not think you will need to learn to love the chase, my grandsons. But you might remember to let others feel that they can be great at the game as well. When our children were quite young Joan and I told them to watch out for their classmates as well. If someone was new, or being left out of the game, select them, invite them to join in, too. Deidre tells me she remembers being told by us as a five year old that if she were going to invite most of the class to her birthday party, she must ask all. We have proud memories of our children's' early development, seeing each of them live these thoughts. Indeed the dedication to this book includes them as unacknowledged co-authors of many of the thoughts; without responsibility for them, of course.

The point for you is that fully living in the world takes purpose, and purpose is about more than just us. The juice in the fruit of life is heart and grace, every day. In a Christian context we were asked: *"For what does it profit to gain the world and lose one's soul?"* The highest use of what we learn is to judge what is the best, the right, alternative. Simply put, the values I wish for you mean doing the right thing. Ok, but what do we mean by "right"? Well, it is a major point of our entire discussions. Let me give you another clue.

It is wiser not to be *"bad,"* with its short-term allure but long-term defeat of your purposes in life. And let me add that bad is a word you should not be afraid to use. We cast shadows wherever we stand, and we influence those around us.

So take the good and honest acts we find in our journey and promote them. We have been speaking of values. Let's not fail to notice that when we see worth on the fringes or hear beauty in subtle vibrations, it aids us in more easily recognizing the sacred around us. What do I mean by *"sacred"*? Good question. Let's start with a dictionary meaning: *"revered, blessed, holy, honored, valued."* Notice that word, valued. How do we find the valuable, the sacred? Some find values in the rituals and messages of religion, or in the idea of the sound mind in a sound body as preached by the ancient Greeks, or Plato's ideal of the education of human nature, or the golden mean of Aristotle (*"virtue balanced,"* in contrast to such instincts as courage in excess, called *"recklessness"*, or deficient courage, also called *"cowardice"*. Indeed for the Greeks, it was a combination of the *"vigorous virtues"* of mind and body that seemed the essence of life. The pursuit of principles intertwines with all we will be discussing. It mirrors what we hunt every day. Civilizations have always recognized and emphasized that actions should be based upon basic moral principles, which might be briefly summarized by the golden rule of doing to others as you would have them do to you. We will not shy away from this direct question of what is right and what is wrong, but we will leave the deeper conclusions to our final chapter.

You may notice on our walks that you seem so real that the way you dress, your appearance, is of less importance than usual. But let us also consider the opposite view. Traveling on a short cold winter day past a stand of leafless deciduous trees can be a colorless bleak experience, while just a quarter of a mile away a pinewood forest glistening with the sun shining on snow offers reassurance that beauty also dwells in the stark winter. The poet Mary Oliver tells us that trees are not just for decoration but can be a book for study. Yet the affect of trees upon us does depend upon their arrangement in nature. In a similar manner, *"the presentation of self in everyday life"* is important to us because we care about, are reassured by, what others think, or as Thomas Jefferson put it in the American Declaration of Independence, *"a decent respect to the opinions of mankind."*

Recent studies of evolution and human behavior demonstrate that social relations are of immense importance to people. Managing others' impression of us is a fundamental component of our natural history and our present success in life itself. It is we who define ourselves for others. We will be treated in the way we allow ourselves to be treated. Said another way, your own perception of your position in the world, how you see yourself, greatly affects how others treat you. You create the impression to which they react. I can still clearly remember my first work day, sitting in a training session at the downtown Pine Street New York City offices of Price Waterhouse & Co. We all were just out of college, similarly dressed in dark suits with white shirt and tie. At noon as we were leaving for lunch, our instructor, a senior accountant a good four years older, informed us that there were 20 of us and 19 hats on the coat rack now; that there would be twenty hats on the rack after lunch. We would soon be sent to visit some of America's largest corporations to audit their records and provide recommended improvements in business methods and internal controls. The fact that we had been students at colleges and universities a month before would hardly impress our clients, and close attention to our dress was deemed necessary to impart a level of comportment and confidence. To this day, I often wear a dress jacket to meetings and to dinner out, although in the Adirondacks, a suit jacket with jeans can be considered semiformal dress.

Research has further shown that putting on more formal clothes made those studied feel more powerful and altered the way they saw the world, enhancing their aim and accomplishment: appearance begets reality. A renowned New York judge, Benjamin Cardozo, offered a judicial decision a century ago based on the opposite context. *"The antics of the clown are not the paces of the cloistered cleric,"* he opined, in deciding that a funhouse proprietor was blameless for the injury suffered by a visitor who lost his balance.

One military leader offered another perspective. He has stressed that first character, next presence, and lastly intellect are what he looks for in senior military officers. In his view, the appearance of command outranks intelligence. He might not be right; I think his second and third places are in the wrong order, but it is useful to remember first impressions are long lasting, and you will usually be seen as you present yourself. Abraham Lincoln suggested that *"Character is like a tree and reputation its shadow."*

There is a story about Lincoln, who as President of the United States rejected a job-seeker and gave as his reasoning, *"I don't like his face."* When an advisor complained that no man is responsible for his face, Lincoln responded, *"After forty every man is."* The point, of course, is that we choose to smile or frown, or put on an air of gravitas or clown, and the habit becomes our look to the world. It has been said that when young our first President, George Washington, trained himself to play the role he wanted to live. Our appearance, in all its ways, is an early and continuing part of how we are seen as us. In Shakespeare's *Hamlet*, Polonius gives this now-famous advice to his son, Laertes: *"the apparel oft proclaims the man."* All this is true in its way. Yet, ultimately, the self we offer the world should be our best self, based upon the truth of our character and what we are trying to do. Those who most matter to you will instinctively know and honor you as yourself. As we have been saying, our task is to be real, which is best first discovered in the experiences and inspiration of the natural world; but there is seldom harm in dressing it up.

There will also be times you find a need to mask some feelings and intentions as you go through life in this world because, as you now know or will soon learn, not everyone will always wish you well. On your journey, you will be probed and tested by bold assertions or aggression by some, who covet position or possessions. If we imagine how others may act, we can often prepare our response, whether to welcome or even to recognize the possibility of wider embrace, tactical retreat, or strategic attack. So, part of life is being prepared to respond to others, to rehearse, and if necessary, reject the initiative we confront, after prudently taking any available high ground.

"This hour I tell things in confidence,

I might not tell everybody, but I will tell you".

— Walt Whitman, *"Song of Myself"*

Family stories are important because they are our first stories, creating connections and shaping continuity for our lives. They give us a sense of who we are when they capture meanings that are passed along, which reinforce our identity, telling about those with whom we spend our lives. We hope it is a story of happiness and gratitude, but it may be one of overcoming obstacle; it is our story nevertheless. What we can take from these stories are things we admire and want to emulate, and those we resent and reject. In either event, they become the habits and values of an independent mind.

"The secrets I tell you are for your ears alone."

— Walt Whitman

We have been talking in general about what happens over many years, but now let me make it more personal, a more biographical moment. Your Aunt Deirdre graduated from college in 1996 and went to work in Northern Ireland for a year. Northwest Ireland is the land of your paternal great-great-grandparents. While there she bought me a CD in a pub, from a folksinger named John Spinelli, knowing I would be entranced by a lyric that goes: *"That's how I am, not too bad, not too bad, don't tell them what you're thinking, they'll think you're mad."*

I found these lyrics appealing, perhaps descriptive of a reticence found in Irish culture "not to put on airs" or speak about one's emotional self, and use them here to introduce you to a general idea. I have a similar natural reluctance about braggarts, but I have begun telling you what I am thinking and to fully do this it is necessary to be candid: what has been the most important in my life are your grandmother, Joan, and my children, your dad, Darrin, Aunt Deirdre, and Uncle Brendan. It has been fun traveling life together, and now you join us as an important part of the story. And you are, my grandchildren, *"your grandmother's prayers and your grandfather's dreams,"* as Sweet Honey in the Rock sings.

The list of most important events in my life include those resulting from three life-changing decisions: to go to New York University School of Law in 1964, to move our beautiful young children to Lattingtown Harbor, Long Island in 1972, and for Joan and I to retire to the Adirondack Mountains in 1998. It is interesting to me that two of these decisions concern a sense of place, which you might notice is a continuing theme of this story.

"I am the Lorax. I speak for the trees."

- Dr. Seuss

I also want you to notice another theme because it is useful to acknowledge that these essays are not just my own thoughts but indebted to those who came before. As Isaac Newton put it, we see as far as we do because we stand on the shoulders of giants who have come before us. Indeed, in seeking the truth about life, we choose from the stories inherited from all the civilizations. We also all learn from each other as we pass along together.

"The child is father of the man," William Wordsworth, an English poet, wrote two centuries ago. To me this means that we tend to grow in the shape that we are bent in childhood, so early impressions are important, but also that we learn as much from our children as they do from us. I still think of fresh lessons learned from my three children such as environmental sustainability, the concept of the selfish gene, and so much more. Indeed, Joan and I have gone on to spend much more time outdoors in these later years than we did growing up in New York City as a result of the example of our children. Your father was one of these children so there is co-authorship, in a sense, of many of these thoughts, and I am serving as historian in presenting a synthesis of them to you. My hope is that some of them will become yours. Let me add that, in another sense, they belong to you; and when you assimilate and use them, it is not copyright infringement or any unauthorized intellectual borrowing but your legacy that you are building upon. I hope you do.

While we are reminiscing, let me make several other points about habit. I was recently re-reading a book called *The Island of Maneskootuk* by our very good friend Carol Scofield. We visit their island in Maine every summer for a few days. A short quote from Robert, the other half of this team, demonstrates the everyday nature of the fact that it takes fortitude to keep our daily routines: *"In years gone by I would wake up and jump in the lake rain or shine, Memorial Day to Labor Day ... I always hated getting out of a warm bed and into the cold Rangeley Lake, but coming out I never regretted that I had taken the plunge."*

I met Robert when we first moved to Lake Placid. Our next-door neighbor Bill Stowe had recruited us both to glean potatoes, the small ones left lying in the field after the farmers were done harvesting. This story might suggest the eccentricity of our group; I hope so. Bill and Barbara are the third couple we go with to Canada every January. Our annual trip started at that time because Bill had noted that the trip would be a bargain, with the Canadian dollar only two-thirds the value of the American. This side tale lets me introduce another book that discusses habit. Bill wrote a book, *All Together,* that recounted the rare circumstances that led to his winning a gold medal in crew (in the men's eight) in the 1964 Tokyo Olympics. The title of the book is the phrase the crew teams use for their united effort, from picking up the boat to moving it along the water, and stresses that the habit of cooperation in all they did was essential to win.

Speaking about reminiscing, you will note, my grandchildren, that I am not writing autobiography. But this discussion does encompass family stories, so I think it best to mention the collection of people who preceded you in your lives—us—as I note another matter. I have not spent much time speaking of my early life and do not intend to, other than a few brief comments here. We have a very large family whom I love and want you to know. I also still have many friends from my early years and onward. I look forward to your meeting many of them, or their children or their grandchildren. We all start this accumulation of friends and acquaintances growing up, in my case in Queens County, an outer borough of New York City. It provided constant activity and change, and an impetus to be where the action was, part of my motivation to become a lawyer. I have said on other occasions that these early years held a great many laughs and a great many scars as well, which I hope provides you with the sense that I prefer to always look forward, not back. We also had a great many friends from Locust Valley and then Lake Placid who are part of our lives and memory. It is my hope that you will also consider them, and their children and grandchildren, as friends and resources to help and to be helped by you as you travel your path. I ask you to think of these family and friends as a part of your legacy, with a confidence that they will want to help you if they can, and are deserving of your help if you can. But your primary focus is to take your path with those you meet on your journey.

My ancestry is mostly Irish, and they are a storytelling people. The other half of your heritage is your mother, Megan's family. I cannot tell you the story of the people of Alsace-Lorraine or their migration to Cincinnati, Ohio, but I hope you learn and share those tales and lessons of their past. Of Strasbourg, the capital, the beautiful wine valley and the Route des Vins; and the beef, lamb, and pork with juniper berries, the cabbage, sausages, and other wonderful food celebrated in this land two hours from Paris and so close to Germany.

While we are speaking of memory in this personal context, let me take a tangent to another personal story suggesting life as continuation. Finn and Cormac, when your Dad was about three, I began pulling the sled he was sitting upon downhill. I had forgotten Isaac Newton's first universal law of motion being that bodies at rest tend to stay at rest. As the sled moved forward, your Dad did not and rolled head over backwards into the snow, butt up like a V, and face fully buried in the snow. I lifted up your dad; he looked puzzled, as if he might groan, *"Good grief!"* like in a scene from Charles Schultz's *Charlie Brown* cartoon. (By the way, please notice here the autobiographical suggestion in the same first names of character and author.) Anyway, thirty-plus years later I was visiting you in Maine, Finn. Mom and Grandmother Joan had gone off somewhere, maybe shopping in Bar Harbor. You were about two-and-a-half, and we were out on the sand pile. I suggested we go for a walk, and you said we should bring *"the guys"*, a teddy bear and a soldier, I think. We pulled them in the wagon to the destination you suggested, *"the hot rocks,"* which was a red gravel driveway up the road. On the way back, Finn, you wanted to ride in the wagon, and I asked if it was safe and you assured me it was. I once again had forgotten the Newtonian first law of motion with the same predictable result. The wagon moved forward, you remained at rest and rolled backward over the wagon hitting your head on the pavement. I had to carry you home to explain to your returning mother why I was listening to the assurances of a two-year-old. I think our personalities bond in sharing such anecdotes with both of you in this book.

Let us take a look at the essence of what we have been doing. These small stories have a larger purpose as well, to convince you that the distinctive, relevant, fulfilling life is not something that just comes along. The pursuit of happiness is an active verb, persistence in things large and small. The best life is something that you think about as you live it. We will soon look at these expectations with more density, but as we move into the future there will necessarily be thicker fog obscuring the lens. For now I have been giving you my answers to common themes as you begin to develop your own story, informed by you your own time, the witness to your life, and the author of it. Does what I say include my own presuppositions and prejudices? Of course; it is my take on experience. I have suggested your successful choice is to embrace differences as opportunities, to see if they lead to new insights. Nothing ventured, nothing gained. Knowledge is cumulative, and it is often contradictory. When we look, listen, or feel, we are gathering knowledge; but the point is to not just accumulate it but to fuse it, putting information together in new ways.

As we move from events already lived or imagined it would be more than rare to always think and say the right thing. It is impossible, of course. But trying to do so is still a talent to be cultivated. As we observe and then think about something, we can circle round and round until no more improvements can be recognized. When someone comes along with a loftier view, or a more precise perception, perhaps they are right, perhaps they are wrong. They might even be standing on your shoulders. But if your tentative conclusion is that they have hit upon something that is valid, then embrace it and them.

Let me add something I have already implied but is worth emphasizing. As you take risks, you should not be afraid to make mistakes, since it is only by being willing to do so that we can really learn. Good judgment is obtained by prior bad judgment, as the clever saying goes. In other words, mistakes are the tuition we pay, and the pursuit of the perfect is the paralyzing enemy of the possible. When you did not achieve what you set out to do, absorb the criticism and retrench. And remember what should be the consequence of this: do not be hard on yourself when you are wrong, in a social context or anywhere else. It is not only tolerable, it is natural and, in the larger sense, good that you are willing to take the chance. We need to be accountable and to hold others accountable, yet if we, and they, fail from time to time, we learn from our mistakes. You win some, you lose some; you learn from it, and you live with it. Embracing our disappointment is a key to accomplishment, for as it has been said, particularly when starting a project, *"Success is enthusiastically going from one failure to another."* Einstein declared, *"Failure is success in progress."* In a slightly different context, Ralph Nadal, a current tennis champion, gave us an imaginative way of understanding this: *"Losing is not my enemy...fear of losing is my enemy."*

Yet, as always, there is more to this issue of embracing mistakes that is worth contemplating. When we are on a task in a class, on a job, or anywhere else, there is nothing more frustrating than to have someone refuse to confront their lapse, or continue to explain and justify it. If you failed, you failed, even if there was a hurricane. The only response is: It was a mistake, and it will not happen again. The lesson is not "Don't make mistakes," it is "Don't make the same mistake twice." A colorful New York City mayor of the 1930s, Fiorello LaGuardia, when asked by reporters about a mistake he'd made, defused the crisis by candidly responding, *"When I make a mistake, it's a beaut."* Moreover, when you ignore your mistakes, you are demonstrating that, at the least, you are not concerned enough to do anything about it. At the worst, you are blissfully unaware. This was memorably emphasized in a story of a college coach who reportedly asked his underperforming star athlete, *"Son, what is it with you, ignorance or apathy?"* to which the student replied, *"Coach, I don't know, and I don't care."*

Let's take a look at another general situation, one where you find you are in a predicament. There is an apocryphal story I sometimes told clients: a bird was sitting on a tree branch, freezing in a severe Siberian winter when a woodsman came along and *"fixed"* the problem by placing the little bird in oxen dung lying on the ground. The bird began to warm up and sing softly when along came another woodsman and seeing the bird's *"plight,"* placed the bird back on the branch where it promptly froze to death. Now the moral of that story is that whoever puts you in it is not necessarily your enemy, and whoever gets you out is not necessarily your friend, but whatever you do when you're in it, keep your mouth shut. Sometimes this is not bad advice from an attorney. But it is not always the recommended way to manage a public crisis, for which the most successful strategy has often been to address the problem at once, show the courage to admit that a mistake has been made, and correct it. A cover-up has often been far more toxic than the initial error, indeed even leading to the resignation of presidents.

We have been looking at how we interpret life, and a respect for truth is the legacy we are promoting. We do not have to accept a grim account for the way things are, but we must recognize when they are grim. If it is toxic, it is toxic. Yet we do not have to be crushed or adopt a defensive posture; we can shift the approach.

We have been noticing, again and again, that there is usually another side to every issue, much like the comic characterization of *"two-handed"* economists who always say, *"But on the other hand..."* For example, the desire to be both broad and deep does have its price, since pursuing many choices leaves less and less time to study any at length. So, as we have also been saying and will say again, you need to find what you want to do, choose that path, and pursue it at the inevitable price of not taking another direction. We cannot be very good at everything; we might as well then gladly give up one way as we go with light step, anticipating the adventure of another course. Maybe it *is "a road less traveled,"* as Robert Frost put it, maybe not; either way, it becomes our way, to which we allot our life. Our prior experiences may come back around to meet us in the future, as we travel far from our original area of exploration and specialization. Indeed this is inevitable since we must have some expertise and specific knowledge if we are to be taken seriously in any forum. We often expand our experience with representations, by stories, pictures, music, dance and then consider how and why these things move us.

We started by looking for and feeling the movements of life, listening to sounds, finding spontaneity, and discovering direction. It is a delightful experience being with you, and this rapid introduction will continue a conversation about "mastering wisdom's heritage" so you become the *"charming cultivated youth"* (to use the language of Alexander Pushkin, the great Russian poet) that I think both of you already are. We are seeking lines of inquiry but not pursuing them as far as we can take them. In his autobiography, Anwar Sadat, the daring Egyptian military and political leader of the last half-century, said that every man's life is a search for identity. But this is not a somber process, and let me suggest that establishing connections between thinkers and thoughts can be at its best when we find it casually, perhaps with laughter, in the enchanting play that is your life.

You will be off to your higher education one day soon enough. That is our next subject and we will have the courage to imagine how it might go. But first let's take a look at a few more stories before we move on.

Your application to a college or university, which will come far sooner than you now expect. I want to talk to you frankly about those words dreaded by high school students: "We regret to inform you that your application has not been accepted." You may receive one or more of these since there are more talented students than vacancies at our best colleges and universities. This is the moment to mention an article in *the New York Times* by a college admissions director of an Ivy

League school, who spoke about how difficult it is to find the diversity that so many schools look for in their student bodies. I do not mean this paragraph as coaching by your grandfather on how to game the system. It is one more paragraph on how to live your life. The welcome problem of the admissions offices is that there are talented and intellectually curious students from all over the world applying to these schools, with high grades and SAT scores, and outstanding extracurricular activities and recommendations. All of this is good and necessary, but the resumes become indistinguishable from each other. What characteristic can shine through that makes the difference? In the article we are speaking of, the author points to a student who was recommended by his school custodian, who wrote of the student's thoughtfulness with "a refreshing respect for every person at the school regardless of position, popularity, or clout." Now I do not know if you really will be getting a letter of recommendation from your school custodian, my grandsons, but I want you to focus upon the main point, which is to be a person that deserves to be helped because this is what you do for others.

A year before I applied to law school, I ran into a young man who was working on a civil rights march about to take place in the South. He told me he was beginning Harvard Law School in the fall. I asked about his grades, LSAT scores, and the college he had attended, and none were particularly impressive to me. So I asked why he thought he was accepted. He replied that it might have been that question where they asked were you ever arrested, and he had answered yes, three times, in civil rights marches throughout the South in 1963, a very crucial time in civil rights protests.

It reminded me of an experience several years before as a young accountant with the New York office of Price Waterhouse, a respected public accounting firm. The partner on our assignment told us that the way to earn the respect of corporate officers was often to first earn it from their secretaries, because that is where corporate executives get much of their information. There is a similar story about Felix Frankfurter, a law professor at Harvard inviting his law review students each year to a party at his home to which he also invited the women from the then-sister school, Radcliffe College. Frankfurter kept the women after the party and inquired about the law students before selecting the two they liked best to be law clerks for United States Supreme Court Justice Louis Brandeis for the next year. This was not a whim. Frankfurter knew that Brandeis was under extreme pressure and that all the law students were more or less equally talented. He wanted to provide Brandeis with law clerks who had the more easygoing personalities that attracted the women college students. The same point appears again in what I believe is an actual story of a college ethics professor whose first quiz of the year asked the name the cleaning woman who worked in the hall from which the students entered class every day. When they complained that their answer should not count toward the final grade, he replied that yes, it should, since the woman's hard work made their education possible and they should care enough to know and appreciate it.

This is a short history of everything I wanted to tell you and would have if I had the time and opportunity. I have already enjoyed the delight of starting the conversation with each of you, but the truth is, these thoughts can be more complete by writing them and you can revisit them, if you choose. They were and are really stories, and I wish more of them were about what we will have shared over the next twenty years. But now is now, and that is where we are at the moment. To end this phase of our discussions in your young life and to foreshadow our future discussions, I suggest that what you can profitably watch for is the complicated lesson that cooperation is the successful long-term strategy in the competition of life.

We are now about to move into a new time, and forward we will go.

PART II

A Dozen Years Later

"All that we see or seem

Is but a dream within a dream."

— Edgar Allan Poe,
"A Dream Within a Dream"

CHAPTER 5

A University

Finn and Cormac, you have grown, and it is time to move into the wider world for a new narrative, *"a time to get civilized,"* as Mark Twain put it. The future is always full of possibility so we will be uninhibited in our imagining. These next two chapters will offer a more speculative account, which may seem ambiguous and even contradictory, but so is life.

We talked about many things when you were children. Now is the time for you to choose the place for your higher education, while you continue the introspective journey of understanding your life.

It is also the time to transition from the predominant question of our earlier chapters: What am I trying to do? Now is the moment in your life to emphasize another undertaking, the study of people, more fully developing your relationships with others. This has now become as important as being conscious of your objective. We all play off each other in the back and forth of life's interactions, and this play is especially formative during the time of your advanced education. You will travel for the rest of your lives with some of the people you meet at university. How do we find the people with whom we begin to explore these relationships and connections? One way you can do this is by first focusing upon purposeful things that engage you, choosing activities that you find challenge mind and body. Energetic, joyful activities enhance your well-being and promote an embracing spirit of life. Those who are interested in the same pursuits are those you want to be with. In your search, let me strongly suggest that although losing a sense of self may be attractive to a monk and may provide serenity to those overwhelmed by life, when young and looking for a voice, you will find that affirmative confidence is far more attractive, especially when coupled with an interest in and attentiveness to others. We all want to be with those who love life.

With this thought in mind, we'll move on to a university and imagine we see two students, a young man and woman, leaving a literature course. The professor had spoken of the legendary Helen of Troy as an example of beauty's power as romantic motivation. What is *"beauty"*? The ancient Greeks had different perspectives depending upon whether they were speaking of the attractive and pleasurable or the good and holy, and they knew and spoke of both. The philosophers and artists of Athens spent a great deal of time reflecting upon the standards of physical beauty with its proportions, ratios, and symmetry, ultimately based upon biological standards of the Greek people. It has been three thousand years since the Greeks imagined Helen to be the world's most beautiful woman as they sought to define ideal beauty. They identified the secret to the exquisite in proportions, calculating the width between the pupils of Helen's eyes at half the distance from her ears, and the height from eyes to mouth at one-third the distance from hair to chin. It was a face of classic beauty with high cheeks and brow whose perfection *"launched a thousand ships,"* as Christopher Marlowe described the start of the Trojan War in the Greeks' attempt to rescue the abducted Helen.

We will later return to the ideals of these ancient Greeks as foundational concepts of Western civilization. Their big ideas have had immense consequences. They are part of your legacy if you will take it. Of course, this is true for everyone else in the West. I note this anecdote briefly now to introduce several ideas that we will return to, again and again.

First, such ideals are immensely important motivational factors in human history, a theme that will reappear when we later revisit the ancient Greeks and the development of core Western ideas. This development remains a work in progress.

Second, I mentioned Helen of Troy here also to make the point that every sentence, scene, and story does not always, immediately, or directly lead somewhere. This is the way life is: a scene starts one place, and we soon end up at an entirely different place. The landscape may shift as the story and concept evolves. Indeed, your study at university should raise questions to which you do not find immediate answers, and beginnings that do not lead to a definitive end, while you explore a wide world of differing times, thoughts, and places worth emulating and pursuing.

Third, there are fundamental human questions that are faced generation after generation, and so, in this sense, there is a pattern to history, or as Mark Twain put it, *"History doesn't repeat itself but it often rhymes."*

Our story will now diverge as our two students move along the path toward their music and dance seminar, and their conversation veers from discussion of the Ancients. It is the young man who changes the subject and speaks of a poem he has imagined but has not yet written.

His poem tells the history of a people, beginning with a tribe residing in a forest far from any other, living among predators of great stealth. For their protection, the people evolved over time so that they could hear the rustle of each leaf with one ear and the breaking of every twig with the other, and tell the source of every wind from the sound of its movement against grass and brush. As they walk and talk, the two students seize upon the idea of communicating the story of these people as a project for their dance seminar, focusing on the theme of the movement of people through place and time, beginning in this faraway forest. They imagine combining subtle melodies in Act 1 that would be danced with two distinct, simultaneous movements. As a soft sound rises to a crescendo, physical dangers would be suggested when the music ends with the sound of loudly breaking wood. The dancers would then move across the stage, following one pattern of sound, as a second rises and another group of dancers begins to emerge alongside the first. Each group dances to separate melodies, which echo a soft rustle as an end to the first act of <u>The Rustlers</u>. This first act suggests and symbolizes the early preoccupation of men and women with physical safety, while also suggesting the search for higher meaning through music and dance.

From the progression of physical movement of man through early times in this first act, our student poet suggests an ambitious leap in the next act. Act 2 would move from an elemental concern for safety from the conflicts found in nature, all the way to the Sixteenth Century to portray the redirection of human concern to the conflict of cultural beliefs. Our young poet, now also a choreographer, thinks to contrast the evolution of planetary theory with the long historical suppression of unacceptable beliefs. He would do this by looking back four hundred years, to the time when Galileo Galilei was looking through his telescope at the four moons of Jupiter. As Galileo gazes at the skies, four dancers would begin circling four moons to four soft and clear strains of celestial music, rising as if to the heavens. Galileo had seen that, other than our moon, celestial bodies do not revolve around an unmoving earth. This insight signified that the earth, and we, are not the center of everything. This was a most heretical assumption at that time because the common belief of Judeo-Christian religions was that God created man on earth as the center of the universe. The scene in Act 2 could be brought to a stark end as an imposing figure in a red robe abruptly enters upon the stage to dramatically halt the music. This would show a cardinal suppressing the "*heretical*" idea that man is neither the center of the cosmos nor the object of God's focus. In an ironic comparison one could consider the dancers flying through space like the planets with the cardinal trying to hold everything together as if he were the earth holding the planets together against the newly proposed belief. The dance would end as two Greek choruses appear on stage chanting contrasting messages: "*mea culpa, mea culpa, mea maxima culpa*", "*for my sins, for my sins, for my most grievous sin*", followed by a counterpoint chorus, just as clearly chanting: *"nevertheless it is the earth that moves, the earth moves, the earth moves."*

Our co-authors think that this play, The Rustlers, need not end with this conflict between theology and science. Galileo was placed under house arrest by the Pope and his scientific papers banned; but the prohibition of his writings was lifted by the papacy three centuries later. A final Act 3 might begin with the house arrest of Galileo, with the dance then moving forward to more modern times, portraying the scheme of modern science with dancers representing the planets and stars that have been rapidly flying away from each other since the Big Bang.

The idea of this play about Galileo, stifled as he speaks of celestial bodies circling the stars as they do our sun, foreshadows discussion of a major theme, oppression and rebellion, but it is not more than a mention here, more or less a one-dimensional picture of censoring dissent. The subject will later reappear, and as we revisit the concept, we can become aware of a far wider view, just as ideas and understanding initially developed in university should become deeper and more sophisticated as we go, which is how we develop wisdom.

The progression of this dance proves both far too complex and too subtle for our students to produce on stage. If this story is ever to be given an ending it will have to be in your imagination. If you do think of finishing this piece, my grandchildren, I will give you advice, which I do not always follow: less can be more. Being too clear when you write these stories of the mind can be a recipe for tediousness; elusiveness can be more tantalizing and more readily capture the imagination.

In the meantime, let's say this dance project earns our protagonists an A for performance art. They go out dancing that night and soon become "an item." And what do I think of such diversions from serious study? As a grandfather, I feel more or less like the actor Maurice Chevalier playing a Parisian judge and raconteur in the musical Can-Can, who commented: *"I may not approve officially; but what are you waiting for?"*

But, as in all things, moderation. It is easy to arrive at extremes, to step too far. There are far too many examples of going way too far, such as Janis Joplin, the haunted rock singer of a half-century ago who in the troubled love song "Me and Bobby McGee" sang, *"Freedom is just another word for nothing left to lose."* She threw away her life on drugs. I will be suggesting throughout our talks that affirmation rather than alienation is the path to take at every turn.

This has been a free-flowing, far-fetched tale. What I am emphasizing is that, to the thoughtful person, everything we see or do amounts to interpreting experience. Your future will be the stories you tell as you select paths leading somewhere you wish to go. It will be up to you how far you dare test the limits, take chances. We are now really just playing with the idea of playing with ideas. A point to learn as you explore the new is to adopt a dual inquiry: What is real? What am I trying to do?

In our talks when you were younger, Finnan and Cormac, we looked at parts of the world, whether in the woods, on a mountain, on a beach, or anywhere else, in order to catch glimpses of what is real. We recognized that we can find truth without asserting it as the only truth. How do we know if an idea is true at all? One way is to test our assumptions, especially when they seem obvious. Testing what we have taken for granted is effective across the spectrum of human activity. In our discussions, we have not been reluctant to jump from supposition to supposition, subject to subject.

The world and your life are made up of assumptions, and in any field, we can find thousands of assumptions. We will examine this idea that there are underlying suppositions in everything we think and do. It is one of the primary points of our entire conversation and, in my opinion, of university life. Let us look at a concrete example, a current economic issue, as one example from the real world. Economists who try to improve the lives of poor people in economically underdeveloped countries found that to make a positive impact they needed to allow communities to make their own decisions about what they need and less to do with the interventions that the bureaucrats had supposed would be effective. This may seem obvious. The plan they implemented a preconceived "logical" remedy, small loans to individuals, whether anyone wanted it or not. Closer study revealed that loan recipients might buy a TV rather than invest the money as development agencies had hoped. Yet the TV made a great difference in their lives. A similar lesson could be learned from public health campaigns. Operating under the notion that recipients are likely to become dependent upon aid, malaria prevention campaigns charged a small fee for a protective mosquito net. But people refused to buy the nets. If the nets were provided for free, however, they were used, and the nets had the intended result of preventing malaria. Preconceived notions about preventing dependency were strong but also wrong. We might be on to something when we explore alternative approaches, such as asking the people we are dealing with what they actually need and want. It may be the unexpected option that has merit, even if we do not anticipate the conclusion at the start.

Yet there is another side. Effecting longer-lasting changes in people's lives requires more than satisfying immediate desires, so considering the outcomes when using limited resources may be warranted. There seem to be three sources for such decisions: from the top down when some standards prove necessary, from the bottom up to allow individual voice and choice, and consensus-based decisions based on what is recognized as the collective good by the entire group, if that turns out to be required. Decisions for the long-term expenditure of resources may be required for the third choice when support as the only be available when agreed upon outcomes are measured and improvements made. The point here is that it depends on the question at hand; each alternative may have benefit, and we cannot just prejudge all.

The conventional economic model, which assumes a rational economic individual, has been demonstrated in a series of behavioral studies to be insufficient and incorrect in predicting the economic decisions that people make in everyday life. The free market model, in which the laws of supply and demand are able to best allocate all of society's goods, is wonderfully powerful as an economic model, but it has its limits. In country after country, it has been shown that people in poverty commonly feel powerless, as their aspirations are blunted by a history of struggle and deprivation. When basic needs are unmet, leaving no margin for error in life, then an individual's economic behavior is dictated by the need to simply get through the day. What might be considered wise choices, such as investing in the future by spending money on education, are often not seen as viable options. When I was dealing with harried businessmen in my law practice, a popular yet crude view of the general problem was that *"It's hard to soar with the eagles when you are in mud up to your ass with the alligators."* We will later revisit this idea of assuming the logical expectations of people within in the *"real world."*

For now, we can be conscious that just assuming traditional "facts" does not always lead to the solution. To say it another way, the habit of questioning certitude is to be welcomed in life. The process of offering substitutes, by definition, presents options and thus other possible answers. As with the ambiguity of poetic images, taking contrary positions allows us to observe the assumptions underlying our initial view. We really do not know which is better until we try.

> *"A cat's meow, and a cow's moo, I can recite them all.*
>
> *Just tell me where it hurts, and I'll tell you who to call."*

> — Bob Dylan, *"The Mighty Quinn"*

We have been bringing together different themes. Part I of this book spoke of the essential need to remember what we are trying to do, and now Part II adds that we need accomplish it with others. We observe patterns and decide which to explore to determine whether they are true, if we will use them, and if so how. We begin our quest as individuals yet society and culture set the background against which we think and live. The choices we make as individuals are bound up in those made by those who surround us. Most of what we do is accomplished with others. Our goals and efforts converge. Cooperation is the necessary element, external to ourselves, in realizing what we want to do. By working with others, we are able to find and combine alternative ideas and approaches that help refine our own.

How is this so? Earlier we spoke of nature as a common playground, where we learn to cultivate natural, necessary, and fruitful habits that stay with us for life. We found that meaningful stories motivate us to act. As we pay attention to ourselves, we notice that our great advantage is that we are built to be connected to each other. We are social beings. Collective action requires organized associations, often termed *"political."* We soon notice that pooled resources are ordinarily necessary for successful effort. This requires a degree of trust, that others will act reciprocally or predictably and that, at the least, they will not harm us in any way—not steal our stuff, taint the common water well, or kill us. Later we will discuss this predicament of dependence and organized cooperation in subjects often distinguished and studied separately as evolution, civilization, history, economics, law, psychology, negotiation, diplomacy, war, literature, science, art, spirituality, and religion, but which are all really one subject of interdependent pursuit.

We will now turn toward looking at our feelings as we consider how we come together with others. I think emotional commitment is fundamentally necessary for consciously living together. Life is personal. Human nature is the result of evolutionary survival through cooperation and living on through our descendants. We want to be accepted and viewed positively by others. They do, too. We are all motivated to influence other people; our quality of life depends upon it. We are alert to those who take advantage or help, and when we first meet new people, we are likely to see if we trust them even before we judge their competence.

This subject of *"emotional intelligence"* is well explored by Daniel Goleman in a book with that name and in follow-up works that stress caring interpersonal relationships as providing the ultimate meaning in life. We invest our attention in those we think deserve it, and they sense this attachment. Yet possessing social intelligence is more than just being in relationships. It is also being adept at reading and responding to other people, sending emotional messages to others, by gesture as well as word. These actions and reactions guide our social relationships and provide the insight to deduce someone's thoughts and sense their feelings, and to find the clues from looking at peoples' faces and eyes, hearing their voices. This sophisticated skill comes from observing the hesitation, the enthusiasm, how they directly interact or avoid us, from hearing the words they actually use, what they do or do not say, or hesitate to say, or rush through as if seeking to avoid detection. Let me give one more personal example here. On April 1, the year that you, Finnan, were just turning five years old, you called Joan and me on FaceTime to report, *"Momma was taken by a bear while we were on the way to school. She is gone."* You could not look us in the eye until you arrived at the punch line: "April Fools!" Even from a young age, we display certain patterns of behavior when we are not being direct with people: we cannot look them in the eye. May it always be so, except when playing poker or negotiating, of course.

The ability to precisely assess situations and people is immensely useful. So, the other half of all this is reading other peoples' thoughts and motivations, and understanding that someone else's preferences or actions may not be our own. Both reading others and psychologically identifying with them are crucial to success with people. In a useful illustration of this last point (how transmitting messages to a group can turn a situation around), Goleman tells of an American army colonel whose troops were sent to visit a local Iraqi cleric in the aftermath of the 2003 invasion to arrange the delivery of relief supplies. As they approached the mosque, they were quickly surrounded by an angry mob concerned for the safety of the imam. The colonel instantly recognized the danger of the moment and to defuse the threat, ordered his men to one knee, to turn their rifles to the ground, and to look up and smile. Most of the mob began smiling in return. The soldiers then slowly backed away, smiling the entire time. Some of the crowd patted them on the back, an incredible instantaneous turn of events. I would give the colonel a medal for that action, which he deserved at least as much as if he had won a firefight. The fundamental point is that people have evolved to connect, an instinct that is hardwired in us. We profit much from learning about how to proceed in these human relationships.

Somewhere between our rational thought and emotional life is the juncture of how we act and react. Our momentary emotional desires may urge us toward the easy way out, to skip the task, to stop work on a project, to slack off, to take it easy, to be distracted by life around us. We have been talking about building habits that toughen us up and lead us to act in our long-term interests. But exactly how do we control our actions at this juncture of decisions, senses, and emotions, my grandsons? How do we get beyond mere reflex? How do we control the tension between instinct and rationality? How do we take a deep breath and go forward to succeed?

Daniel Goleman points to a crucial way we can think and act in *Focus: The Hidden Driver of Excellence.* Our ability to focus upon a specific task amidst all the distractions and disturbances around us is one of the most important predictors of success in a career and in life. The capacity to focus, the selective attention needed to beam in on a single target while ignoring the multitude of other stimuli is key to achieving what we want to do.

We can be distracted by either sensory or emotional pulls. We can tune out and push away the triggers of sensation—of sound, taste, smell, sight, and feel—to the margins more easily than we can the emotional signals from our brain. The emotional turmoil of a romantic breakup, the angst and anger from a recent fight, the haunting of life's humiliations, and anxieties that we cannot forget can all be unwanted but dominating intrusions that prevent the total attention it takes to get something serious done, sapping our chance at real accomplishment.

Building the habit of concentration is thus one more secret of success. Turning off the physical and emotional distractions, all of them, can also lead you to be unflappable in a crisis, to be the "go-to guy," *"If you can keep your head when all about you are losing theirs and blaming it on you,"* as Rudyard Kipling put it in the poem *"If."*

By now, I hope you are beginning to hear the next step in our thinking echo in your mind: "On the other hand…" There is always the symmetry of the other side, just as Oscar Wilde added *"even moderation"* to the Greek dictum *"moderation in all things."* Those who focus intensely can lose sight of everything besides their task and must ask themselves about the larger goal: What am I trying to do? If you have reached a dead end, the failure to drop one's focus and move on to something else can lead the mind into repeating loops, to useless anxiety in a hopeless pursuit. Countless repetition of a useless activity becomes compulsive disorder. We must then disengage from the chaos. Our well-being requires that we recognize reality. When it's done, it's done. So we can learn from ourselves about ourselves.

Finding order in the chaos allows us to use our intellectual energy to build the structures for our life. Our conversations, my grandsons, are anecdotes, not systematic analyses. I am not giving you a university lecture based on my life experiences. I am trying to convince you to go get your own and to live your own life well. Along the way, we are trying to catalog how you might do that, which requires you to notice what helps you and what hurts you, and what to do about it. When we talk about big ideas and concepts, you will notice they are made up of smaller ones. So we keep eyes, ears, and minds open. We are fortunate to have traditions from the past to learn from. Were they right? Not always. That is what you want to think about and talk about, but it is useful to consider a model that has worked before.

Much of your early learning at university about human actions comes from studying history and literature. Sages, clerics, and even some political leaders have been preaching values like compassion for millennia. This is a place to begin careful consideration of how people react to the differing contexts life offers them. What clues can be found to help us on our journey?

Let us take things a step further, as I hope is becoming our custom. We are talking about more than just tolerance of, and by, others. We arc looking further, as we become aware of the feelings of others, as we develop relationships with them. We express concern about others and expect them to be concerned about us. To understand this sympathetic impulse between people, we can learn from both the ancient classics as well as modern behavioral studies. To skip either is to lessen our understanding.

Thomas Cahill, in commenting upon his book *Sailing the Wine-Dark Sea: Why the Greeks Matter*, noted that the compelling story told in Homer's The Iliad, of the Greek march to war with Troy three thousand years ago, reveals an idealistic but savage hero with scant evidence of concern for the pain of others. Indeed, the gods seem often to take the place of deliberate, conscious decision by human actors. What we hear from the ancient Greeks is not *"I think"* but *"the gods told me."* Yet in *The Odyssey*, there is abundant expression of compassion for others' suffering throughout the long homecoming of Odysseus from the Trojan War. Why? It is thought that Homer wrote these tales some three hundred years after the actual events, adapting them from the stories handed down in the oral tradition over the intervening generations. It is believed the story of the soldiers' return recounted in *The Odyssey* was begun to be told about two hundred or so years after those of *The Iliad*. Cahill suggests that there seems to have been a dramatic shift in the psychological culture of the ancient Greeks in the centuries between the telling of the departure to war and the creation of the tale about the war hero's return to Ithaca. This claim of a dramatic psychological shift toward compassion among the ancient Greeks in a relatively short period could be of immense importance to understanding the capacity for cooperation among men.

This claim of a newfound sense of empathy in ancient Greek culture may contain some truth, yet we should put this in perspective by considering other theories. In a recent book, *Just Babies: The Origins of Good and Evil*, Paul Bloom, a behavioral psychologist at Yale University, found that there is apparently inherent, hardwire, capacity in the brains of one-year-olds to distinguish and react to helpfulness and selfishness in the actions of others. In one experiment, infants watched puppets rolling a ball to each other: one puppet rolled the ball back to the sender, while another ran away with the ball. The infant punished the offending puppet, by taking away a treat and smacking it in the head. These newer behavioral studies suggest that some sense of fairness and justice is within us, even when very young.

Finn, in addition to considering ancient Greeks and modern behavioral studies, we can look to a somewhat reminiscent experience in our family that touches upon the innateness of our sense of fairness and offers a way to understand the subject from a personal perspective. When you were slightly older than the infants in Bloom's study, our whole family was at a belated Christmas celebration. Your Mom showed your Dad the daily reports from your pre-nursery school, which described a happy, healthy, even ebullient you—until December 17 when it was recorded that *"Finnan bit Jackson in the forehead today because he was angry that Jackson took his blanket."* In your grandfather's opinion, given your young age, it seems justifiable aggression in the circumstances.

Let's go back to the broader subject: How do we develop our sensibility and talent for interacting? Let me hazard a guess: the concern we express to others has to be perceived as real, which for most of us means it has to be real. If things are going well in your interaction with another person, chances are you are smiling, or better yet, laughing. When smiling is a natural habit, this joy is catching and your face exudes a quality that makes others want to join you. Other obvious and very useful elements of our social interaction are voice and body language, harmony rather than aggression, interest not boredom, sincerity not deceit. If you really look, you can notice in interactions around you a pleasing coordinated timing of animated expression when someone establishes rapport with another person; you see this in men, women, boys, girls, even dogs and cats, when they are on the same wavelength. When peoples' emotions are in harmony, you may notice that even their postures may match; they may lean forward, evidence of mutual sympathetic enthusiasm. Friendly conversations are often punctuated by mirrored movements, similar words, and expressions of agreement.

If we look at our close relationships, I think you will find that trust, cooperation, and loyalty are cornerstones of interaction with family, friends, neighbors, community, tribe, religion, nation, and all with whom we are close for many good reasons. We choose to incorporate others into our sense of ourselves; values resonate and are shared between us. There is a sense of reciprocity and that most elemental sense: fairness. There is a lot at stake. Think of our armies whose soldiers take the greatest of risks, death. The necessity of dependence leads to the advantage of unity. If each soldier, out only for himself, hesitates in the face of an opponent's fierce, immediate action, there is a predictable collective downfall for all on our side. In ancient times, military strategy relied upon the superior ferocity of its infantry to break through enemy lines and inflict casualties on fleeing troops. Bravery has become one of the qualities by which we are judged; demonstrating it shows that despite any apprehensions we are deserving of trust. So it is too with friendship and love. And this expectation applies to friends and lovers as well as warriors. Of course, things are not simple. This commitment to others is so important that it goes beyond conscious self-interest to an innate psychological sense of our own self-worth, our honor, our soul. We instinctively feel bad if we do not live up to expectations, our own as well as that of others. Your grandfather is not brave enough to try to definitively define what love is here. There is a lot to it, including physical attraction, admiration, commitment, a history of life together and its consequences, the adoption of common viewpoints and ideals that goes beyond what's in it for me at the moment. In fact, if all there is to life and human relationships is some transactional equivalency, "I pay this and I get that," then we will all be much the poorer. I suspect that out of such emptiness depression and even suicides are born.

All of this compassion and commitment, which is the essence of our humanity, evolved over millennia. This psychological loop, the emotional expression, the intimacy of a shared mood, and the sensibility of others, is captured in the soul. The point I am trying to emphasize is this empathetic tendency can be studied and enhanced. In other words, we can learn to do better, which brings us back to our earlier acknowledgement that practice and habit matter. The emotional attention given to others may be just as important to our success as all the many, many thousands of hours of formal education, study, and hard work. It's sort of the second secret to success.

If we think a little longer, we come to a further realization about the power of fully recognizing this emotional understanding. Feelings that are directly expressed are perceived by others and, as we noted, are often unconsciously mimicked as they feel our joy or sadness, fear or exhilaration. This interaction between people is often intuitive, as we look people in the eye and feel close to them, when we care and we sense their sincerity. Often those most adept at reading the emotions of others will also most strongly feel those emotions themselves. This heightened emotional sensitivity was wonderfully captured and caricatured in a political cartoon in the late 1990s during the presidency of Democrat Bill Clinton, one of our most intellectually and emotionally gifted leaders. In the midst of his threatened impeachment by the Republican House of Representatives, the very aggressive special prosecutor expanded the investigation to Clinton's alleged lying under oath about a sexual affair with a White House intern. The Democrats mounted a daily public counterattack against the investigation, which had been stretched in both time and scope by the Special Prosecutor. The cartoon showed the famously empathetic President standing next to the harried prosecutor, with the caption *"I feel your pain."*

I hope this detour gives you a sense of what is at play in personal connections and interactions. It took me a long time to fully grasp the importance of personal interactions in achieving anything with others. The fact is that emotions are at least as real to us as our thoughts. So while we seek perspective, we also recognize that we must work with feelings as well as minds to convince others and overcome resistance.

Yet, as always, ambiguity is never far away; there is always another side to the story. It is worth noting that Goleman observes that the famous eighteenth-century Scottish political philosopher David Hume found a remarkable inclination in human nature *"to bestow,"* that is, to project, upon other people the same emotions we observe in ourselves. Of course, this is not always true. In the extreme case of sociopaths, they not only do not feel our pain, they don't even feel theirs and couldn't care less about it. So we come to the rule that every rule has exceptions.

> *"We speak of what we know; the sailor of winds,*
> *the plowman of bulls; the soldier counts wounds,*
> *the shepherd sheep".*

— Propertius, an ancient Roman poet

This Chapter has been a more or less lighthearted attempt to construct *"tomorrow's experience."* What do we think is going on in these flights of thought? Our minds are continually trying out models of conduct. I think an imaginative leap into other places lets our *"ghosts"* communicate expectations; we can then consider what to change as we think forward. Experiences are associated with actions, places, objects and the ideas that flow so we think about a date, a success, a fear, an ideal which becomes a sort of a movie of the mind within the context of our lives, as we urge ourselves to accept or to move away from that scene.

Let's pursue this thought further. We are seeing our thoughts as the creation of stories. When we become interested in a story, whether of us or of others, the narrative begins to take on importance for us and we anticipate possible future paths. Especially when we have gone beyond the superficial, these tales begin to become "our own" as we think about them. We become vested in this narrative, which impels us to make choices that further this narrative; when we accept them, they become a part of us. This intellectual exercise has an emotional side, often a hint of the romantic associated with exciting quests and strong passion.

When I talked to your father and his brother and sister as teenagers, we continually used that G.K. Chesterton phrase *"furniture of the mind"* for thoughts we fell back upon again and again. I want to push this notion of our mental adoption of ideas another step, to look deeper at an under-examined psychological truth. When we deduce something from the facts before us, when we comprehend something that has not been directly stated, because we have discovered this knowledge, it more readily comes into our thinking as "our own." The process of discovery excites the mind, as we come to see what we had not been able to see before. For an example of this idea from the physical realm, think about our earlier walks in the woods when you were young children first looking at nature. Details suggested what may happen next, such as two small streams approaching and becoming a loudly babbling brook, as the possibility that a rabbit and a fox we have just seen may reach the same juncture at the same moment. We see a future that may be immediately before us and of which we are to be a part, even if it is as an observer. If it happens, and is important to us, the psychological wonder is an image that has moved past the edge of consciousness to action and reality captured in memory, maybe forever. This discovery can be of any nature or kind, can entail hard facts, words, or feelings, and still become a crucial part of our thought process, an important part of us.

Let me suggest that this sustained imagination becoming memory can be expanded. Memory and imagination become "documented record" when we write about what we have experienced and thought. As we ponder what we have seen, finding connections in a more formal search, it provides possibilities far greater than we first imagined. It is as if having reached the wide view at the top of the mountain, we now triumphantly see the entire mountain range. An early simple example might be keeping a journal of what we do in life and reviewing it later; it is good training for more important examples.

Two events in the first half of the nineteenth century come to mind here. A young Frenchman came to the United

States to study prisons and took the opportunity to write about the society he observed in what became *Democracy in America.* An Englishman signed on after university as a naturalist on a small British sailing ship circumnavigating South America, and from his notes he wrote his conclusions about changes in the animal life he saw *in The Origin of the Species.* Thus Alexis De Tocqueville and Charles Darwin took their opportunity to write two of the most important books of our civilization. The central truth of *The Origin of the Species* is that evolution is the predominant force for change in the development of life. We will be suggesting throughout that this process of evolution is both a biological and cultural process. *Democracy* is a remarkable look at us Americans in our early history, explaining to us how we reacted and still react to our unique environment. Both deserve your serious study, but this is a good time to also notice that opportunity is found in unexpected places, if we will make the most of them, seriously pursuing to conclusion the ideas we encounter. Attitude matters. And history seems to be moving ever more quirky.

Our scientific contemplation of space in the universe is proceeding with rapid velocity. You can visit a transportation museum in Rockland, Maine and look at an exhibit of two man-made objects that aptly demonstrate this progress. There is what looks like a large and flimsy kite hanging from the ceiling that is a replica of *the Kitty Hawk,* which the Wright Brothers used in 1903 to fly hundreds of feet in this first powered fixed-wing airplane. Below, on the ground, is a copy of a ten-foot-long space capsule used for America's first suborbital flight into space less than sixty years later. Less than another sixty years later, in 2015, man sent a spaceship to the outer limits of our solar system, passing Pluto on its way toward outer space.

Back to the University

Well, let's return to our young student protagonists at the University who we imagine are busy with their studies. He has taken a survey course of the beginnings of modern physics, and how a thirty-four-year-old nineteenth-century Scottish professor, James Maxwell, accomplished the first great explanation of the unification of physics, showing that electricity and magnetism were different expressions of the same force, light. In 1905, twenty-six-year-old Albert Einstein wrote his five great papers, which introduced, among other ideas, the theory of relativity. His special theory of relativity suggested that when the moon is passing in front of the sun, gravity will pull, that is bend, celestial light of the sun toward the moon, proving that light and matter are differing versions of the same thing, made up of atoms.

Einstein's theories also evidenced that time and space are curved. If you fly west on a plane to Los Angeles, when you get there you are a little younger, a very, very, little bit younger. Does this mean that the arc of the future is bent so that it circles back upon the past? Can we measure the slight arc of the curve and thereby calculate the length of time itself? I would not bet upon it, suggesting that logic and the human mind have limits.

At about this same time in the early 1900s, another great German physicist, Max Planck, presented a theory that energy comes in discrete particles, or quanta, and a race was on to understand subatomic particles in the universe. Then in 1964, the speculation of thirty-five-year-old Peter Higgs, also Scottish, predicted the existence of a new particle that would explain how other particles got their mass, a strong force that holds the nuclei of atoms together. The idea is that space is filled with an invisible field of energy, which attaches to some particles moving through it, the particles, the Higgs bosons, make up that field. On the Fourth of July 2012, a super nuclear detector in Switzerland "confirmed" the existence of this particle that made matter, *"the God particle."* Forty years after he had proposed this idea, Professor Higgs won the Nobel Prize in physics. What it did not answer is why it all began: Why there is anything in the universe at all?

In the 1980 public television series and book *Cosmos,* Carl Sagan stated, *"We are star stuff, contemplating ourselves."* Our science student's next advanced class explores this existential question: What is life itself? The subject of quantum mechanics examines the foundation on which modern physics and chemistry are built, as it provides a remarkable picture of the very small building blocks of the universe, the atoms and tinier subatomic particles that can behave like waves, and light waves that can behave like particles. I do not claim to understand all of this, but without this understanding we would not have computers, the Internet, smartphones, lasers, CDs, DVDs, MRIs, satellite navigation, and modern electronics, which today constitute one-third of the world's gross domestic product, the economic measurement of the value all the world's goods and services.

Our student's study includes quantum entanglement,

the "*spooky*" fact that particles generated or fundamentally linked can remain in communication no matter how far apart they may be, even at the other end of the universe. This entanglement allows them to simultaneously signal each other, even far beyond the speed of 186,000 miles per second, which "should" be the fastest the signal should be able to travel under Einstein's theory of relativity.

Moreover, once the entanglement is observed (that is, measured), it ceases. In *Life on the Edge,* Jim Al-Khalili and Johnjoe McFadden tell us that this measurement of quantum entanglement lies on the edge between the classical and quantum physics. They say this edge is "where all life lies."

These discoveries lead us to re-examine the question, What is life? To answer that, the authors of Life on the Edge first take us to Voyager 2 and its visit to the moons of Jupiter, for mankind to once again learn from these Galilean moons. Voyager 2 began its journey in 1977. The authors tell us that clues from their moon rocks give us hints of *"running, jumping, flying, navigating, swimming, growing, loving, hating, lusting, fearing, thinking, laughing, crying, living stuff."* The authors then go back to the ancient Greeks, to a question posed by Socrates: *What is it that when present in a body makes it living?* Socrates, through Plato, answers: *"A soul."* In itself, giving it a name does not describe or explain the phenomenon. But the authors note that classical Chinese philosophy similarly believes that living beings are animated by a life force called qi ("*chi*") that flows throughout them. So, this phrase is given as a biological description of the soul. Life on *The Edge*'s long exploration of life begins with a young robin migrating from Sweden to the Mediterranean and continues through many topics, from photosynthesis to enzyme action, and from quantum noses to quantum genomes, compasses and maybe even quantum brains. They co-authors conclude that understanding the ability to make new life from scratch would provide a response to physicist Richard Feynman's famous dictum: *"What I can't make, I don't understand."* We are beginning to suspect that in the right environment of water, the minerals in celestial rocks and the release of energy led to amino acids and the first simple life cells. But even if we were to discover how these laws of science work, it does not take us close to who or what made these rules—and why?

Our student wonders how the natural world came to be, and how a person can adapt to new assumptions. His mind has released itself from the precise rules of the moment to where thoughts take off. Ideas scatter, flying like stars moving through the universe with no one knowing where they might lead. He began with the concept that scientists now think they know that we live in an expanding universe that originated in the hot, dense *"Big Bang"*. You might then think that the attraction of matter, that is gravity, might then slow things down and pull everything back together again in a big implosion. Apparently you would be wrong. Many researchers now believe that the resulting stars continue to recede at a faster and faster velocity as the expansion of the universe is speeding up, suggesting the universe is on its way to becoming a vacuum of non-being. Galaxies distant from Earth are moving away faster. Scientists have made an educated guess, a startling theory, to explain the phenomenon. As we spoke of a short time ago, they suppose that most of the universe that is not matter is weak dark energy and dark matter, and then there is matter and anti-matter, annihilating each other when they meet, all resulting in the universe expanding away from its original center. So while the gravity of matter was drawing things together, something else was pushing them apart, and this something is so powerful that it forms much of the universe. This seems a subtle interplay of, well, everything, and every choice may seem strange, with only one of the alternatives likely ...... maybe. So although scientists discovered the Big Bang that created our universe, then a *"God particle"* as explanation of how it continues to exist as matter, and a theory of quantum physics that might explain how life itself might exist, science still seems to need answers.

I do not pretend to be able to even remember all of the above sentences, my grandchildren. While speaking about science, which is very obviously not my field, I can only convey a very general sense that we cannot fear to go where we do not have a complete map, or we may not get anywhere. Even when I speak of other subjects from greater personal study or experience, I am only, at most, suggesting a higher degree of confidence. Even while we are learning from prior generations, new facts and theories offer other suggestions for our understanding.

Science fiction writer Isaac Asimov has noted that our experiments are interesting even when they do not give us the expected results. When our student was studying science, sentences became equations. But if our student's graduate degree were in literature then data, analysis, theories, or models would not break a code or provide a model but merely provide the genesis for a different kind of book. It all seems to depend upon what we are trying to do. If we imagine our student is without supporting data, he might be closer to a higher grade if the degree is in the arts and our young speculator is writing as a poetic prophet in following the dreams of Einstein. While we are on this very fuzzy thinking, we might remember once again what Albert Einstein famously said, that doing the same thing again and again and expecting different results is the definition of insanity. So we need to learn the lesson, whatever it is, or move on.

Our student has now gone on to write poems about the cosmos, entitled <u>Fullness and Particularity,</u> about creating something out of nothing, of a universe started by a big bang, which does not answer the question what caused the big bang. He begins by pursuing an internal logic, which if understood would tell us why it all exists without beginning, perhaps suggested by some *"singularity"* as Professor Stephen Hawking has called dark holes in the universe. The poems are free-flowing, a temporary commitment to a point of view inspired by a vast landscape and structured to feel the wide universe, with repeated idioms adopted and then adapted to particular local landscapes. After a theme was mined for all noticeable sources it was left in a bewildering play upon the paradox of the immenseness of space which might enhance our view of separateness, or oneness. Suggested choices might imply moralities, or at least existential conclusions for men and women. That is, the poetic search is for the source of matter, energy, space, and time, the ever-organizing principle that made it all. In short, a search for God.

This leads in a circle back to the question, "Who made

God?" the source of the source. Looking back beyond the stars, past the big bang, to the organizer in the void, to the seemingly inevitable beginning consciousness called *"God,"* left only a word for an answer.

There are poems in our student's collection about matter turning into energy and back to matter to help internalize our sensibility to our place in a vast universe. Like all interesting literature, it is a reflection of dreams and fears. Our student next explored the micro view of it all to question, but not explain, that if we were to allow for a *"Star Trek"* style of transporting people into energy and back to matter, then what happens to the life process, the qui, when this collection of matter is energy? What happens to the soul? Is it on an edge, and where is that? Eventually he leaves the poems without conclusion, as is often best, indeed inevitable, if we cannot go further. It leaves the reader with mysteries to contemplate.

Moving along with the search, our student then looks at calculus to measure where we are and how fast we are leaving, change over time, chunks whose variations can be measured. Heidegger's *"uncertainty principle"* provided that by merely measuring moving particles we change them, so our perception of the world must change as it happens. The point of it all seems that change is inevitable. This suggests that, perhaps, there is no perceptible certainty at all in life as we can know it. At the least, as we measure it, new information may change what we think we know. All this may also be enough to give one a headache, but as you have surely noticed more than once by now, I strongly adhere to the belief that imagination adds zest to the play of searching for answers, and exhilaration while we are synthesizing ideas to see where relationships may be. This is part of a wide undergraduate search, before selecting a particular course for detailed study. Yet eventually an intellectual pursuit has to have purpose if you are to continue to invest time. If it does, the system of thought may become a part of our life work. If not, we discard it, as it is now time to do here.

> *"I love mad youth, I love the crowd, glitter and joy without a cloud.*
>
> *Alas in my pursuit of pleasure, how many years have slipt away?"*
>
> – Alexander Pushkin

We have, or at least I hope we have, already adopted the framework of thought in which experience shapes much of what we think and these speculative flights deserve only so much of your time.

But what about just reading about life, say through fiction? Novels allow us to move beyond surface ideas. In them, we can see the range of how people think, feel, and act, and can be a way to try out risky ideas, the marginal, the extraordinary, and the bizarre. By now it has become widely recognized that reading classic literature also contributes to making us more socially sensitive and empathetic. This should not be surprising since you step outside your own mind and get the insights of people of different ages, races, times, and places. Fiction, unlike life, may have exact beginnings and endings as the story provides substitute experience, different from living life itself but similar enough to affect us. A well-written novel is appreciated because it also leaves much to the imagination; inferences make us sensitive to nuance and the complexity of emotions. Some years ago, my close friend Jerry, who has helped by editing the first half of this book, used to say that we were more interested in novels when younger because we were trying to figure out the world around us. You might say that we are now more presumptuous in thinking that we have now done a lot of that, thought it through, and think we know more of the questions if not the answers. This, of course, is an underlying assumption of this book.

We already began speaking about evolutionary psychology, but let me emphasize that our emotional responses can be primed in reading literary classics, as if discoveries within everyday life, and so become interpersonal social skills. How is that? As we noted, fictional characters in great literature present differing versions of reality and alternative responses to life. Classic and often-read works are our cultural literacy. All are not reliable; they need be sorted out as in the lives we actually live. The lesson is that we learn from both experiences and comparisons, from the good and the bad.

And as great literature shifts perspective, we see the scene from a second or third point of view, which lends psychological sophistication. It reveals how people respond emotionally. We learn how they can move us by a good word or gesture, by retelling a story, by a lie. There are multitudes of motives for how people navigate their world. Most have many reasons why they do something, and we see when and how they act according to *"the better angels of their nature,"* or the opposite.

We recognize that literature often provides moral guidance, in the questions it asks, if not always the answers it gives. We see for ourselves that people are not always good or generous, pursuing what they can gain from other people for themselves. It can provide us with the negative example that hardens a steely resolve within us to act differently.

So, reading sensitive explorations of peoples' lives puts you into another person's position and allows you to understand other points of view. It is not so different from the reasons that the classic education for Europeans of prior centuries included *Plutarch's Lives of the Noble Greeks and Romans*: *"to recognize their mistakes, to have some of their character rub off"* on the reader and become their own. As Plutarch asked, *"Whom shall I set so great a man to face? Or whom oppose? Whose equal to the place?"* He gave us Alexander and Caesar, Cicero and Demosthenes, and many dozens of such *"noble lives."* A collection *"not of histories but lives,"* the thoughts and experience of such great men have been central to the Western canon, which in turn reflects recognized values, of which the most widely embraced has been termed *"the golden rule"* of mutuality, the biblical maxim to *"do unto others what you would have them do unto you."*

Taking the discussion of values to a more nuanced level, it has been said and I agree, that the object of life is not to be on the side of the majority but to find our own way, yet to escape finding oneself in the ranks of the insane. Our sources include the writings of many others, and we celebrate differences among all the choices the world offers. Yet these differences may be vast. Ralph Waldo Emerson wrote in the first half of the nineteenth century and Frederick Nietzsche fifty years later; both faced their issues in the different cultures of early America and late nineteenth-century Germany. In *Twilight of the Gods,* Nietzsche stressed that it is you who are responsible for the expedition of your life, as did Ralph Waldo Emerson very differently in *Nature,* and *Self-Reliance.* Both authors suggest that you need to search for your own voice; they would say listening for greatness, and both are well worth reading closely. But let me foreshadow what is to come with a clue for you at this time. The self-affirmation of Emerson, not the alienation and subsequent madness of Nietzsche, is the successful choice.

And Then?

Well, life has moved along swiftly for our two student protagonists. She writes "The Threat," a story of the journey to the United States, a passage faced by all our immigrant ancestors with the courage, heartache, joy, successes, and failures required of the journey. The central character in this iteration of this universal story is Francesca, a contemporary young woman, who travels from Central America with her young son through the desert and finds a life cleaning homes in Locust Valley on Long Island. Life is good, but she has a plan and sends her wages home to her husband and other young son. A few years later, she returns to her native home to find her husband and a new woman have spent all the money. Francesca makes a second bet on a better future and another trip though the desert with both sons. There were perilous moments as "coyotes" guided her for cash as she again enters the States and makes her way back to Long Island. She eventually gets a green card, gaining the ability to stay as a legal resident of the United States, to own her home, with two grown American boys, and to a secure the rights of residency. Her spirit has brightened the lives of those with whom she comes in contact, and years later she attends a wedding in the author's family.

Why do I tell you this story? Is it true? It can be, if we are not too precise about relations and generations. Our focus is upon rejecting temptations to accept life as it is and withdraw into community, tribe, or nuclear family. Ultimately, it is about us learning that we have choices to shape our experiences and create new significance. If we fail to listen to these voices, what are our chances of achieving anything? As boys at play, Finnan and Cormac, you invented new worlds. You were very good at that, imagining and accepting all kinds of things with new places to play, which habit can now serve you well to better plot and correct life, to fill dreams. Knowing that the world will let you sit there doing nothing should be inspiration enough to go see the new, and to grow. Progress depends upon this doing, and success requires belief in self. I hope you will learn from this never-ending tale of immigrant striving.

But I also want to emphasize once again that in literature and in life, ambiguity is never far away. Thousands and thousands of immigrant children have fled across our southern border. The United States cannot possibly allow all the millions and millions and millions of people who dream of coming here to do so. Yet children of unlawful immigrants grow up here in the only country they have ever known. If they had the good fortune to be born here, they are already American citizens under the United States Constitution. For some of them and for their parents and older siblings, it is nerve-racking living in the shadows. Our political leaders need to find a way to cooperate to address this dilemma. So far they have not yet found the will; but it is their job, and if they do not, shame upon them.

So, what happens next to our students? One thought leads to another, and they then seize upon jointly writing a slightly more contemporary version of a celestial accounting than Galileo's moons. They next write <u>The Judgment of Jefferson,</u> a novel and then a play about one day, July 4, 1826, the day that Thomas Jefferson and John Adams both died, exactly fifty years to the day after the Declaration of Independence. As he approaches paradise, John Adams learns that he is to try one more case for the defense. Earlier in the day, Thomas Jefferson had moved from detached amusement to melancholy realization concerning his recent rejection at the gates of St. Peter and is appealing what he sees as a bureaucratic mess. He has chosen Adams as the best possible person to explain his case to God.

Adams begins at once. He outlines the heroic task of the American Revolutionaries and their vital contribution in taking the ideals of the Enlightenment forward to organizing the new political world, including the momentous words of the American *Declaration of Independence* written by the defendant. Adams speaks of the other majestic words of Jefferson such as *"No man is born to ride the backs of others"*, and addressing slavery notes that Jefferson admitted, *"I tremble for my country when I reflect that God is just."* Conceding that Jefferson did not fully live up to all the revolution's ideals of a just humanity, Adams concludes that while it is desirable to achieve everything you should, in measuring a life it is critical to do enough, with all our human frailties, to achieve what you can and make a difference, and this Jefferson has nobly done. There was great anxiety among the heavenly spectators about the weight of slavery on the record of the great man, who even when faced with death freed only those slaves who were his own children by his enslaved mistress. Then judgment was rendered by the tribunal: defendant, Thomas Jefferson, the third President of the United States, and John Adams, his attorney, the second President of the United States, are both found guilty and damned as heretics.

It is Jefferson who files another appeal, at once, to the highest authority, exclaiming that tolerance of our faults, not vengeance, has been the higher ideal the divinity has given to our civilizations from Hittite, Mesopotamian, Babylonian, Assyrian, Egyptian, Persian, Greek, Roman, Jew, Christian, Catholic, Protestant, Muslim, Buddhist, Hindu and on and on. It is an understatement to say that is not totally true, but in a better world will be. The decision of the Lord was reserved for another day.

CHAPTER 6

Post-Graduate Education

"Hello, darkness, my old friend, I've come to talk with you again."

— Paul Simon, *"The Sound of Silence"*

Well, my grandsons, while we are trying to take account of the wide world, obvious and brief suggestions creep in about some somber perspectives on life, the depressing as well as the uplifting.

"Slumber sleep, my fairest baby, slumber calmly, sleep...

I will tell to thee a story, pure as dewdrop glow"

— Mikhail Lermontov,
Cradle Song of the Cossack Mother

"Margaret, are you grieving, over Goldengrove unleaving? ...

> *Ah! As the heart grows older, it will come to such*
> *sights colder."*

— Gerald Manley Hopkins, *Spring and Fall*

Remember back to when you were young and your Grandmother and I invited you both to spend the night with us in the big bed in the back bedroom. It was early fall in the Adirondacks. We awoke in the early dark as you both looked with wide eyes, confused emotions, scared but excited. The snow hares had been returning to Boulderwood Way that summer. Food is a factor in the fluctuating populations of all kinds, and as night follows day, the coyotes soon returned as well. On this night a fitting series of wails floated up the hill on the brisk air signaling predator hunting prey, a central story of animal life, now as it always has been. We spoke of basic truths of existence: that at night, rabbits are hunted, and some die so that others, such as the coyotes, may live. You already knew this, having seen it with the fox and the vole. You also undoubtedly recognized instinctively a not-so-nice fact, that it is better not to be the prey.

The next night, the eerie sound told us the coyotes were back and that not all the snow shoe hares had perished. We again listened, with the realization that it was the time in your lives to grasp this dark truth about the world. None of us can avoid that the other side of life is death. My task, in the time I have left, is to share with you what I think I have learned about this in three-quarters of a century of life.

The predator–prey relationship developed over billions of years. As best as paleontologists can determine, life began as single-cell organisms in the sea, with algae following simple soft-bodied life forms evolving over hundreds of millions of years. Eventually, during the oxygen-rich period of the Cambrian explosion 65 million years ago, life became dramatically more complex. Animals began to move around more so that they could pursue their prey in a scheme of evolutionary advancement: life taken, life given. But not without struggle. The advantages of better eyesight, sense of smell, strength, and speed evolved, as did defenses such as camouflage and hard shells. Quickness in space and time mattered. The fight for comparative advantage between animals has gone on ever since, in an unforgiving evolutionary battle for survival and dominance. Humans, as animals, have been full participants in this battle, and the immense advantage of their intelligence has led them to dominate the world—and often each other. For the rest of this book, I hope you will keep in the back of your mind the questions: Will it always be so? Does it have to be so?

There is purpose in taking a long view of the journey and the struggles between birth and death and in prudently plotting our path. Yet there is a dual perspective to our model for living. Since life is lived one day at a time, it makes little sense to dwell daily upon the deterring risks of life's darker side. Said another way, embracing a desirable dream serves to move us toward larger, long-term goals. A Unitarian minister emphasized the duality of our view, setting off the present objective of noticing the roses and smelling each day's coffee with this observation: *"The fact that you, like everyone else, will someday die is currently uninteresting."*

We Wear the Mask

> *"We wear the mask that grins and lies, it hides our cheeks and shades our eyes, this debt we pay to human guile; with torn and bleeding hearts we smile."*

— Paul Laurence Dunbar,
"We Wear the Mask"

Now is a useful time to examine some of the underlying themes we have been pursuing, to consider where we have been before we move on.

While outdoors we have been creating a mental map as we look for reality in examining the natural world. We tried to remember that the first lesson is always to remember what we are trying to do. We concluded that one theme is the power of self-belief, that optimism and confidence give us motivation. We should not be afraid to appear awkward as we find our way, or to risk being wrong. For example, I think I did this in the previous chapter in speaking of dance and cosmology, of relativity and quantum physics, subjects of which I demonstrably know little. The entire search of this book began with looking for repeating patterns, structures, and relationships as the basic building blocks for lessons for life. We did this with sharp-eyed practicality yet with a poetic romanticism because life is poorer without both. Then we recognized that our expectations and habits become our stories and, collectively, our culture. So the question we ask ourselves is: What do we want our way of life to be? By aiming high and working hard, we're likely best able to answer the question.

Foundational ideas we looked at were:

- We take the reality of nature personally;
- we bridge the gap between instinct and logic;
- we define our identities by the stories we tell ourselves (often about ourselves);
- we become what we think we ought to be;
- we have to throw away old thoughts and habits that no longer help us;
- we need not just accumulate facts and feelings but fuse them together in new ways;
- we look for differences that provide opportunities;
- the imagination and ambiguity found in poetry and elsewhere give us a powerful way to see variations, to question the certitude of assumptions, to glimpse the soul; and
- evolution gives us a model for understanding life and thought.

We will be tackling this last concept of the evolving nature of life and thought as we go forward.

"Imagination is the beginning of creation. You imagine what you desire, you will what you imagine, and at last you create what you will".

— George Bernard Shaw

Society has never seen its task as doing our job for us. What we must do is find the story we want our lives to be even as we are telling the central features of that story, not so much just to comprehend but also to apprehend newness and incorporate it in our lives. In the space between chaos and stagnation, we find something to show for life on earth. For many of us, cooperation in guiding a baby from potential to fulfilling life can be a large part of this story; but I am suggesting more when I say an active, rewarding life.

For now, we have been talking much about imagining. What is this all about anyway? Let's look at some examples. *"Tus was"* is German for *"become someone."* This was the advice the mother of Marlene Dietrich gave her young daughter early in the twentieth century. As a biographer of the actress explained, Dietrich tenaciously imagined herself into the enigmatic, sexy, independent entertainer and movie star she became and who settled in America where she was outspoken against the rise of the Nazis in Germany in the 1930s. She had quite a vision, and she fulfilled it.

It takes more than just imagination to succeed—also determination, and more. It is more than just a desire to achieve regular successes but also a stubborn insistence in going on and eventually achieving a higher goal. The goal itself is up to you, but let it be an interest with passion, akin to what one-time dean of New York University School of Law, Arthur Vanderbilt, a former judge, *called "a fire in the belly."*

In recent times in our culture, the phrase *"reinvent yourself"* has often been used for imagining new possibilities for our lives. This powerful concept is highlighted by Richard Reeves in President Reagan: *The Triumph of Imagination*. The author, a declared liberal, clearly liked the conservative President and saw him as a man of decency with an optimistic sense, who looked at life and the Presidency as what he wanted it to be. My grandchildren, I saw these same qualities when I met the former President. I picked up the then Governor Reagan at O'Hare Airport in January 1976, shortly after he had narrowly lost the Republican Presidential nomination. He was speaking to our client at the Chicago Ambassador West Hotel that very cold evening, and I had the opportunity of spending time with him, and I still have our photo taken together. To this day, I consider his policies wrong in overemphasizing reliance on one's own resources to get ahead: this policy left out those who never had adequate resources, including sufficient ability to muster the necessary motivation to get to the starting line. Yet there is no doubt that this President's vision held attraction and power. He dreamt big, had captivating ideas, was not concerned about laborious details, and pressed for what he wanted, thereby far exceeding the expectations of his critics. Many conservatives consider this man a political saint. While I do not agree with many of his conclusions and solutions, I do agree, my grandchildren, with Mr. Reeves's opinion of the man in that I liked him, his easy-going manner, and his optimism.

Despite strong conservative convictions, which were persuasive because of how strongly he believed them, Reagan had a willingness to compromise rather than treat politics as religious dogma. And those he disagreed with were not his enemies. Another description of a different President by former New York Governor Mario Cuomo is equally fitting: when Cuomo nominated Bill Clinton for President at the

Democratic National Convention in 1992, he described Clinton as *"someone smart enough to know, strong enough to do, and sure enough to lead."* I might add to this, with all his considerable faults *"likeable enough to get elected."* By the way, your Grandmother and I went to President Clinton's inauguration in Washington, D.C. in January 1993, and to the New York and Tennessee Balls that evening. I know you will notice that I am beginning to "drop" names, facts, and events, but you are our grandchildren and these are family stories I want you to know.

Now, let's move the conversation back directly to you. When you arrive at University, you find it a place and time to challenge the conventions that we and others assume about the world, and the way it is. This is the time of life when you can seriously pursue studies at a place with ample resources to do it well, at a pace that allows you to laugh as you learn. Our story of the University serves another purpose. It is meant as a strong reminder to be aware that a thought, a sentence, can start a whole story flowing, with all sorts of possibilities. Only some will prove fruitful, but it is not likely you will know which unless you engage them. You might also remember the paradox that while pursuing these divergences is not a waste of time, time is finite. Soon enough, you will have to decide among many potential choices. Soon enough, you will need to abandon those paths that do not lead where you want to go. The time has also come to understand that in this world we live in the present moment, and we need to play the bad hands we have as well as to learn to make the most of the good hands we are dealt. Let's say that another way. There is almost no perfect time so you take what you have and work with it to achieve what you can. Success is so often achieved by making the most of the opportunities that the crisis of living bring with them, but great success comes from exploiting the opportunities to their maximum. We begin by chasing opportunities, often found in fleeting images of the mind, or symbols embedded in what we study.

> *"In foreign land with faith unshaken, I kept my country's ancient rite;*
>
> *The captive bird from cage forsaken I loose when dawn's spring festal light.*
>
> *I feel the breath of consolation: 'Gainst God why should I murmur now?*
>
> *At last on life in all creation, I could with freedom's gift endow."*
>
> – Alexander Pushkin, *A Little Bird*

Metaphors and analogies can be found everywhere, on campus and off. A birdcage could be a symbol of nightclub follies in Paris or South Miami Beach. The release of a bird from its cage for the great Russian poet Alexander Pushkin was a symbol of freedom inspiring a fight against oppression. Beethoven or the Beatles, Dvorak or Dylan, inspiration can be found in any genre when thought and effort accompany talent. Indeed, in a fascinating talk about his songwriting process, Bob Dylan recently said, *"They didn't get here by themselves... It's been a long road, and it's taken a lot of doing. These songs of mine they're like mystery stories, the kind that Shakespeare saw when he was growing up. They were on the fringes then, and I think they are on the fringes now."* This reference to William Shakespeare is particularly apt, I think, because of the Bard's ability to capture and incorporate into his plays apparently every thought, fact, and personal and historic event he came across.

Let's take *Romeo and Juliet* as one small example. The story was an existing Italian tale, but the play's magical, transformative language and psychological portrayal of the tragic and romantic archetypal young lovers is all Shakespeare's genius.

So anything can be a possible source of inspiration, prompting new ideas and ways of seeing things—and it can be catching, which is a good reason to be conscious of with whom we choose to spend our time.

From Literature to Politics

Meanwhile, our students continued to pursue their studies. There is a time for studying the Ancients, for they give us lessons for our time as well as theirs. At other times, more can be learned in the present. Our young scholars have noticed that a long-standing theme of Russian poets, for example, is the implications of small actions, that individual acts can bring more than self-respect; the actions of a few sometimes changes our collective future.

Our students have now begun to focus their study. Their courses begin to center on political dissent, on resistance and rebellions through the ages, some of which have been brutally put down while others successfully changed the status quo. It was a story of revolt throughout the ages. The second book of *the Old Testament* tells of Moses leading his people out of Egypt to the Promised Land, at a historical time not too long before the Greek city states, also bordering the Mediterranean Sea, invaded Troy.

What can we learn from the numerous and disparate instances of dissent against oppression, besides the obvious point that sometimes uprisings succeed and sometimes they did not? Well, one point is just that, some revolutions do succeed and sometimes they alternatively lead to incremental change. Aiming for Mars may only get you to the moon but that is still an extraordinary accomplishment.

Beyond the grand goal, history has demonstrated that once an objective is reached, to achieve peace thereafter, stability and order must be established in the wake of chaos of conflict. The stability that men and women need might come from an alliance between the ancient Greek city states, for example, or a coalition among the military leaders that eventually led to a *"Pax Romana"* across the Roman Empire. Peace could also come from cohesion provided by acceptance of a unifying religion, as Christianity did to the new kingdoms of the first millennia A.D.. Order might also be imposed by a treaty, such as in 1648 with *the Treaty of Westphalia*, which established sovereign geographic boundaries of new nations, and ended decades of religious wars. It might be a principle of a balance of power between alliances of nations, proclaimed at the Congress of Vienna in 1815 by Austrian Prince Metternich after the defeat of Napoleon. Another attempt at crafting a balance of power by a League of Nations created by *the Treaty of Versailles* after World War I did not prove successful in ensuring "peace for our time," but it did provide the model for the subsequent United Nations established after World War II. The UN's existence did not end conflict, wars, genocide, or resource extraction but it has provided a framework for many more limited successes, which it would seem foolhardy to throw away.

Such institutions can provide stability which lessens upheaval and makes incremental change more possible. There will often be internal conflicts where a prevailing class uses the power they have taken, or kept, to control a disproportionate share of resources. Nevertheless, the arrow of history seems to point in the direction of ultimate cultural progress toward more peace, as societies evolve toward greater opportunity, freedom, and justice. We Americans view our Revolution as a culmination in history, yet we obviously are still evolving toward "a more perfect union," a form of government to which we suggest all others should aspire as an ideal, and a possible antidote to more easy wars between peoples and nations. These are noble words and ideals, but how are they more fully realized?

Studying Dissent in Modern Times

Well, Finnan and Cormac, events can be Googled or further researched whenever individual facts seem sufficiently interesting. Yet "*history*" does not have all the answers that can just be looked up. It is said that studying a subject in depth serves the purpose of teaching you how to study any subject.

What is important is to understand how to explore a topic seriously, to its core.

This seems a good time to insert mention that *"great men"* often seem clairvoyant after they have seized upon a great idea or achievement but not before. A wonderful example is Isaac Newton who spent his life pursuing three different themes, physics, alchemy and religion. His study of physics through the principles of mathematics, the optics of light and the laws of motion gave us a brilliant foundation for modern science. His pursuit of the other two subjects did not. So we pursue seemingly important ideas with big payoffs not really knowing which will provide the brilliant insight. Persistent pursuit on a path of thought or action sometimes proves the decision brilliant, but only after a long series of events that are fortuitous.

We have been moving back and forth with the particular subject of dissent and revolt and we are now going to spend what may seem an inordinate amount of attention on this reappearing issue of dissent. Our effort is meant to demonstrate the value of long-term pursuit of one subject, to see how you go about trying to get close to the impossible goal of fully understanding the matter. We do this by circling around the subject again and again, each time with a differing and hopefully clearer vision. Dissent and political opposition seems an interesting example of staying with one subject and viewing it through many lenses, so we will go on with the subject.

As we do so we seek coherent themes and great effort finding the process that is of greater import than just facts. To get a sense of how this enduring effort works we might consider Walter Isaacson's observation that Leonardo Da Vinci spent sixteen years working on the smile of *the Mona Lisa*. He describes Leonardo's painting of the lips as an incomparable intertwining of motion and emotion. As you walk across the room at the Louvre you see her from differing angles and the lines of her mouth smile back at us in differing ways.

Such a deep dive into a topic provides the opportunity to be sufficiently informed to be able to measure interactions between the parts, which allows us to construct a model that best exposes what happens, how and why, and what we should do about it.

Back to the University

Let us imagine that our students at the University are now mulling the Russian poetic praise of rebellion. Their professor had recently written a textbook tracing the chronology of citizen revolts of the past half-century, which led to a discussion of their comparative contemporary European and Middle Eastern history classes.

The Squares

I still have memories while in high school of the spontaneous Hungarian uprising against the Soviet Union in Budapest in 1956, which led to the Soviets' disastrous suppression of the revolt. Protests of the Prague Spring in Czechoslovakia in 1968 led to similar results, as Communist tanks once again rolled into city squares.

Yet later, in the 1980s, growing opposition to Soviet rule in the Eastern European Communist States finally led to the collapse of the Soviet Union. It was not sudden, but it was dramatic. Soviet satellite countries had long been ruled by ruthless leaders who controlled all aspects of political, social, and economic life through the Communist Party. Yet the party was dependent upon the support of the masses of workers for legitimacy and fiercely silenced oppositional voices and eliminated negative publicity. Across the Eastern bloc, this decade saw resistance against harsh Soviet central rule, which met with some success when a critical mass of demonstrators existed. Then, as the people achieved some little freedoms, they demanded more.

Solidarity, the only non-Communist Party trade union in the Soviet Empire, was formed at the Gdansk Shipyard in Poland in 1980. One year later, it represented one-third of all the workers in Poland. With substantial public praise and private support from an influential native Pole, Pope John Paul II, it had early success in loosening the authoritarian grip of the Communist regime. The consequences of subsequent revolts in the 1980s among the East European countries in the Soviet bloc culminated in 1989 with a successive wave of countries overthrowing the Communist Party and the USSR. It began with elections in Poland in the summer of 1989 and continued with protests in Hungary, East Germany, Bulgaria, Romania, and Czechoslovakia with its *Velvet* (*"Gentle"*) Revolution. The subsequent fall of Soviet Communism in Russia itself came two years later, in 1991.

How did that happen? It is said that *"success has many fathers."* In each of these countries, the story was similar:

a few dissenters with a plan, eventually leading to massive protests by hundreds of thousands. Some people were still being arrested and shot as the states crumbled, but ultimately governments fell. The case of East German offers a wonderful window onto this story of progress toward freedom.

Germany and Berlin had been split into regional sectors by the victorious Allies after WWII. Fifteen years later, at about the same time that I was graduating from college, the crippled economy in the Soviet zone led the East German Communist government to build a wall to keep its citizens from leaving. In 1961 President John F. Kennedy stood before the Brandenburg Gate and gave his now famous *"Ich bin ein Berliner"* speech, in which he stated that the United States and the West never had to build a wall to keep people in. In 1987 President Ronald Reagan famously gave a speech in that same place in Berlin, concluding with an exhortation to the president of the Soviet Union: *"Mr. Gorbachev, tear down this wall!"* But these were not the words that brought down the Wall. In *The Collapse:* The Accidental Opening of the Berlin Wall, the author Mary Elise Sarotte tells the mostly happy and fascinating tale of a dull television press announcement on November 9, 1989 announcing a new law would permit East Germans to travel more freely, which the spokesperson read was to *"immediately go into effect."* After the news was reported by the West German media, dozens and then hundreds and then thousands and finally a half-million people came to the East Berlin Wall. As night became morning, the insistent pressure of increasing numbers at the Wall could not be stopped, and the guards let the masses cross to the other side of Berlin.

In fact, the East German government had not intended to relinquish control of travel in and out of the country. They could never survive if people were free to do what they pleased and had planned to carefully control visas and passport applications to limit travel. But their clumsy statement, attempting to convey the promise of more liberty than was actually permitted by the new law, and a phrase on the TV news that was taken out of context gave viewers throughout the country and the world the mistaken impression that the Wall was now open. Following government confusion, contradiction, ineptness, and inaction, the crowd in Berlin got out. Then across the country, people crossed into West Germany, resulting in the loss of all government control. Newly available evidence, which the author of The Collapse drew on in writing the book, makes clear the accidental nature of the opening of the Wall. It also reveals that about a few dozen provincial East German dissenters made a major contribution to the immediate events that gave us the birth of modern unified Germany.

It has been cynically, but more or less accurately, said that *"power comes out of the barrel of a gun."* Yet public exposure can sometimes be equally effective. In Leipzig, East Germany, months before the collapse of the Wall, a handful of young students, workers, and clergy arranged prayer marches at churches in the central city. Finding a platform to stage a public outcry made the difference. These marches were widely publicized, growing to 100,000 marchers, demonstrating the sheer power of mass protest, and foreshadowing the end that was soon to come. There were widely publicized appeals for nonviolence by the marchers, both in Leipzig and then across almost all the Soviet controlled countries.

The peaceful nature of the protests proved crucial to preventing a response of corresponding violence by the state. It wasn't that the cold-blooded East German Communist Party leaders feared looking hypocritical, they were inevitably used to it. But if thrown into the spotlight, they risked criticism from the majority of the country. This made brutal crackdown unfeasible in the eyes of the bureaucrats. So, the key tactics of the reformists were nonviolence and public exposure. Crucially, protests were launched in venues where public meetings could not be easily be prohibited. Prayer marches from churches and rock concerts fit the social context of the place and time, providing settings where dissenters could gather in groups.

It was a story that began with a remarkable determined few with a plan. It grew to a half-million marching to the Wall who could not then be kept from going into the West. The same result followed throughout the affiliated European socialist republics as the year ended. The public watched the protests grow from marginal to massive, and in a blink, it was over for the calcified Communist regimes.

Two years later, the Soviet Empire ended with the resignation of Mikhail Gorbachev in 1991. This was six years after Gorbachev had become head of the Soviet Politburo in the middle of a decade of political turmoil and economic decline of the USSR. Gorbachev had instituted the reforms of *glasnost* (openness) and *perestroika* (restructuring) to try to save the Soviet system; they were real reforms, but they proved too limited for the raised expectations of those who had a taste of freedom throughout the Soviet Empire.

Finnan and Cormac, a month after the fall of the Berlin Wall, I was in Budapest with your father, and your Uncle Brendan, fulfilling my long-standing wish to celebrate New Year's Eve in Budapest. The anticipation of a historic freedom could be sensed in the people in the streets. We can tell you personally of the exhilaration of the many people we met at three parties that evening, and of the college and high school students, about Brendan's and Darrin's ages, who were celebrating New Year's Eve, dancing, singing, and drinking bottles of wine around bonfires, all night long, on and along the bridges over the Danube between Buda and Pest. It was wonderful.

Months before the uprisings in Eastern Europe in that summer of 1989, a revolt of students and other dissenters had broken out on the other side of the world, in Tiananmen Square in Beijing. But power still revolves at the top in China, and as has been previously noted, ultimately comes out of the barrel of a gun (as stated by Mao). A decision was made, the dissent was crushed by the tanks of the Chinese army. Condemnation by the West and television exposure of its brutality added to the outcry in Eastern Europe that fall. Yet discussion or even mention of the events in Tiananmen Square is suppressed to this day in China, a quarter-century later.

I had been in Tiananmen Square two years earlier and never would have guessed that this could happen. It seemed China had passed a political and psychological benchmark by this time, and free market reform was clearly the future as well as the purpose of our lawyer delegation's visit. But there had been some evidence of recalcitrance, even schizophrenia, in the demonstrable public attitude of the Chinese lawyers and bureaucrats at *the First Economics and Law Conference* in 1987. In the daily meetings at the Great Hall of the People at the Square, the Chinese delegation wore Western-style suits and ties one day. When there were stories in the next day's English-language newspaper about the hasty slide from socialist ideals, there was a dramatic change the following morning in the attire of many of our host delegates; they conspicuously wore Mao-style jackets, without collar or tie. Nevertheless, in the summer of 1989, the crackdown on the dissidents was inexplicable, also inexcusable in our minds. Trying to understand the rash brutality of the tanks in Tiananmen Square, you began to fathom that the Chinese Communist Party was ready for economic, but certainly not real political, reform. With their long history without democratic institutions, one felt that *"East is East and West is West, and never the twain shall meet."* At least not yet.

Two decades later, in 2011, the uprising of students and workers in Tahrir Square in Egypt seemed a seminal moment of the Arab Spring, which had begun a short time earlier in Tunisia in what was called *"the Jasmine Revolution"* of 2011. It was said that the students in these countries had been using a blueprint for peaceful political defiance found on the Internet: *From Dictatorship to Democracy: A Conceptual Framework For Liberation,* written a decade earlier by Gene Sharp of the Albert Einstein Institution in the US. This manuscript distilled its essence in a quote from Charles Stewart Parnell during the Irish Rent Strike against the British in 1879: *"When you have made the question ripe for settlement then, and not till then, will it be settled."* What this means, of course, is that when enough people publicly share ideas with the gravity required, then the environment will be ripe for change.

This intensity of the people in these uprisings in the Middle East was captured in a scene in a documentary our two students watch. In one scene, an elderly Egyptian standing in the street in Cairo exclaims to security police: *"Better you take me than my children and their children, then my grandchildren's children."*

In 2013 the scene of world dissent shifted as Ukrainian demonstrations arose in Independence Square in Kiev; a voice was heard on the TV news: *"It is hard to make a movie when the director is always being arrested."* These protests in Kiev were really a follow-up to *the Orange Revolution of 2004*, which had led to the ouster of an incompetent and corrupt leader, only for the country to hear many hollow promises followed by more of the same from incompetent or shady politicians. There were Russian entanglements again in 2014, and a takeover of the Crimea in the southwest as Russians in the Baltic city and Ukrainians began to divide. This seems a never ending story, which continues as I finish your book. On and on, this theme of protest, sometimes successful but often not, continues, a reminder of the human inclination to resist suppression. These scenes of uprising seemed a promising premise to try to explain movements of people and protest through time.

What if you were going to university at this time? Let us now imagine that our two students have decided to go beyond studying the past and to pursue the current escalating uprisings, so prevalent in the Middle East at this time. In effect it is writing a term paper about real and serious events as they happen, trying to find solutions for a very messy situation as it develops, not being afraid to seek answers that even the leaders of the world are finding elusive at the moment. Call it an A for audacity. And why not?

Our protagonists speak to other students in their history class and soon have a discussion group they call "*The Squares*", which they form to take on this big theme. One thing swiftly leads to another as their professor joins the group and soon an informal group becomes a seminar. The scholarly blueprint on the Internet, From Dictatorship, advised how to conduct peaceful sudden protests designed to slow or avoid government crackdown, and its plan had been widely adopted by the Egyptian students and others in their initially successful protests leading to the overthrow of the longstanding, dictatorial Mubarak regime. This map of possibility leads The Squares seminar to study the methods that have, and have not, been working for current revolutionaries. Recent protests had been a repeated cycle of: public protest by thousands of people; then attempts at greater government control; followed by new censorship, spying, and repression; then further protests by more disgruntled demonstrators of democrats, workers, true believers and other dissidents. Sometimes there was some success, sometimes not.

Our students notice that ultimately, a successful uprising always relied on more than a few people, which meant that widespread publicity proved crucial. Occasionally the former leaders attempted escape from the country. Other times a threatened government conducted arrests and show trials, amid fears and new violence. The daily question was how the revolt might succeed among the opposition, propaganda, competing elites and interests, armies, and conflict. Those in the seminar found that anything could happen after a crisis develops. The old regime may survive for a while disguised under new leadership but then come to a head; and the change can be incredibly swift and brutal. In 1917 three hundred years of rule by the Romanov czars in Russia vanished in just three days. In August 1991 three-quarters of a century of Soviet rule ended in a tense, comparable amount of time in the streets of Moscow.

The consuming question for our students becomes: What happened to the activists' efforts and why?

The Middle East, unfortunately, provides neve-rending study as they focus upon ambiguity between the assumptions of those proposing change and what actually was actually done and happened. In a word, a lot of lying was going on. The Arab Spring had initial successes but more conspicuous failures. After Mubarak, the Muslim Brotherhood was the most organized of the protesters and easily won elections, but at threats of increasing restrictions and hints of the usurpation of all government power by religious groups and imposition of Sharia law, there were more protests. The Egyptian Army seized control, and democracy quickly deteriorated. Politically limited government with *"power in the people"* was more a foreign than locally grown idea and could quickly feel stale. An Egyptian army general exchanged his uniform for a business suit and assumed power as "president." Dissidents were arrested, the option of moderation was ignored, and elections were delayed at the risk of infuriating millions of dissenters.

It was difficult for the students to remain optimistic as the Arab Spring quickly chilled. There had not been a prior culture of collaboration. Rather there was an underlying long history of war in the Middle East between the two branches of Islam, Sunni and Shia. This produced a violent rupture when geographic boundaries that had been imposed by the colonial powers a century earlier were no longer enforced by a controlling government. Without an imposed order, violence accelerated and became alarmingly worse in many places. There were new, continuing armed conflicts between factions in Libya, Iraq, and Syria, then the rise of radical Islamist militants of ISIS spreading throughout the region to Yemen and beyond to who knew where or when next? All that seemed left of the Arab uprising was the hope that something could be done again to renew this brief glimpse at democracy, or at least civil peace.

How could it be put back together? What was going wrong? The study of history suggests that convulsions of civilization do not just appear, they happen first in peoples' minds. As elsewhere, the discontented and energetic young are often the catalyst, the vanguard of change. But what was also at play were minorities who are majorities in regions with boundaries that extend and advance, retreat and change. The Holy Land and neighboring region has a long, long history of conflict, so often intertwined with imposed religious beliefs. Merely asserting a claim to the right for democracy in the twenty-first century would not, by itself, prove enough for the people in power to share it. Power, belief, and money are not easily given up. Nor was religious freedom easily shared especially where arbitrary national boundaries had been imposed by European colonial powers in the early days of the twentieth century and remained a hindrance to overcoming fear and an acceptance of the other groups necessary to share freedom in one land. The misinformed, the demagogues, and the intimidators among a mob of protesters accelerated tendencies for all to fly apart. Mixed with this were the expectations of the young, angry at being denied the opportunities they saw at their universities and on the Internet daily. Unequal distribution of resources that excluded the young from what they valued most had been a primary reason for the uprisings and provided continuing hope for the future. Yet escalating tensions among the populace did not inevitably lead to a sharing of prosperity among those who took control. Every faction believed itself to have exceptional status, which did not promote democratic behavior of the victors, or prevent them from acting in ways that they would have viewed as unacceptable by "*the others*." It was a laboratory, presented with ever-new experiments in places with too many differences, too many pockets of religious intolerance, even the rejection of modernity itself by some self-proclaimed righteous but very violent people. With brutality regularly on display, the university students unfortunately never run out of places and peoples to study.

During these turbulent times the Study Group meets weekly to deliberate the questions, divide up the research, and collaborate on drafting working memos for class. The next month, the study group critiques where they seem right or wrong and consider what leverage is now available to the people they are studying as the next phase for their proposed plan of action. The students had first adopted Gene Sharp's premise that for a non-violent solution to be successful, it was critical for dissident groups to strengthen determination to press on early, while simultaneously adopting a long term plan based on nonviolent methods. As they explored the consequences of alternatives, they come to understand that a strategic approach must rest upon some form of eventual stability. The lessons they have learned from history have shown again and again that this is not a trivial point since any vacuum of power or questioned legitimacy could be exploited. If a way could be found to overcome everyone's differences and to serve everyone's perceived needs then there might be an acceptance of peace. At the beginning what mattered was not a mere possibility of change but the stubborn decision of some to take the risks that were necessary to create an open society and the steps available to avoid fracturing.

Yet, when an old regime collapses, it is the reality that infighting is far more likely than not. After Czar Nicholas I was deposed in 1917, the new democratic government lasted but a short time before the competing Bolshevik takeover of Russia. The truce between Nationalists and Communists in China did not last beyond the defeat of the Japanese in WWII. Following the week-long war against Saddam Hussein in Iraq in 2003, the Shia and Sunni Muslims never seemed able to share resources or power in any way other than for temporary convenience.

The students know that they need to ask what the actors were trying to do, to glimpse their reality, to identify what reciprocity might provide a diplomatic solution. This is the lesson of game theory, that a "tit for tat" approach can be a long-term winning strategy. A cynical view of real politics holds that three methods—logic, bribes, and threats—and that twisting laws and regulations and spying are part of this game. But we can also directly look at a different approach, a more narrowly held view: *"Could the world of tomorrow be one of negotiation not missiles?"* as former Iranian President Ayatollah Rafsanjani had asked.

A series of barbaric, retaliatory acts might not be in the best long-term interests of all the actors. Indeed Mahatma Gandhi, Nelson Mandela, and Martin Luther King, Jr. showed that the opposite goal of reconciliation, focusing upon rectifying injustice, could be successful for an oppressed minority, if supported by the cultural values and underpinnings (such as universal justice) held by a majority of the society.

The students pursued the question of whether the actors in this drama in the Middle East are nationalists and patriots? Did their culture suggest some hope for peaceful democratic elections? Had they planned for the many small steps along the path to achieving the mutual benefits of cooperation? Was that even possible, or were they involved in an intractable and irreconcilable conflict? In the Middle East more often it seemed just that *"heretics have no rights."* There are times when chaos reigns and only force matters. ISIS proved it here.

Equilibrium can be central to the success of democracy and seems to require recognizing the rights and demands of the people and the unacceptability of the naked display of power by a superior force. Geography and prior history matter a great deal since if you can be easily crushed because of exposure, or you have a history or prior passivity of the people then chances become slim. One of the more sophisticated lessons of the end game was seen in the experience of South African Nelson Mandela in the early 1990s. After the conflict had apparently come to and end in South Africa, former enemies were forced to work together as new leaders chose reconciliation as the path forward, rejecting retribution, "*an eye for an eye*," which would make for "a nation of the blind," as Martin Luther King, Jr. put it. The choice was not ignoring resentment and fear but rather promoting a reconciliation process. Unless the acceptance of the population was resolved in some way, the victims of Apartheid could not get beyond the fear that the butchery might return while those who had been in control feared that the victims might enact revenge and thus prompt a return of violence.

But let's put aside the question of finding peace after war and get back to the issue of breaking from the status quo at all. The fact is that it takes enough people to recognize and accept the political possibility of radical change. Networks of small groups begin to see and live within the context of subcultures, to do what is necessary to bring to the surface frustrations of the people in order to motivate sufficient numbers to take risks necessary to take power from the existing government. What is particularly interesting is that this radicalization process ordinarily comes by degrees. Pushing forward too fast against dictatorial power runs greater risk of provoking brutal response and bloodshed. The overall reality is that all sides need to calculate the risk, and it is fruitful to contemplate the disadvantages that can come from pushing too far, too fast. The East German story is a superb example of how it can begin. But also promoting some cohesion among the people seems necessary for it to ultimately work. It is presently an ongoing story.

The time comes when our students' Squares seminar must be brought to an end. Continuing historical awareness and religious and cultural understanding have been critical to an analysis within the context of economics as well as politics. But things were even more complicated than just that. To achieve an end game within the framework, there were other pieces to the puzzles that needed to be addressed. The students have come to recognize that solutions would take more than projecting their current understanding and feelings onto the goals of many disparate players. Some of the Middle East participants may have heroic vision, but many, maybe most, are alienated and dysfunctional, others marginalized, and some just wanting to be left alone. So the students decided to consult the experts, that is, to survey the scholarly literature and current periodicals. What they find emphasizes that context matters, a great deal.

In this way they find a counterintuitive concept. In the push and pull of political decisions, eventually all states must look after their own citizens' interests, as their leaders find this necessary for their own best interests. Many Middle Eastern countries that experienced recent turmoil nevertheless seemed resilient. Conversely many countries with longer periods of a calm façade created by a tight control over its people and economy by an authoritarian regime might just conceal deep structural vulnerabilities. Stern centralized decision making in the Libya of Gaddafi and in the Ba'athist countries of Saddam Hussein's Iraq and Assad's Syria were comparable to the rigid Soviet Union. In the Middle East, dominance had been used to suppress tension, sectarian as well as religious. The lack of diversity heightened the fragility of these countries. The psychological reality is that when a lid is put on debate, grievances fester. These nations become subject to threat from the political right or left. A rightist coup is far more likely when political and economic control can be taken from a centralized government than when decisions are being made throughout wide geographic and economic sectors of a people. When economic and local decision-making has been dispersed, then the people will have been primed to resent political control that leads to favoritism, corruption, and inefficiencies. Privileges granted to favored entrepreneurs by the former government creates concentration, which hinders other people in naturally specializing in what they do best. There is a concomitant loss of comparative economic advantage. Aversion to risk and disorder and a lack of a history of adapting to criticism, complaint, and objection add to the fragility and to the weakness of an authoritarian centralized society. If there are large debts owed to outsiders which the State had used to curry political favor, then the foundations of a civilization can become shaky indeed. With dissatisfied masses, a seemingly stable state can find itself vulnerable to a revolutionary strike from the political left or the right, either of which can swiftly end the old police state.

Using this measure of centralized control, Egypt, Saudi Arabia, and much of the Levant in general currently may consist of fragile countries, candidates for overthrow. And when looked at from this perspective of flexibility, surprising alternatives scenes can also be seen. During a summer job as a law student, I briefly visited Lebanon and the American University in Beirut in 1964 when it was called "*the Switzerland of the Middle East.*" It seemed an oasis of peace on the Mediterranean until the subsequent intrigues and hostilities of the following decades dragged Lebanon's Muslim, Christian, and Jewish neighbors into what became a swamp of violence. The shooting goes on in Lebanon fifty years later, between Lebanese, Israelis, Hezbollah, Syrians, and Iranians. Yet the model discussed above, this analysis of fragility and the sustainability of Middle East governments by authors Taleb and Treverton in *Foreign Affairs*, suggests Lebanon may likely be a survivor. Years of civil war decentralized the state, yet it brought about a more balanced sectarian power-sharing structure. It has a free market economy with concomitant diverse commercial decision-making. Lebanon's small size, like ancient Venice or modern Singapore or Dubai, makes it more like an ancient Greek city state, easier to administer than larger nations, which can add to its durability. There is some protection for an existing state that may seem in disarray but is functioning.

But the students came to understand the critical importance of the society accepting the rule of law if there was to be sufficient trust of the people to provide the necessary stability for that civilization to function.

Change is hard in the Middle East, and there will be more uncertainty, fear, and worse before it is over. We do not know the future, but after a half-dozen years of downward trajectory, it is looking bleak at this time.

It has been suggested that flexibility seems to be a

characteristic that can save a nation, if it can extract itself from large, all-consuming circumstances such as war. To bring down a dictatorship, an immediate task is to strengthen independent social groups and institutions and their determination, self-confidence, and skills of resistance with a strategic plan. As Charles Stewart Parnell called out during the Irish rent strike campaign in 1879 and 1880:

> *"It is no use relying on the Government. . . . You must only rely upon your own determination. . . to help yourselves by standing together . . . to strengthen those amongst yourselves who are weak . . . to band yourselves together, to organize yourselves . . . and you must win . . . When you have made this question ripe for settlement, then and not till then will it be settled."*

The students' Squares study group did not know how the conflicts in the Middle East would end, but they could identify extraordinary moments and gain considerable insight. They have learned to identify their own biases and to see matters from others' perspectives. They had learned that the steps taken should be pulling in the same direction, and it is necessary to be able to explain the mission to colleagues as well as those you are trying to influence. Leadership was face-to-face, one-on-one, as well as to large public audiences with differing economic and political interests. In the long run the revolts of the Mid-East Squares.

Yet the semester and life at the University is over. In our scenario we imagine that some of the student group elect to go on to graduate study in diplomacy, a field that is not likely to become unnecessary. Whatever the study or the choice, University life must come to an end.

"The doctor alone learns".

— Frederic Nietzsche

How much imagination do we have, anyway? Does this idea of the University students participating so deeply in "the real world" sound unrealistic, my grandchildren? It seems not.

Your Dad and Uncle Brendan had a somewhat similar experience when they were both at Swarthmore College. They went further and became active players in the drama as they formed with a group of fellow college students to protest logging announced by the US government on federal land. They divided up the scientific research and federal environmental law and regulatory process and filed formal objections with the United States government. These appeals objected to what they saw as indiscriminate clear-cut logging. They continually proved so successful that the New York Times quoted a Congressman objecting on the floor of the House of Representatives to their successfully stopping the cuttings. The goal of the students was to prevent unwise logging in the national forests and to make the deliberation process a better one. As far as I could determine, this was the result. Years later, your dad gained experience with the new Federal objection process where the government now proceeds with a collaborative procedure adopted to seek the common ground that all interested parties recognize as a superior way to proceed. Actively managing adjustments rather than a post-facto appeal process to await alternatives is practical recognition of the power of cooperation.

The process of studying dissent:

We have been looking at how we can pursue a task, examining how we can push it along, step by step, toward a goal. The grand point has been to demonstrate to you an example of the educational advantage of pursuing any subject in depth.

Our recent examination has been about the dissent of many in search of independence in Eastern Europe and the Middle East. But we will not end quite yet, my grandsons. In our talks, our custom has been to swing back and forth from the particular to the broad general theme. We have just spent a great deal of time both figuratively and literally in the forest, looking in great detail at parts and sequence, seeking clues to how history might be affected by details.

You could just as easily have selected Lech Walesa and the Solidarity Union that began at the Gdansk Shipyards of Poland in 1980, and contrast him with Pope John Paul II who inspired Walesa and so immensely helped throw off Soviet oppression in Poland. It is said that the Pope wrote a secret letter to the Soviets threatening to resign the Papacy and join the Polish Resistance if Soviet tanks rolled into Poland. This is as great and noble a tale of the same general subject as can be told. Great fortitude accomplished a heroic success comparable to those of the Ancient Greeks. If you combine all these stories of post-World War II Europe and the

Mediterranean, it would be a mighty work, comparable to a great Russian novel and worthy of a doctorate thesis. But all this is a story for another day.

And as to our protagonists at this time?

> *"Have you broken trail on snowshoes, musked your huskies up the river, dared the unknown, led the way and clutched the prize?"*

— Robert Service, *"The Call of the Wild"*

Our students' years at university have been an astonishingly heady time and immense opportunity. Their lives have been shaped by what they did and remember. But, as Mark Twain once observed, twenty years from now they may also be disappointed by the things they did not do; uninformed and unformed by what they did not do, they also do not know what might have been.

However, what was once novel has started to become usual and to grow old. All things must end, and graduation is close. There is a prize to be had, and there comes a time when paths diverge. Prospects narrow as choices must be made. All cultures have a story of *"drums drag"* or doomsday coming someday, which become a conversation between our two students as they prepare to graduate. They were doing the same thing yet expecting different results and realized this was Einstein's definition of insanity. They had begun "writing songs that voices never shared" as Simon and Garfunkel had put it in "The Sound of Silence."

So bags are packed and ready to go. As the strands of

University life begin to pull apart they each went on to Portland for their new lives, propelled by their careers, one in the Northwest, in Oregon, and the other in the Northeast, in Maine. Time goes on, and so do their separate lives. What was this ending all about?

> *"What—not upbraid me,*
> *That I delayed me,*
> *Nor ask what stayed me*
> *So long? Ah no! -*
> *New cares may claim me,*
> *New loves inflame me,*
> *She will not blame me,*
> *But suffer it so".*

— Thomas Hardy

> *"Should your complexion*
> *Be less than perfection,*
> *Is it really the mirror*
> *That needs the correction?"*

— Edmund Burke

There is no blame: the styles of people and their lives change. They are young, and our protagonists now move on, as we transition once again.

But wait a minute, maybe we should lighten up. Whose life is it anyway? Maybe this is the moment and she is the one, my grandson, and maybe it is a different ending.

"Hey Jude, don't let me down,
You have found her now go and get her.
Remember to let her into your heart,
Then you can start to make it better."

– John Lennnon

PART III

A Transition

CHAPTER 7

What's It All About?

"The time has come," the Walrus said, "to talk of many things:

Of shoes — and ships — and sealing wax -- of cabbages -and kings —"

— Lewis Carroll, *Through the Looking Glass*

At about this time I hope you might begin to wonder: Why don't you speak much of the practice of law? I do commend it to you if it is what you want to do. But as I have said before, life is not compartmentalized, and much of what we have spoken of is relevant to the study and practice of law as well as life. Like everything else the question is: What are you trying to do? Then, there are related questions such as: What price are you willing to pay to do it? Where do you draw the line in living your life?

By now I am confident that you will not let me get by with mere bold assertion that the law is just life being lived so let me briefly explain. What is the law anyway? It is where we, as a community, draw the line, the rules that that society has chosen to enforce. The law seems to work best when it evolves from what we together think are fair and just relations between us citizens at large, achieved through consensus and cooperation. When the expectation of cooperation is not enough, sanctions restrain and incentives promote conduct. What behavior we should encourage or retard is question of policy, what we should want people to do to realize that aim and what programs give us that result.

As we have been saying, the law is supposed to be based upon facts that we, as a group, recognize and agree upon. So we may indeed say that knowledge is power. Driving the discussion of law is its play with the culture, that is the accepted norms of the people, shaped through the political process of governing. As said, law is at its best when it is accepted as the expectations of the people involved in seeking *"a more perfect union"* for *"life, liberty, and the pursuit of happiness,"* as our Declaration of Independence tells us. These rights, expressed in laws, protect persons, property, agreements, customary commercial transactions, and divisions of labor; and they prohibit wrongs enumerated as our collective obligation to uphold, for our mutual safety, health, and prosperity.

The rule of law, rather than the arbitrary pronouncements or prejudices of an individual or small group of leaders, is central to any free society. We cannot be free without it. Our law is based upon written federal and state constitutions and statutes and the precedent of prior judicial decisions. Political conservatives insist this should be based upon the words actually written in those documents. Political liberals insist the law must also be based upon interpreting those words by taking into account the fundamental values of our system, including external factors that shed light upon the words adopted, and prior decisions interpreting them. It is undeniably partisan to pretend only one of these approaches is sufficient to interpret and uphold the law. In the early twentieth century, United States Supreme Court Justice Oliver Wendell Holmes, Jr. argued the source of our collective rules for civilization: *"The life of the law has not been logic; it has been experience."* He also said about the Constitution: *"It is an experiment, as all life is an experiment."* What exactly did he mean? Patterns of behavior, if they prove successful are repeated enough that they become the acceptable tradition based upon the grand assumptions of what we want as our way of life. At times we must choose which basic value is paramount in the particular circumstances. Whether, for example, justice trumps liberty or the other way around. The effects of such acts of interpretation have been debated over the centuries, and the consequences are felt in each age. We will briefly look at this view of law in our later discussion of the <u>Lochner</u> case.

Supreme Court Justice Felix Frankfurter's titled his autobiography *Of Law and Life and Other Things That Matter.* I do not view the practice of law as the central essence of my, or your, being. In speaking to you in this book, I compare my effort to pointing the way to the law in a manner similar to a Wyeth painting of Jersey cows, called *Brown Swiss.* The cows themselves have been removed from the scene; only their footprints appear in the painting, which shows instead the farm. This composition is a means to an end and reminds me of my real property law professor in our first year at New

York University School of Law. This class was known to us students as *"Black Ralph's mystery hour"* because of the paucity of explanation by our Professor. At the end of the full-year course, which began with the early history of the English common law of real property, we had only proceeded as far as the *Statute of Uses* passed by the British Parliament in sixteenth century. The Professor's only explanation was, *"Not much has happened in real property law since then anyway."* Lest you think that this was a dereliction of duty, I will add that he was soon named the Dean of Vanderbilt Law School, and it would be inaccurate to assume that he did not care. First, as lawyers in training we needed to quickly appreciate that we could not vigorously promote and defend our clients' interests by sitting around waiting for someone else to do it for us, or to tell us what to do. I also agree with his other implied premise, that our job is first to understand how legal concepts have changed alongside societal and cultural shifts, so that we can consider how they and we may evolve in the future. We can look up the details, the specific rule or statute that effected these changes, in a law library at any time it is relevant. What we most need is to understand and fit our case into the fabric of society. In other words why we are right as anyone can plainly see.

Having completed a university education, you will look differently at questions. Professors seem unable to resist telling their graduating class, *"You are now entering the real world."* I prefer the equally quoted *"Life is not a dress rehearsal."*

Either way, the reality that time is passing is always with you as you now move on to the rest of life. As time passes, memories will reappear and it seems an apt time to propose that in one sense, you can view your real world as your family's timeline. Your parents loved you as no others have, as they shared the task of guiding you, even when you did not want to be guided. In past times, grandparents were guardians of history and transmitters of tradition. Today we grandparents also have a more enviable role, as cheerleaders, to provide confidence in your fullness whatever you decide to do. But we retain the role of passing on the lessons that have been learned before you were here. Your awareness of your place in the family timeline blends with your grandmother Joan and my limited access to you as grandparents, which heightens our strong urge is to be a presence in your lives, and to stop you for a moment and tell you as much as can be told, while we still can. This has been the purpose of this book and we continue on, to some more lessons that I think I have learned in three-quarters of a century of studying life and people. So we will be moving into more of a monologue as we conclude these last few chapters.

As we continue this endeavor, I think it is time to address what might be lingering questions in your mind. Hopefully, you will not find me *"often wrong but never in doubt"* since you recognize that nothing said between us is conclusive. It is meant to inspire you on the start of your own adventures. Let me also acknowledge that at about this time you may be asking yourself: *Am I taking the fun out of your life by denying you the opportunity to find all these questions for yourself?* Do not worry about that at all. Every answer comes with new sets of questions trailing behind. You are merely getting a head start on some questions here, as I stress that our behaviors and emotions trace back to evolutionary patterns, some having developed in response to problems faced by ancestors in distant times and so, in some cases, may no longer be useful to us. Indeed, some behaviors conditioned by our past may now be harmful, and it is time to jettison them. As we have also been discussing, a good deal of what we do is influenced by the stories in our minds, and we can make sense of how you and others think about questions and their context by paying closer attention to these stories. We are looking for insights into human minds.

We have noted that stories reappear in our conversation. These restatements emphasize recurring themes, with the repetitive process much like a trial lawyer who uses this technique of restatement to assure that no juror misses points that are too important to be overlooked.

While I have been reflecting for the past half-decade upon these questions, I have not heard of anyone advising his grandchildren in this way, by writing them a book. So let us not shrink from another question you may also be asking: *Are you ahead of your time, or out of your mind?* Well, we won't worry about it since, as I said, this book is not the answer, it is a primer on the questions.

Among the important thoughts of your book is what I see as common predicaments of collective action, what people have thought, and thus done. As we have already discussed, this is ordinarily studied as civilization, philosophy, history, economics, law, literature, art, evolution, science, psychology, spirituality, and religion, but these are all really one subject. We will not be dividing the world into sub-disciplines.

There is a place and time for such microscopic examination, at University and afterward—but not this day, when we will take a decidedly historic perspective. Our approach is to look at the humanity of people as well as the identity of individuals, rooted in their experience, rather than the discipline of scientific experiment. The current sermon was and is about curiosity and wonder providing the impetus for study of moments and movements, organized communities and paradigm shifts, by looking at the ideas of the people behind them. This is what we have been pursuing and now conclude by following our marvel at this world to how we lead our lives in the trio of ultimate subjects of politics, economics, and spirituality. It might help if you keep an eye out for what you see as your preferred quality in life as we go forward. And forward we go.

We are proceeding to where my thoughts have taken me, but let's note that we have recently been making a shift from the earlier chapters. Before we move on in our more-or-less conversational mode, let me suggest that while we speak of the broad world, this book has been a connection between us. If you will accept it, reading the story can be taken a step further as a family tradition, a habit of drawing on life-enhancing inspiration from those you choose to think of as spiritual ancestors, be it Plato, Voltaire, Jefferson, Darwin, Lincoln, Gandhi, FDR, Einstein, or anyone else.

As we form and reform ideas that are useful to us, we find much the material for these ideas by reading, and trying to make sense of how it fits in. The first question to answer in the process is, as always: where have we been, where are we going, what are we trying to do? We have seen that we profit from looking at both ancient and modern societies and thought since we humans have been asking many of the same questions for a long, long time. The ultimate search is for lessons to apply when we answer that question in making personal decisions or implementing government policy—and to share them with enough people so they can also see the need for and advantages of enhancing our patterns of living.

From antiquity to the present day, the same issues are examined in different ways across varied fields—philosophy, psychology, religion, politics, economics, science, and behavioral studies—because as humans, we all share a biological and psychological history that also shapes our present experiences. The subject, ultimately, is us.

The Greeks were not the first to think about life; like us, they learned from those who came before. But they are the first deep thinkers to which we in the Western World have full and ready access, and when we begin there, we can observe as they first asked the questions and how these changed for the Greeks and those who have entered the conversation for the past thousands of years. This is why they are so interesting. Indeed, it has been said that the study of philosophy since Plato has been merely footnotes, since the important questions were posed by Socrates and recorded in writing in Plato's dialogues. Plato's exploration was Socrates's method of questioning, as problems were propounded for solution by the students of Plato's Academy in the beginning years of the third century B.C.E. Plato had been appalled by the spate of violence that erupted in Athens between oligarchs and democrats after the end of the Peloponnesian War with Sparta in 404 BCE. He advocated strong rule by law. In *Book I of Laws*, "an Athenian stranger" asks: *"Now who would be the better judge – one who destroyed the bad and appointed the good to govern themselves, or one who, while allowing the good to govern themselves, let the bad live and made them voluntarily submit? Or third, I suppose, in the scale of excellence might be placed a judge who finding the family distracted not only did not destroy anyone but reconciled them to one another forever after, and gave them laws which they observed and was able to keep them friends."* To this Cleinias, the Cretan, answered: *"The last would be the best sort of judge and legislator."* But here the dialogue is just beginning as they follow what truth and justice require us to say, and that war is not the best state of affairs. The pursuit of being free and governed by just laws goes on through *Book XII of Laws,* and ever after.

Plato was not optimistic that the people of the City could govern themselves when so much self interest of the citizens and demagoguery of the politicians inevitably to follow. There have been echoes of success to this question but it was the United States that finally affirmatively answered the question, until now at least.

Even today when standing on the Parthenon in Athens you can feel the ghosts where democracy was first practiced, peer down at the cave where Socrates drank hemlock after being condemned *"for corrupting the morals of the young."* You can look upon the hill below where the apostle Paul delivered his Letter to the Ephesians and at the Theatre of Dionysus, where the long tradition of Western theater began twenty-five centuries ago. It is stirring and relevant to see where art that moved people and mattered was created. For example, in 425 B.C.E. Aristophanes wrote and performed *The Acharnians* about a resourceful charcoal maker who bypassed the corrupt

Athenian politicians and pompous generals to make peace directly with the Spartans at a crucial time during the thirty-year war. The play's timeliness has as much to do with the folly of war itself as lampooning the generals and demagogues who perpetuate it.

The philosophers and artists of the golden age of Greece came from the same long oral tradition of Homer, yet they certainly did not all agree with each other. And you can agree with Plato or not, but we pursue these ideas to our great advantage if we watch them evolve from Homeric legends to today's vital questions, and see that it is still the same inquiry.

From my point of view, the most important moment in the history of Western civilization after classical Greece and Rome was *the Enlightenment* of the Seventeenth and Eighteenth Centuries, when the repercussions of Copernicus's revolutionary assertion that the earth revolved around the sun (not the other way around), played out. All of what had been known and all certainty were thrown into question. Instead of certitude based on a belief in the gods or a God, emperor or king people were offered a belief in reason, to understand being and meaning, a system of belief that is fundamental to the world we know now. The old order of monarchy and church, of nobility and rigid social hierarchy, began to give way to freedom of thought and tolerance.

We learn from everything we experience. Part of the incredible power and the intellectual appeal of the Enlightenment must have been its newness as the broad sweep of the intellectual Eighteenth Century led on into the Nineteenth century. The rational examination of life gave way to also consider the emotional romantic poetry of young lovers of life such as Lord Byron, Percy Shelley and John Keats. Cadence and art became important messages in the dramatic music of Bach, Mozart, and Beethoven. I have never studied music, but I know you both do and will, Finnan and Cormac. I urge you to think of how in this age of loud, electronic, and digital communication, you might learn a new way to convey your thoughts, perhaps in the form of more subtle message of music that softly builds tension, develops themes, and expresses a satisfying, convincing message.

But again, back to one of our themes, lessons are found everywhere as they come round and round.

The experiences of those who came before do not dictate what will follow; they do provide perspective and some context to continue as you go forward.

"Those who do not engage in the passions of their times may be judged not to have lived."

– Oliver Wendell Holmes

These last chapters look at historical, political, economic and moral issues, not as definitive or survey courses but rather from some thoughts, some of which you may use as pegs to hang concepts as you find your way to put your view together. It is a whole new world out there, every day, and it is your world.

PART IV

PART IV

CHAPTER 8

Life's Circumstances and Its politics

"Many cities did Ulysses visit and many were the nations of whose manners and customs he was acquainted. ....Tell me, too, about all these things, O daughter of Jove, from whatsoever source you may know."

— Homer, *The Odyssey*

We look to both past and present from our personal point of view to identify points of reference, which serve as pegs upon which we hang the puzzle pieces we are assembling as we create a view of the world. Then we see if we can marshal evidence to support our present perspective, and organize what we have into a story that we understand. Ultimately, what we are doing is developing our thought-out understanding of our culture and our world.

From stories of history we glean questions to frame further investigation. In this progression, the vital habit of the mind is taking a long view. Once, when your grandmother and I were hiking the Adirondack High Peaks, we saw the water bottle of a passing hiker with the saying: *"You are not lost if you don't care where you are"*. You have to pick a direction. Should you take up sailing, you will quickly learn that if you tack listlessly in your boat without any general direction, you may be on the water for a long, long time.

Again, it is those with an extended view that see the big picture, and thus think large. It is not a coincidence that those who continually pursue their subject continually become our counselors. As you come across these experts you may accept or reject their conclusions, but you should closely inspect the basis for their opinions. *"Facts"* are weapons for many, as they manipulate them for their, not necessarily your, purposes.

In daily life today, we will find the beliefs of the collective often trump a careful consideration of what is really happening. People are pulled to go along with their group, while ignoring inconvenient facts. Yet facts must be rigorously examined if we are to deal with reality and its consequences. The former Democratic United States Senator from New York, Daniel Patrick Moynihan, famously said, *"We are all entitled to our own opinion. We are not entitled to our own facts."* This is being readily ignored today, yet we cannot live rationally in a world where *"what is"* cannot be recognized as it is, without the spin.

Yet yesterday's *"truth"* is not always today's. A problem with most humans is that we are bad at letting go of what happened yesterday. Resistance lurks in our predisposition but, despite our reluctance, things will change as we go forward. The great Economist John Maynard Keynes said it well: *"When I get better information I change my opinion."* Would we want less from someone who is betting our money in the stock market, or our future by their decisions? So let's refine our question and ask: What is true, today?

Magical Thinking and Bridges

Passions have been high many times before in our nation's history. The country is deeply divided today. It was so shortly after the founding of the nation, and never more so than fourscore years later when half the country went to war against the other. Labor strife and strikes during the industrialization of America soon cast a darker shadow of communism and anarchy, resulting in violence in the early 20th Century. There has also been the strain of civil disobedience. Civil rights marches and riots in the 1960s were followed by the protests against the Vietnam War. Yet fundamental to our society is respect for law, and for the constitutional balance of power among the branches of our government...

All sides present the facts as they saw them and want us to see them, yet there has been a tradition of compromise in the United States. Now something may be changing, as it seems possible in 2017 for compromise to be called betrayal while the majority of citizens may not even care about truth. I find this difficult to believe but it seems that this is becoming so. In a recent issue of *The Atlantic*, Kurt Andersen talks of *"a promiscuous devotion to the untrue"* among Americans today. Paradoxically we find the information age upon us so that almost all information seems available yet, on the internet every tribe has a voice using sensationalism to often drown out boring facts in "a cacophony of irrationality." As Andersen puts it, *"we are in a long winter of foolishness."* He reasons that, because we are free to believe anything we want, it is concluded that all beliefs are *"equal."* It is becoming our "God-given right to be right even when we are wrong." The incredible becomes credible.

Wrong. Truth matters. Someone may tell you that you can jump off a tall bridge and not get hurt, but a leap from that height will result in injury. Regardless of how many people believe otherwise, the known consequences will come to pass. It is important that our language be precise to express what really will happen. We must also understand the purpose as well as the expression to understand what is being said and merely claiming will not change the laws of nature. Magical thinking has consequences too. There is the dreamer of dreams who works to make his vision possible, and there is the hustler out to swindle the sucker who wishes rather than works, and thinks it will be enough.

Fiction and nonfiction can both get us closer to subtle truths. Calculations and estimates are useful in measuring the world as close as we can. But estimates are estimates, and metaphors are metaphors. As we said earlier, you may be able to catch more flies with honey than you can with vinegar, but if you are not collecting bugs, this observation has its limits. Magical thinking may make a great novel about South America, but it will not hold up a bridge. Even if the majority of people disagree, the engineer must insist upon his measurements. The delusions of the insane are not the best information to lead us. People are free to think otherwise, but as John Stuart Mill reminded us, their rights stop where ours begin.

Judging Facts

When litigating a lawsuit, lawyers face the question of how to present to the jury the facts that support their client's case, and the contrary problem of how to rebut the contradictory claims of the adversary and prevent them from being accepted as the truth. In Anglo-American jurisprudence, there are rules of evidence that have been developed to limit what can be presented to a jury or a judge. These are based on the question: Can it be tested for veracity? One way to test the truth in a trial and in life is cross-examination of the claimed statement. If a witness says something at trial that is contradicted by a prior written or oral statement, record, or document, or that is inconsistent with or improbable given the other facts of the case, then we focus upon these to show the doubtfulness of the claim. This right to challenge the accuser and the evidence has been a central aspect of the Anglo-American law prohibiting "hearsay evidence." The hearsay rule provides that a testimony must be based on only what you personally know or have observed, not the knowledge or observations of others who are not present in the courtroom. There are narrow exceptions to this hearsay rule, when there is sufficient believability of the out-of-court statement. For example, an admission of guilt is usually accepted as believable because the individual would not otherwise say such a thing. Such "a statement against interest" is deemed enough reason to allow the jury or judge to consider the veracity of the witness's testimony as to the accused individual's confession. This can lead to some seemingly puzzling situations. A co-criminal can be called as a witness to claim the defendant told him he committed the crime, and we allow the testimony. But if fourteen bishops are willing to testify that they do not think a person would have committed the crime, it is not admissible. The saving grace is that opposing counsel can cross-examine at length the accuser as a hostile witness; in order to discredit the witness, the defense counsel can probe when, where, and why the witness heard the confession, the witness's background, and the motivation for the testimony, such as any hostility or promised leniency. But there is no basis to question the clergymen about the facts in the case; in our example, they know none, they merely have an opinion.

All societies are bound up in this quest for veracity and reality. Familiarity with the cultural background of a people is elemental to understanding their perceptions. Their way of doing things was developed over a long time and cannot be fully understood with just a snapshot of a contemporary moment. You need to know with whom you are dealing. Experience has shown us we also need rules, procedures designed to arrive at a fair conclusion. In the United States Constitution, this is called "the due process of the law." In our country, the aim is to decide fairly, based upon these rules and laws and not be ruled by the arbitrary decisions of men. Underneath it all, we should always remember that the ultimate values of our culture, and thus our aim, if not always our practice, is to actually arrive at the truth, not just check off a box indicating that a rule has been "observed."

We have noted the power of cultural ideas in the early written tradition of Western civilization as found in *the Iliad* and *the Odyssey* of Homer. Greek ideals included not only truth, beauty, and art, but also of courage, honor, dishonor, and respect for the gods. Ideals can be as powerful as facts, and history tells us that the Greeks took these bedrock values seriously. So, for example, we might suspect that a brave man would be admired and thus believed more than a coward; the Ancient Greeks might also expect that he would be a believer in the gods of their City over an alien. These ideals of the ancient Greeks was so linked to their common destiny in the story of the Trojan War that it prompted the city-states to unity of action over half a millennium later in the Persian Wars that defined their civilization. We have visited the development of this story and now return to it.

This idea that these ideals impacted the fate of a unified Greek people, was later promoted in the history of the Peloponnesian War, written by the Athenian General Thucydides in his first-hand account of this later thirty-year civil war from 431 to 404 BCE. An underappreciated, but to me incredibly dramatic, story, it is well worth your attention. Thucydides saw this newer Greek war between the city-states as immensely important: *"A war like no other."* He weaves into his account of the conflict between Sparta and Athens a contrasting theme: that they had united a half-century earlier to repel the enormous invading armies in the two Persian Wars. He speaks of the common effort, heroism, ideals, and gods who came together in historic effort that had saved their peoples and culture from Persian conquest. His emphasis of the long, shared heroism of the Greeks seems to have enabled Thucydides to successfully convince Sparta to later spare Athens at the end of the war, "a feat like no other". The City's critical defensive walls were torn down, but Athens was allowed to survive as an incorporated ally, thus allowing the subsequent Socratic dialogues told in the Academy of Plato, the philosophical works of his student Aristotle, and exploits of his student Alexander the Great. The Spartan dominance of the Greek world was short-lived, and Greek and Persian alliances and breakups continued for another half-century, through the end of the classical period. But the possible immense loss of Athenian culture did not come to pass; and the ideals of the Golden Age of Greece has been the prime heritage for Western civilization for at least twenty-four hundred more years, that is, until today.

Of course, this was not the only attempt to influence critical moments in history. I think that you will find in the study of men who achieved much that there is so often a long-standing purpose, and they find different ways to achieve it.

To grasp what Thucydides was trying to achieve, we might look to a more recent wartime leader, Winston Churchill. The Prime Minister of Great Britain during World War II also led a life-and-death struggle for his nation. After the defeat of Nazi Germany in 1945, the British electorate, as is often the case, voted the old warhorse out of office. But the man's indomitable character would not let the fight go on without trying to greatly influence it. Churchill gave a speech to students at an American college in Missouri in 1946 and with one phrase focused the Western world on the danger of *"an iron curtain"* of Communism descending across Europe. He had previously opposed the dismantling of the British Empire and the long-overdue independence of the British colonies, which he saw as a threat to his country. Churchill had been writing a history of Britain from Roman times through the colonial period and modern times in *A*

History of the English-Speaking Peoples, which was finished and published after the War. What do you imagine might be happening here? Obviously, it is just what it says, a political history with the emphasis on English speakers; but to my mind, we cannot ignore the attempt to more firmly bind Great Britain, the United States, Canada, Australia, and New Zealand with a common cultural heritage and ideals in a new and dangerous world. His book was part of a larger effort by postwar Great Britain to engender public recognition of *"a special relationship"* between these countries. Churchill's A History might not have had that much to do with that result, but it seems clear to me that it was a praiseworthy effort at an informal alliance of English speakers. Even if it was a form of propaganda the goal of such an alliance has held for well over a half-century and still going strong.

The concept of using a sense of identity and common purpose to forge a people together is a powerful one, where these two venerable leaders, Thucydides and Churchill, employed the ideal to achieve very specific aims. These two examples, which stretch well over two thousand years, emphasize how an idea or a suggestion can so effectively take hold in the minds of a people.

We might look at another important trend in the power of ideas that is discernible in the rent strikes and monster marches led by baker O'Connell in Ireland in the first half of the nineteenth century. These were peaceful mass marches, one at Tara Hill, north of Dublin, where it is estimated more than one-quarter of the Irish population assembled. Rows and rows of men marched in civilian clothes; they protested without weapons, but there was the sense that these circumstances could change. The tactics proved powerful persuasion, and Britain passed legislation to emancipate Catholics in 1829. By the 1840s Catholics were allowed to vote, to serve in Parliament, and to own land. Actual full emancipation took almost another century, but that is another story.

Henry David Thoreau's abhorrence of the enslavement of other human beings as well as of our country's imperialist invasion of Mexico in 1848 motivated the moral tone of a lecture he gave in Boston on political dissent. The following year, he published this argument as the essay *"Civil Disobedience."* At the time, the Irish Catholics were immigrating to America in vast numbers. Thoreau would thus have known about O'Connell's mass protests for Catholic civil rights in Ireland in the preceding decades while formulating his assertions of the right, the obligation, and the potential power of citizens to oppose the unjust actions of their collective government.

Thoreau's concept of civil disobedience, in turn, influenced Mahatma Gandhi, who in the early 1900s, after studying law in London, traveled to South Africa where he successfully protested discriminatory laws and practices against Indians living there. While Gandhi may have adopted the moral sense of Thoreau's civil disobedience, he had studied law in London and no doubt also knew of O'Connell's mass marches across the Irish Sea a half-century earlier and their successful political achievement of emancipation. When he returned to India to continue protests against the British, Gandhi translated Thoreau's ideas into his concept of non-violent resistance as *"respectful disagreement."* He continued to employ his non-cooperation tactics for over thirty years until ultimately achieving Indian independence after World War II.

Noncompliance with the methods and structures of English control was effective both in nineteenth-century Ireland and in twentieth-century India. Why were the protests able to succeed? British political decisions and hypocritical justifications for oppression, such as the notion of *"the white man's burden to civilize and convert the heathens"* during the centuries of colonialism, were often cynical selfishly *"realism"*. However, the moral philosophy underpinning Britain's laws and political organizations made them susceptible to accusations of hypocrisy because of the distance between professed beliefs and actual political actions. Of course, the willingness to address this distance between professed ideals and actual practice was achieved when the benefits of continuing repressive policies and institutions began to be outweighed by the public outcry and costs. Such dissent and refusal to cooperate could not have been successful against a more brutally oppressive regime, such as the Nazis who were most willing to suppress and exterminate entire peoples in the 1930s and 40s if it served their interests in any way.

This idea of non-violent protest with both moral and political dimensions traveled back around the world, again to America. Gandhi's ideas were picked up by the young Reverend Martin Luther King, Jr. in the American Civil Rights Protests of the mid-20th Century. MLK, Jr. was instrumental in the series of marches and related sit-ins, protests, and acts of civil disobedience on behalf of blacks, first in the southern United States.

Round and round it went. And the story once more returned to Ireland.

Your grandmother and I spent St. Patrick's Day in 1982 at a celebration given at the United Nations by the Irish Consulate. The speaker was John Hume, the Northern Ireland Catholic political leader at the time, who was vigorously trying to promote a peace process for the eight northern counties of the island. After the dinner party, a group of us invited Mr. Hume to join us for a drink in New York City. He agreed but asked where; when a law partner mentioned *"The Quiet Man,"* Hume immediately replied, *"No, no. A Provo place,"* displaying a remarkable bit of barroom knowledge, which was apparently deemed necessary for a Northern Irish politician to avoid conflict even in faraway New York City.

This, of course, underlines the deep level of political animosity that can exist, even or maybe especially, within the same tribe, such as the Irish. Two other personal examples come immediately to mind. One afternoon, around the same time period, another law partner and I went out for a drink with his wife's cousin, who had come over from Dublin. He was the President of a subsidiary of a British construction equipment company and had recently flown from Dublin to Belfast in Northern Ireland to solicit business from a large builder. He had made his presentation to the President of the Protestant contractor, who confirmed that the equipment was just what they needed and the price was the best. But the North Ireland contractor declined to place the order because "his company did not do business with foreign corporations". What he was clearly saying is move your subsidiary from Dublin back to Britain if you want our business.

Your Aunt Deirdre encountered the same mindset a dozen years later, right after she graduated from college, while working in Derry in Northern Ireland. Derry is known there as *"Stroke City"* because of its split identity and its split name: while the Catholics know it as *"Derry"*, the Protestants call it *"Londonderry"*. *"Stroke"* is the British term for the mark *"/"* that we Americans call a slash. She had taken a job with a not-for-profit community organization trying to promote cooperation between the two religious groups and quickly found that it could be done with the five-year-olds that attended the school but not with their parents.

The British–Irish conflict had been festering for a thousand years, but particularly after the American Civil Rights marches of the 1960s, new "troubles" began in Northern Ireland between Protestants and Catholics, with British soldiers in the middle. The minority Catholics regularly quoted Martin Luther King, Jr. during the series of violent clashes. The long-standing dispute was settled in the late 1990s, with the assistance of the United States, Britain, and the southern Republic of Ireland. The ensuing elections provided jobs for the leaders of the two disputing sides: the Sinn Fein, political wing of the Irish Catholic Republicans (the IRA); and the Ulster Protestants politicians. When both parties, long suspicious of the other, began reneging on the agreement, the financial subsidy that supported the new legislature ceased, as did their pay. This time, with a re-focused attention of everyone, they found a way to find enough trust in compromise to allow reconciliation and reinstitution of shared governing. Over time the peace has mostly stuck, although at this time, twenty years later the successor leadership on both sides is having some difficulty holding it together.

To return to our theme, there was a price of blood to be paid during the moments of political resistance in the United States, just as in Ireland and India, as well Central Europe and the Middle East. In the 1960s in America, where we are deeply proud of our ideals, the media's revelation of the brutal hypocrisy of accepted violence associated with enforcing Southern segregation proved to be something the American people would not allow to continue. It was an idea whose time had once again come: that is, change came once many people were willing to take on the required risk. To rephrase (as I have often done for emphasis), a powerful ideal triumphed when there were people willing to make it so.

Ancient Greek poets and generals, and American, Irish, and Indian protesters, anti-imperialists, and democrats all profited from a powerful idea; but its influence can depend upon both place and time. A common dictum about the power of an idea whose time has come emphasizes this factor of timeliness. It is worth also recognizing that some ideas may need to be aged. We note that English poet Percy Bysshe Shelley described poets as *"the unacknowledged legislators of the world,"* which assumes an inherent germination period for the acceptance of new truths.

Not all moments of independence have an immediate and uninterrupted lineal descent from the idea. Sometimes they await the opportunity. Between the two World Wars, Ireland took advantage of the political landscape to declare itself a Republic, entirely independent of dominion status within the

British Commonwealth and thereby avoided participating in World War II. In 1944, when twenty-five thousand American troops were stationed in Iceland and while Denmark was occupied by the Nazis, the Icelandic People decided to complete a process initiated at the end of World War I, to declare formal independence from one thousand years of rule and influence by Copenhagen. The time had come.

It has been said that fights over history are about claiming the future. Plato held that those who tell the stories rule society. Why? These moments always have context: the real or assumed explanations for why things are, or have been as they are, and thus why they should change. The advantage to motivate or dissuade, to cast an appearance of inevitability or at least justification for what they seek has its power. *"Cui bono? To whose benefit?"* asked the Roman Orator and Statesman, Cicero.

We are looking at the progress of a people by focusing upon the thoughts behind the action. Motivation is often the most important thing to know if we are to fathom what is really going on. This leads us to look at the interests of those involved in order to understand what they will do, or did if we are looking backward. In either event, we must then go beyond just what people want, to the leverage they possess to do something about it, that is, the power to act, to change or maintain things as they are. To do this intelligently we must ask: what advantage do they have? Geography is sometimes destiny. Do they have an ocean or mountain protecting them? Is the wind at their back, or do they have a strong defensive position on the heights? Are they fighting a headwind, a lack of resources, or other weakness? Is there inertia to be overcome, a general feeling of people that this is just the way things are?

Our examples have often related to politics and war and so let's conclude within this context. Motivations for war are basic: traditional rights, fear based upon past experiences, survival, power, land acquisition and greed, differences of religion and ethnicity, support of an ally, hate of the perceived difference of others, a dispute initiated and from which neither side knows how to back away. Knowing the reason conflicts begin says nothing about the consequences. Unleashing primitive responses in conflict can shatter the core of human beings, bodies destroyed, spirits devastated by immense horror. In a word, consequences that are at odds with the *"benefit"* envisioned at the start.

So history suggests that given human nature, conflict and tyranny have not and will not become a thing of the past, without help, and this becomes our cultural task. This seems a moment to continue with a brief recapitulation of history from the eccentric view of your grandfather.

I dwell in possibility.

— Emily Dickinson

Ever since Charles Darwin gave us his report of the HMS Beagle's voyage, people have been examining the fossil record of life in sedimentary rock, the development of animals of like kind, and the similarities and progression of species evidenced in ancient bones.

One area of interest was Darwin's assertion of natural selection as the mechanism for passing on superior genes as those who adapt survive and prosper. There was some trouble at first in understanding how running faster on the savanna from a predator, or in pursuit of prey, could be passed on to descendants. The answer was found in the studies of an Austrian monk of the second half of the nineteenth century. Gregor Mendel crossed tall and short pea plants and found that each plant had a gene from each parent plant and the height of offspring plants would not be the average of the parents but be either tall or short. He also found the tall gene dominant and the short gene recessive so that the pea would be tall unless both parents were short. This meant that babies born with a favorable adaption are more likely to survive. Thus, qualities that might be considered odd but were advantageous could be passed on.

Darwin's proposition that these environmental adaptations would be gradual was also often true, but species were also found to be susceptible to environmental changes. Chemical and radiation changes in the environment have large and far-reaching effects, and this changing environment could prompt great and more rapid change in species if the resulting adaption promoted life and flourished. Later discoveries of quick mutations, jumping genes of corn for example, also explained dramatic species change.

More recent discoveries aided by understanding of genes and DNA that have focused upon many of man's more recent predecessors have enhanced our certainty that this evolutionary process also happens culturally as well as biologically. Socio-biologists have been demonstrating this in study after study of this past generation.

The traditional story begins ten thousand years ago when hunter-gatherers found wild grain plants in adjacent places such as Jericho, the Tigris–Euphrates Valley of Iraq, and the adjoining areas of the Middle East. This birth of agriculture during this transformation in the Neolithic Age provided a sufficient supply of food for the first time in the history of man and even today half the world carries on similar forms of agriculture.

To grow a surplus of these crops, and to store and disburse them, required organization, and modern culture grew from those grass fields. As we evolved to higher states of civilization, stories about our successful efforts, of being together, became important. We began to recount how we understand our experience of the world, and we learned collectively from it.

We saw the power of cultural change when we talked about Homer's two epics, *The Iliad* and The *Odyssey*. There was a great shift in the empathy expressed by the ancient Greeks in the short span of about a hundred years. From the two-dimensional emotional characters found in the story of *the Iliad* to a people able to feel empathy even for the enemy in the story of *the Odyssey* as told only one hundred years later was an amazing evolution in the culture in such a short time of one century.

Our main point here is that the culture of a society, the way people act, can change rapidly. And as I have been suggesting the arrow of history suggests that a key conceptual modification is toward greater cooperation.

In *The Turning Point*, Fritjof Capra explores this proposition that cooperation is a complementary alternative to the existing model of aggression as the organizational basis of life. Such a conception, that we can cooperate rather than overcome others, rests recognizing our interdependence is an alternative to accepting the inevitability of a Darwinian proposition of survival of the fittest. By actually accepting ideals that are prompted the sadness of anyone's child's death we can let culture tame other basic and baser instincts. The point of it all is that, in a world that has grown so interdependent in so many ways, the model of cooperation, by definition, considers the collective cost of critical world issues like global warming and the shared benefit in addressing them.

Robert Wright takes it a step further in *Nonzero: The Logic of Human Destiny*, concluding that the effort can begin anew; *"reaching out to create closer affinities"* as we work together.

In *Identity and Violence*, Nobel Prize winner Amartya Sen also appeals to our commonalities: he speaks of the various different attributes we all share with many different peoples and that stressing these similarities rather than the differences of "the other" can make peace rather than war. He points out that we all have many roles to play and we can either notice the ones that bind us, or the differences that divide us.

Thomas Friedman, in *The World Is Flat*, in discussing our global political world pointed to a conflict between India and Pakistan in the early 21st Century which threatened to quickly escalate into nuclear war. It was abruptly stopped, over one weekend, when international corporate clients convinced India that its future economic growth and prosperity depended upon their continuing uninterrupted business, which in turn depended upon peace with the neighbors.

Let us turn from looking at the rational case for cooperation, to an emotional look at the other side of the picture.

> *He did his very best to make the billows smooth and bright, and that was very odd because it was the middle of the night.*
>
> — Lewis Carroll, *"The Walrus and the Carpenter"*

Life can be grim. Sometimes it is the spirit of people that makes the difference, and this seems a good time to focus upon the emotional side of such habits of mind. For the moment we will try to feel it rather than think it.

For example, I am confident that you will be naturally repulsed by those who intimidate others and try to crush their aspirations. The more forceful the bully, the more fervidly we are aroused in opposition. A most obvious example Is blatant racial prejudice and its most crippling allegation: You do not belong, you cannot belong. *In All God's Dangers: The Life of Nate Shaw,* there are two quotes from Ned Cobb, the Alabama farmer who was born in 1885 and died in 1973 on whom the book was based. The first quote from Ned Cobb I want to focus upon is: *"Any way they could deprive a Negro was a celebration."* The second is: *"Some folks don't use the time God gave them, that's why they're liable to come up defeated."*

The rising anger as you read the first statement is balanced by the uplifting sense of an indomitable human spirit in the second. I still hear people today who will tell us that we did not need the Civil War, that the South would have grown out of slavery eventually—or that Gandhi did not need to agitate for all those decades because the British would have granted India independence anyway. War is horrible, but so is apathy and willful blindness. Elizabeth Barrett Browning wrote aptly a century and a half ago of the hypocrisy of slavery in England in *A Curse for a Nation*: "*For your conscience, tradition, and name, explode with a deadlier blame, than the worst of them all. This is the curse.*"

It is in the extremes of human nature that we often see more clearly, and so I think it useful here to consider how people get to keep other people in slavery? The real short answer is extreme fear that only an ever present brutality can induce.

For those who tolerate such continued abuse of others it would be fair to ask if they should be willing to bear the same burden, usually resort to a whipping post. As we flip from our rational to our emotional selves the question we ask has moved from "What we are trying to do?" to also encompass "Who are we and who should we be trying to be?"

In looking at being accustomed to violence there are "traditional views" of fierce warrior peoples, such as the Spartans who spent their entire adult lives living in military camps, the Vikings with their fearsome warship prows which began sailing down from Scandinavian waters in the late first millennia A.D while almost encircling Europe, the Mongol hordes riding out of the Asian plains as far as the gates of Vienna in the early second millennia, the Celts of central and western Europe whom Julius Caesar called "*the Gauls*" and whose descendants are found in places such as France, Ireland and Scotland. The Ancient Romans called similar neighboring tribes barbarians but there was not much more than efficiency to distinguish them from those they saw a need to conquer. Cruel dominance is really a theme throughout history from the Old Testament to today, so what can we make of it? As said above there is a rational case for cooperation. What is the rest of the story?

We can pursue this emotional inquiry from what has become an evolving political viewpoint. *"We believe the family of America recognizes that, at the heart of the matter, we are bound to one another ... that the failure anywhere to provide what reasonably we might to avoid pain is our failure."* This is Mario Cuomo, former Governor of New York, at the 1984 Democratic National Presidential Convention we cannot just all show up at the Acropolis and vote on every issue. John Stuart Mill emphasized that we can best pursue our liberty by representative government. In the early half of the nineteenth century, he examined how we might perfect the relationship between us through a representative government. His foundational point was *"liberty"* since individuals know better than others do what will serve their interest, and what they want to do, and so should be free to decide for themselves. This is bedrock reality.

But in this world there are also inevitable tensions in the many things we share in common. Sharing infrastructure has been with us as long as civilization. These include the canals, granaries, bridges, roads, the common grazing area, security and defense, health and hospitals, libraries, museums, and schools and other public works and institutions for which we need to cooperate if they are to get done. We designate people to make decisions about the construction and distribution of benefits. If we are dissatisfied, we pick other people the next time. J.S. Mill further recognized the more subtle point that man does not just seek the pleasure of sensations but also an overall plan of life which he develops for himself, fulfilled by considering what works in life. Each of us has those plans and wishes. My grandchildren, doesn't this sound familiar? Few Americans would dispute it. The issue is, as always: where do we draw the line between the rights of the one and the needs of the many? With this approach, Mill realized that even if we intelligently pay attention to our experiences, and those of others whom we will next see or sense another valid point, neither we nor they are infallible. He wrote that we need to align the interests of the representative rulers of government and the interests of all the people, while limiting how the state can restrict the individual. I find it helpful to think of this *"alignment"* as *"leverage"*, created by the system of checks and balances by which the United States Constitution constrains elected officials and those they appoint to carry out their decisions for the benefit of all the people. The members of the government are loyal to the government and the people not their boss, even if President.

The question always becomes what works. Two of Mill's central ideas are critical here. First, happiness requires freedom, and second, you're right to such ends where mine begins. We can flesh out this last idea. A plan of life corresponds to our *"pursuit of happiness"* as we develop our own individual concept of a full life, a right expressed in *the Declaration of Independence* along with the wisdom of our Constitution that a majority of others cannot deny us our rights. Polling what the majority says they want at the moment is not controlling.

Your rights to your body, property, and soul end where mine begin. Let me emphasize this concept again, Finnan and Cormac. Whether the rights are personal, political, economic or religious, your rights end where mine begin, and your way of life, sensibilities, monetary gain, or claim to a superior understanding of a god do not trump my individual rights.

Commonly accepted beliefs continue to evolve because all matters were not settled in the late 1700s. Things change, science and society grew, the industrial revolution and the information technology revolution arose, and the discussion never really stops.

There will be differing opinions, interests and groups, and we must find and develop ways to reconcile these if we are to get beyond fighting with *"bloody tooth and claw,"* as the Scottish political philosopher of the late seventeenth century Thomas Hobbes put it in *the Leviathan*. What is required is a process for the laws to balance our rights and our duties to others. The more fundamental the individual interest the more we want strict rules so that some or most of us do not deny others their fair share of basic freedom and prosperity. For, if anyone's rights can be denied then so can yours and those of everyone else as well. In the American political system we achieve this balance through the United States Constitution, and we argue about and it is through both elections and judicial decisions as we flesh out the words selected in the initial compromises of our Founding Fathers.

The only alternative to debate and compromise is to be ruled either by a tyrant, or its collective equivalent, which becomes an oligarchy of the privileged who insist upon greater claim to political power because of birth, wealth, alliances of power, wisdom, or the favor of the gods. In fact, those who refuse to discuss and compromise because they know they are right are really saying just that: they have superior rights granted by some authority or simply lay claim to them, which sounds more like arrogance than conviction. It is certainly not a great way to build the civil trust and cooperation necessary for a well-functioning democracy. And unacceptable in any event.

So what is our optimistic view of democracy? It's a collective effort to organize ourselves, which, ever since the Greeks, comes with the challenges of differing values and ideals; this is especially true in the modern United States. Inclusion of all is needed in our governmental aims and in participation in all our public and political institutions, economy, and civic life. The psychological, or if you prefer, cultural, fact is that we all have to buy in to this political arrangement and believe we own the problem and the solution together. We have to trust compromise.

Affinity as Good Politics and Good Economics

There are so many interesting studies that can shed light and understanding on "other issues" when we take a long and broad view of our subject, an expanding view of cooperation as the successful sharing of life.

Google, whose parent company is now known as Alphabet, is one of the most dynamic, important, and valuable companies in America at this time. It did not exist twenty-five years ago. Every day it provides broader access to more information than existed when it was incorporated. Each year it hires more graduate math students than any other organization in the world. So when it studies a subject, the results might be worth noting.

It recently undertook a study, named *Project Aristotle*, to determine why some work groups continually succeed while others do not. Google excels in analyzing vast amounts of data, and the project examined numerous characteristics of the teams, from IQs and fields of study to project approaches. Finally, they found one behavioral characteristic that proved critical. The teams that succeeded best were those in which the team and its members recognized that their efforts fit in to the larger organizational mission. Members of the team listened to each other. They did not all have equal influence within the group at all times. If someone had a good idea they ran with it. Often a few people dominated a meeting or conversation, but everyone felt they had the opportunity to contribute. The team members understood the team's objectives, were sensitive to the needs of others, and they were confident that there was respect for their ideas. It was a safe psychological environment that allowed the team to thrive. It turned out that good rapport was good economics. I would index this study not only under categories of business and social subjects, but also under political cooperation in every sense. The political message is that we must recognize the great value of agreeing, even if we agree to disagree from time to time.

This value of cooperation should be applicable not only for individual behavior but suggest how our institutions can influence each other in the longer arc of time. In a word, our democratic political/legal system should accommodate you as you define yourself and your life, and mine as I would have it.

Statues Conversing

I recently received my copy of *NYU Law Magazine.* It has a drawing on the cover of two statues of women. The Statue of Liberty holds her torch at her side as she sits by the water fountain in Washington Square Park in Greenwich Village. Next to her is a statue of Justice with her scales by her side and her blindfold worn up on her forehead. Pigeons are at their feet as they presumably ponder the ever-present tension between the competing interests of justice and equality on the one hand and the individual rights of liberty on the other. At its most obvious, I should not be free to throw toxins in the river if it will poison the fish and people downstream. One person's rights end where another's begin. It is inevitably necessary to find where we draw the line. It is not difficult to recognize that if I am a member of a representative democracy, I am complicit if our government refuses to feed our poor children and lets them die of starvation.

We should frankly recognize that these political decisions encompass economics, with benefits to some entwined with costs to others.

There ae always tensions in life and we must wade through them in order to understand where we need find the balance. Thomas Jefferson feared encroachment of political institutions on the lives of citizens. It has been a constant lesson of history and still is. One of the issues rallying the Americans to revolution was that the power to tax is the power to destroy.

Jefferson was deeply concerned that the central government would exert economic power that hindered the rural farmers of Virginia and he saw powerful national organizations, not just the central government, as a threat. Not surprisingly, when Alexander Hamilton proposed the formation of a national bank, he opposed it. He was right that money tends to gravitate toward political power, and political power toward money. A broad outlook must go beyond a slogan about being free of undue government interference, and we must also recognize that large corporations can exercise similar power.

Nevertheless, as our civilization expands individuals have no choice but to join in common efforts. Some old institutions and ways of doing things will fall away permanently. Others are here to stay: we cannot turn from industrialization, the nuclear bomb, the Internet, and information age and we probably do not even want to do so

Of course, we are talking about what actually happens to us all, every day. Our corporations and highly centralized economy leave almost all individuals relying on large institutions for their livelihood and safety. Those who run the large commercial enterprises seldom own them; they are trustees, in a position of trust. Their incompetence, irresponsibility, or greed can reduce many to the margins and poverty.

Does this sound as if we may be beginning to suggest some radical socialist solutions for Americans? I think not. These are almost the exact words Franklin Delano Roosevelt used in his 1932 Presidential Campaign, and he was elected by three-quarters of the Americans who voted. It serves as a clear historical marker in American history from which we should not retreat.

The question becomes how we go forward. If economic growth benefits only a few it will be suspect, subject to being examined and measured by the envious who will always remain a threat. A man who is starving will always steal if he has a choice, and he should. So, peace and stability require some level of fairness in whatever system of economic distribution is adopted.

FDR said that every man has a right to life and this means that he also has a right to make a *"comfortable living."* This was how he explained his New Deal. *"We must restrict the operation of the speculator, the manipulator, the financier. I believe we must accept the restriction as needful, not to hamper individualism but to protect it. These two requirements (of a right to a life and a living) must be satisfied, in the main, by the individuals who claim and hold control of great industrial and financial combinations which dominate so large a part of our natural life. . . . I am very clear that they must fearlessly and competently accept the responsibility which goes with the power . . . instead of each acting for himself, they must work together for the common good."*

My grandsons, these words are from one of our country's most revered Presidents eighty-five years ago.

Now please note, Finnan and Cormac, that after urging you for so long to think for yourself, I have been quoting one man at length, as if relying upon his authority. Well, if you are going to rely upon the words of one person, FDR, a president of thoughtful action, is not a bad place to start. But I do it for other reasons. I wanted to point out the value of framing an argument in a way that both commands attention and surprises when the source is revealed to be someone as respected today as FDR. It is one way to quickly answer critics who indiscriminately dismiss someone as *"socialist"* or some other label with a similar negative image. Identifying this kind of rhetoric is not just an academic exercise. So long after Social Security laws and all the progress since the 1930s, there are still many who would roll back the clock and *the New Deal.*

I chose what might seem provocative phrasing, above, for several reasons. First, I wanted to present a quick answer to the traditional critics who reject any American progressive concerns, be it Social Security, pensions, minimum wages, or universal health care, with oppositional epithets such as socialism designed for the unthinking rather than addressing the issues in a serious manner. Second, I wanted to point out to you the value of framing an argument in a way that both arrests and disarms your interlocutor. Sometimes we can best make clear the values involved when they are emotionally framed. A striking example can be found during the time of the initial American debate on child labor laws. Sarah Cleghorne wrote a short poem called *"The Golf Links,"* which reads in totality: *"The golf links lie so near the factory, that almost every day, the laboring children can look out and see the men at play."* It is hard to argue with that image.

So we can ask: Who will provide the checks and balances, the countervailing power to control our huge corporations, if not the government? During a limited period of our history, labor unions protected some workers some of the time, but their influence is rapidly diminishing. It is largely the government that must check excesses, in business as in all other spheres of life. The government also needs to be watched; the checks and balances of the rule of law and our Constitution are critical to our democracy, as our Founding Fathers so clearly saw, and as we are again so vividly reminded in 2017.

Once again, I will repeat an argument for emphasis. You might assume that emotional appeals such as *"The Golf Links"* are no longer necessary a century later. You would be right that this should be unnecessary, but similar claims are being made in many guises today while debating issues such as a living minimum wage, so it is worth remembering the lessons of historical debates. "Do you not think that a child should have his constitutional right to contract for as long as he wants to work, and for what he is willing to accept?" "Isn't a worker better off receiving starvation wages than no wages at all? You can still hear them in debates surrounding right-to-work laws and the right of teenagers to work for less than minimum wage today. To refer back to our history helps expose the enormity of the unconcern in our land of plenty which I think should prompt you to find it difficult to believe that anyone could still sincerely accept assertions that we are doing people a favor when we pay them less. Listening to today's political debates that repeat these same tired arguments is enough to make you appreciate the power of rituals such as daily prayer, where they repeating something so often that they hope you cannot fail to remember to believe it.

The Law of the Land

The United States Supreme Court is one major battleground in the contest over which ideas will govern us in America. I think it instructive to take time to look at several of their decisions to grasp their impact on the lives of people every day.

Often our ideals of liberty and freedom become litigated issues under a claim of the individual rights of citizens. As we have seen and you will see again, it is fascinating to examine these issues alongside an analysis of the United States Constitution. As I write this chapter, a case decided by the United States Supreme Court (concerning the right of recognition for same-sex marriage) echoes as follows:

> *"The nature of injustice is that we may not always see it in our times. The generations that wrote and ratified the Bill of Rights and the Fourteenth Amendment (providing due process and equal protection under the law) did not presume to know the extent of freedom in all of the dimensions and so entrusted to future generations a charter protecting the rights of all persons to enjoy liberty as we learn its meaning. When new insights reveal discord between the Constitution's central protections and received legal strictures then claims to liberty must be addressed."*

We do not have time to pursue all these lines of inquiry as far as they might take us, and I am confident that they will be a part of your formal education. Since I may not be with you when you are considering them, Finn and Cormac, I am continually suggesting that it is all about stories. Jesus taught in parables; Einstein had his thought experiments; foundation myths hold nations and civilizations together. There is power in viewing these as the chronicles of us. We will now take a look at a few of these chronicles found in decisions of the United States Supreme Court.

Regulating Bakers

A recent article in the New York Law Journal was entitled: *"The Lochner Case: New Yorkers in Conflict.* How old rulings on bakers' hours still influences today's High Court, including Obamacare (i.e. the presently existing federal "Affordable Care Act"- Ed)."

Now that long title references a very important case, decided by the New York Court of Appeals, the state's highest court, in 1904. Its decision was overturned by the United States Supreme Court in 1905. This decision cast a long shadow on economic history in America for a generation.

The conflict was between the liberties of an individual to do what he or she wants, and the right of the rest of us to pass a law that restricts that right for the common good. The question was: *"Can the NY State Legislature pass a statute limiting the number of hours an employee can work in a bakery no more than ten hours a day?* The New York Court of Appeals held that the State had *"the police power"* to regulate the maximum hours worked per day. The dissent argued that this law violated the liberty of the parties to contract for whatever terms they wanted. The New York State Legislature, passed the law unanimously, an almost unheard of unanimity. Had it unconstitutionally interfered with the substantive rights of individuals to contract as they pleased? Could the Court then step in and substitute its judgment for that of the legislature, which is the only branch of government expressly given the power to pass our laws by our Constitution?

At this time there was a developing progressive political movement, with increasing tension between corporations that were growing larger and labor unions emerging as a countervailing power. Underneath the surface of the arguments was the general question of the right of government to regulate if the effect was to redistribute some wealth from owners to workers.

The *Lochner* case had a direct impact on workers who wanted to work overtime, although extra pay for these overtime hours is a story for another day. The fundamental question was whether the United States Constitution should be read to take into consideration changes taking place in society and the economy in the past 100 years. Strict constructionists argue that we must understand the words exactly as they are written and that what the framers of the Constitution meant at the time governs us today. If the Founding Fathers did not mention it, then the government cannot regulate. Of course, this approach of literally reading the words with dictionary in hand totally ignores two essential facts. First, most of the issues decided today contain facts, events, and conditions that did not exist when the Constitution was first adopted. Second, there were numerous disagreements and evolving opinions among the framers, and they adopted a version that was left ambiguous enough to accommodate or papered over differences that no longer exist, of which the most conspicuous example as slavery. To me, the bottom line is that the strict construction approach can, by analogy, be compared to religious fundamentalism, treating our Founding Fathers as all knowing gods.

It is impossible to govern two hundred twenty-five years later without considering the shifting circumstances in this ever-evolving world, the political, economic, and social interests of our times. And we might remember that the whole purpose of the American experiment in government rests upon Thomas Jefferson's seminal assertion in the Declaration of Independence, which he claims is *"self-evident"*, that: *"governments are instituted among men, deriving their just powers from the consent of the governed."* From this point of view, to suggest that we are to be ruled by those who died two hundred years ago seems perverse. The entire history of progress in America rests upon this idea of the consent of the governed, who are, by definition, the living.

In the *Lochner* case, the US Supreme Court considered the common interest in the safety of bakery products sold to the public as well as the safety of laborers working more than ten hours a day. Yet by a 5-to-4 vote, the Court struck down the regulatory law. The language of the justices clearly reveals the holdover of thought from an earlier time. The majority cited "other issues" such as the state's attempt at *"paternalism"* that will *"inevitably put enmity and strife between master and servant."* This decision was based on the Fourteenth Amendment's guarantee of "equal protection of the laws," which had been meant to free men from the drudgery of long toil for the benefit of others. Instead, the Court invalidated the decision of the legislature upon a theory of "substantive due process" and thereby overturned nearly two hundred state and federal laws that had already been passed to protect the public. Less than a decade after the Supreme Court decision in *Lochner*, bakers in New York did achieve a ten-hour day, by union collective bargaining.

Nevertheless, the case continued to be the law of the land and impacted lives for another generation. But the problems of urbanization and industrialization could not be ignored forever, especially as the Depression continued throughout the 1930s. In 1937, the US Supreme Court finally reversed a series of cases and decided that a minimum wage law passed by the legislature of the State of Washington was indeed constitutional. Chief Justice Charles Evans Hughes, a former New York Governor and almost President of the United States, delivered the Court's opinion: *"Liberty implies the absence of arbitrary restraint, not immunity from reasonable regulation and prohibitions imposed in the interests of the community."* As critics had predicted, the floodgates then opened. That same year, the Court upheld the constitutionality of the Social Security Act, and the National Labor Relations Act.

Bakers Back in Court

There is another bakery case before the US Supreme Court at this time. A gay couple is challenging the refusal of a baker in Colorado to make them a wedding cake. The Colorado Court found the refusal a straightforward instance of a business discriminating against gay people, which is prohibited under state law. However, the baker's attorneys have just argued to the Supreme Court that the creation of the custom cake is a form of art: *"An artist cannot be forced to paint, a musician cannot be forced to play, and a poet cannot be forced to write."* As we have been saying, my grandsons, it all comes down to where you draw the line. It was said that the Court is likely to split 4-to-4, leaving Justice Anthony Kennedy to thus decide whether baking a cake, or in this case refusing to bake a cake, amounts to a constitutionally protected expression of religious belief or free speech that is deemed more important than a citizen's right not to be discriminated against. We might ask if shoemakers, haircutters, or chefs should have their sensibilities as to their creativity be equally protected when someone walks into a shoe repair shop, hair salon, or restaurant. I had thought that in the case of restaurants and public accommodations, the black Civil Rights Act of a half-century ago had decided the matter. As I am finishing this chapter The Court found that there had been specific animus against the baker's religion in this specific case and decided in his favor but ducked the underlying question about whether or not the United States Constitution would otherwise apply.

Finn and Cormac, you may want to pay attention to how arguments are selected from various alternatives to persuade the Justices to arrive at a conclusion in these last two cases which round out our list of a few of the long-playing intellectual battles.

Should My Vote Count as Much as Yours?

The next case was just argued before the Supreme Court as I finish this writing. The case is *Gill v. Whitford*. It is on the subject of "gerrymandering," or the drawing of election district lines by politicians to favor their party. The practice has gone on since shortly after our Republic was founded, but it has now arrived at a point where a party in power can use sophisticated computer analysis to create more or less permanent control of government. In other words, elections would often no longer represent anything resembling the will of the majority of the people.

One day, while your father was growing up in Locust Valley, Long Island, our Congressional Representative described to neighbors in our backyard a predicament he was facing. If he wanted to stay within the boundaries of his Congressional District while visiting all of his constituents, he would have to take a boat three times to go from Queens County in New York City and then cross Hempstead Harbor, travel through Nassau County and cross Oyster Bay, and then again take a boat to Suffolk County. It can get much worse with politicians drawing lines to look like impossible-to-solve jigsaw puzzles. To me, this is the antithesis of what our republican system was designed to achieve. The very conservative Supreme Court justice Samuel Alito, in an underwhelming statement called the practice "*distasteful*" in the oral argument a few days ago.

One vote for one man has traditionally been considered a matter of "*equal protection of the law*" for disenfranchised voters as provided in the Fourteenth Amendment. However, the attorney for the Democratic voters argues that the issue in this case is discrimination against voters because of their views, which is a violation of their right to free speech under the First Amendment. He concluded: *"We're here telling you that you [the Supreme Court] are the only institution in the*

United States that can solve this problem, just as democracy is about to get worse because of the way gerrymandering is getting so much worse."

What is the "worse" that can happen? A glaring example was found fifteen years earlier when the same court had to consider a case in which a West Virginia jury had awarded a $50 million verdict against a coal company. The company chairman then spent more than $3 million to elect a particular judge whose vote subsequently overturned the judgment on appeal. It did not take a bloodhound to know that the decision smelled, and this is what the Supreme Court found; the Court reversed the reversal, letting the original judgment stand.

In *the Gill* voting case currently being considered by the Supreme Court, Democrats in Wisconsin won a majority of the votes, but Republicans won 60 of the 99 assembly seats. Two years later, the Republicans won just over half the votes for the state legislature but more than two-thirds of the seats. The same year as the Gill case election, the Republicans in Michigan won 51% of the vote but 71% of the State Senate seats. And the United States House of Representatives has 241 Republican representatives while Democrats have 194, a 10% favorable differential for a 1% voter advantage. When this is not the natural result of demographics or geographic boundaries, but clearly artificially drawn lines that cannot be explained, it seems in direct conflict with the basic aim of the Republic for representative government for all the people. Every citizen in our country should be concerned for the preservation of our democracy when there is no other plausible explanation. This manipulation of voting districts should be subject to challenge in the courts who have the ultimate responsibility for determining when our Constitution is violated. We await the decision of the Supreme Court.

We will look at one, earlier, case, which was discussed in the most recent issue of the New York Law Journal. In 1965, while I was in law school, the United States Supreme Court agreed to hear the case of *Griswold v. Connecticut.* This case is of especial interest, my grandsons, because we can appreciate how many sides there can be to an argument as well as the great importance of fairness in the decision that the Court made.

The Executive Director of Planned Parenthood and its Medical Director, who was a professor at Yale Medical School, were arrested for giving advice and birth control devices to married women in violation of a state law that prohibited distributing birth control devices. Connecticut was the only state in the country that still had such a law. The defendants were fined $100, and they appealed all the way to the Supreme Court. The question was: Did the law violate a mandate of the United States Constitution?

Counsel for the "criminal defendants" claimed protection under the First Amendment's protections of free speech and freedom from religious mandate, the Fourth Amendment's right to freedom from unreasonable search and seizure, the Ninth Amendment's restriction on rights reserved to the people, and the Fourteenth Amendment's right to due process and equal protection under the law. Oral argument went beyond these specific provisions, or any particular language found in the Constitution. It moved on to issues of public policy. Could the State Legislature prohibit conduct because a law had been passed one hundred years ago that seemed patently unreasonable by today's community standards as further evidenced by the fact that that no other State still prohibited when no one could point to the exact words in the Constitution, nor specific intent of those who wrote the Constitution.

The debate centered on growing recognition of an individual's fundamental right to *"personal privacy"*, especially between a woman and her husband or a woman and her doctor, as in the case of *Griswold*. Neither of these concepts are found in the words of the Constitution. Did this mean that the State could do whatever it wanted?

There had never been an explicit *"right to privacy"* found in the Constitution. The difficulty was exposed in the different opinions in the case, which cited a range of reasons for and against reversing what Justice Potter Stewart called *"this uncommonly silly law."*

Justice William Douglas found that provisions of the Constitution such as the First, Third, Fourth, Fifth, and Ninth Amendments provide a *"rational continuum of Constitutional rights"* of which marriage should be considered a part, older than the Bill of Rights itself.

Justice Arthur Goldberg agreed that the right of marital privacy was protected by the Constitution, emphasizing the importance of the Ninth Amendment, which provided that the enumeration of certain rights in the Constitution *"shall not be construed to deny others retained by the people"*. This was startling since the Ninth Amendment had never been so used before. Moreover the U.S. Constitution reserves rights non-enumerated to both the States and the people, and it was the State that was now claiming it was not prohibited in passing such a law. Justice Goldberg explained that one must "*look to the traditions and conscience of the people*" to determine whether marital privacy were such a right.

Justice John Marshall Harlan concurred in the result but not the reasoning. Justice Harlan argued that the Court should acknowledge that it was adopting the principle of "*due process*" for substantial rights, the principle that had previously been discredited after overturning the law that had set maximum daily hours of work law for bakers in *Lochner*. But, he said, the Court should exercise judicial restraint while looking with "*particular careful scrutiny of the State's need to justify the citizens' abridgement of freedom,*" while respecting history, our basic values, and an appreciation of the separation of powers between the federal and state governments.

Justices Tom Clark and Byron White agreed with the majority, with White directly calling the law "*so stupid*" that it violated due process of law since the State of Connecticut could not justify how banning contraception between married couples could prevent illicit sexual relations.

In dissent Justice Hugo Black, well known as a robust defender of free speech and individual rights, agreed that the law was dumb but nevertheless held it was not a violation of the Constitution. He argued that Justice White had it backward, that a law written by a State should be presumed Constitutional unless proven otherwise. He thought the Court had no ability to poll the public to meet Justice Goldberg's proposed test of "*tradition and collective conscience*" in order to find if a law were breaching the Constitution.

Justice Potter Stewart, also in dissent, noted that this was an uncommonly silly law, obviously unenforceable in the bedroom. But he held the law did not violate the mandates of the Constitution. He wrote that Justice Goldberg's reliance on the Ninth Amendment to annul laws passed by the States was exactly the opposite of James Madison's concern for preserving the rights of the States from federal intrusion except for the enumerated powers given to the United States in the Constitution.

There were so many differing opinions that one might wonder if the fist Justice would change his mind by time the last had announced his decision.

As might be expected from such heated rhetoric, this *Griswold* case proved a powerful precedent, and has led to a series of others over the next forty years that have expanded the rights of individuals to be free from intrusion by the government in their private lives. This central point fits well with what I have been saying to you, my grandsons. I will listen to my own conscience. If a majority of citizens tell their legislators that their parents said theirs is the true religion I still do not want that religion to govern my private conduct. Their rights end where mine begin.

Yet I offered this analysis for another purpose: to give you an opportunity to grasp the twists and turns involved in grappling with abstract principles that get us closer to the wiser decision when we nakedly face what is at stake in the very real lives of people. We might consider it an analogy for championing the emotional, perhaps the spiritual, side of our nature, over the cold rational one that follows a pre-ordained premise wherever it logically leads us. This is one of the most important things that I have learned. Following logic to its rigid conclusion, whatever the results can be absurd. Absurdity cannot stand.

Let us take one more view of the judicial process to glean additional perspective.

As we have discussed throughout, we can go off on a tangent and still learn many things that relate to and expand the subject we are studying. When we spoke of federal Constitutional issues, we were really reflecting upon how we structure our society. We spent some time on how we might tailor the argument to appeal to the particular interests of a Justice who might be the swing vote, such as emphasizing the decision's importance for free speech and the First Amendment. Next we moved on to the appropriate but entirely different question of how we persuade individuals with differing political judgments and worldviews of a common ground upon which to build agreement.

We will now turn to one more related subject, the actual presentation of our points.

Once more I will begin with a personal reflection as a starting point. At NYU Law School, as in most others, the law is often taught by using specific cases as reviewed by appellate courts, such as renowned Federal Circuit Courts of Appeal, and the United States Supreme Court. Decisions of cutting-edge issues are often selected for law school casebooks because there do not present any clear answers. The educational value is heightened because it forces the students to draw upon their training and research to balance what should next happen. Cases I dealt with in my law practice included litigating state and federal lawsuits as well as preparing numerous briefs for the federal appeals courts. I also coached the Locust Valley

High School mock trial team for a half-dozen years and observed many of the same lessons. What you come to realize, again and again is that, at every level, the presentation becomes a critical part of convincing. The approach to convince the listener applies to the wide spectrum of human activity, but we will limit our observations to the courtroom here.

First, the decision is likely to turn upon one or two points. So, while you do not want to leave the back door open for surprise defeat, you must focus upon these one or two points in your oral demonstration. Your goal is to convince, so your attention is how you will do that. While arguing the case you can be stunned by an interrupting question for which there is no good answer. Learning to gracefully but directly address that question is critical for your credibility. Admit the negatives at once, then develop the thought of why these negatives nevertheless should not control the decision. The second thing to know, which we encountered when you began at your imagined time at a University, is that the rational will take you only so far so that emotional connection to other human beings is the other important part of the solution. You can't fool all of the people all of the time. Don't try.

But be fully prepared. Before you begin the presentation, argument, or negotiation you will have walked the facts forward and backward in your mind, and are fully comfortable with whatever is to be said of them.

You will have done your research. You will know why precedent supports your presentation or if it doesn't, why it is different or wrong. You will now have to convince the other person or persons. Hopefully, you can draw upon the behavioral psychology and drama classes you took at the

University in preparation for this time. But sometimes the response is obvious and direct. For example, I was in a Federal Court in San Francisco in an antitrust case argument on a motion when opposing counsel told the Judge that the law said a specific thing. Our local trial counsel simply said "The law does not say that, it says the opposite", and cited why. There is no better way to respond in such a circumstance.

You need to recognize whether you are speaking to a judge or professional on the one hand, or a jury or laymen on the other. For jurors or laymen, your statements will be simple. You never want to insult the intelligence of your listener by explaining the obvious, yet you do want to connect all the dots, and to repeat many reasons why this outcome is obvious, enough times that no one will forget it. For a jury of laymen you may find a series of catchy phrases so that they readily understand what you are trying to say. Perhaps one of the most famous of such phrases was used during the widely televised O.J. Simpson murder trial in Los Angeles some two decades ago. A defense attorney, Johnny Cochran, summed held up a pair of leather gloves found at the crime scene and repeated: *"If it doesn't fit, you must acquit."* There were a number of reasons for the acquittal, but this clever phrase did not hurt. The essential point is that any presentation is performance. You should be a genuine, confident person, comfortable and interesting. The formality depends upon the audience, but ordinarily your demeanor should be casual enough that the audience would like to have dinner with you.

It is also a fact of human nature that in the sales pitch, or the trial, you may need a villain on the other side. A vendor may want to stress that he is the local vendor when selling a health food store. To create reasonable doubt, defense attorneys in criminal cases often cross-examine the police investigator and question whether all the evidence was really fully pursued in the investigation. My law partners used to try medical malpractice actions and the defendant doctor's professional sloppiness was a big target in cross-examinations: "The documents do not show that you did all those things for my client, do they?" He may say he did, but if it is not in the documents, at the best he is still sloppy in not documenting it, and if sloppy once then sloppy in other aspects of practice as well?

Let us return to the larger theme of political decisions of the past century that have had a major impact on the actual lives of people. We had used the example of FDR's New Deal to get a sense of what is at stake, and of Supreme Court decisions to understand impact on the public debate.

Of particular interest at this time in history are the two broad opposing camps of politicians who see no merit or virtue on the other side. This movement toward intolerance in political debate has predictably moved us further from a search for the truth. It is destructive. It is time for a change. We should not have to rely upon the final judgment of the courts to continually save us from ourselves. As we have said earlier, the perfect is the enemy of the possible. The more adult approach to recognize that common ground is possible, that our shared interest in our state, nation, and world allows us to find mutual benefits of compromise and cooperation.

We will turn from a legal approach for a moment to look

at the technique of pursuing the idea of a common ground as a way of proceeding. How might it work?

How do we persuade? I served, for a short period, as a mediator in the Adirondacks, and our goal was always to begin by finding some area of agreement. To begin with, since both parties had shown up, so we could have them acknowledge that they had at least one common aim to seek a resolution to the problem. The theory is that you can always find some agreement even if it is only that the parties agree that they disagree. That is a start. Next, we might get them to agree to stay for a set period, say an hour. Then we had them agree to listen and repeat back the other side's position until they agreed that this was indeed what was being said. This, itself, often proved greatly advantageous in moving the parties forward, when they could at least narrow the disagreement to agree on their exact differences. The professionals say that if you want to convince someone, you begin by making sure you understand what they actually believe and can characterize it in a way that will not alienate them. So you may find that you are able to say that you have the same goals but differ in how to get there. You are now on your way. Maybe it is the time of day, not actually the event itself that is the major concern we find.

It is true that people have different foundational beliefs, which shape our value, and color our conclusions. As we have noticed, an emphasis on liberty or loyalty to tradition for people on the political right, or on justice, fairness, or caring about the effect on people on the political left, may yield a different conclusion on how to proceed in political debate.

Professor Matt Feinberg of the University of Toronto,

in an article in *The Atlantic,* emphasized that if you want to convince a conservative that same-sex marriage is a good thing, you might do better if you bypass an equal rights argument and appeal to a commitment to loyalty to one another as the good to be achieved.

You might note here, my grandsons, the emphasis upon the First Amendment right to freedom of speech and association can be directly linked the freedom to vote for those whom we support because we believe in them. We speak about our beliefs and we act upon this and we join with others in supporting and voting for those we believe in.

Professor Feinberg also reminds us being selective about the evidence that you marshal in support of your argument. He notes that the advantages that may accrue in framing an issue in moral terms is greatly lessened if you are quoting from someone from the opposing camp. Thus my above reference to FDR would be tactical only if FDR is such a long-standing icon whose views are no longer considered controversial and confrontational.

In searching for a common path, we first looked for common ground and we then whittled away at the differences. The practice is to put aside unimportant differences to get to some point where we can agree. It might turn out that it was not the activity, let us say immigration, but the quantity, say the annual quota of immigrants, that can be the compromise. The difference between the two sides was then only one of degree. How many people should we let into America?

The *Gold Manifesto,* cited in this *Atlantic* article, makes the point that adversarial debate among philosophers is not the only approach to pursuing truth. There are different methods to finding reality. Moreover, the mind is not a computer. People can more often be persuaded or dissuaded by amicable engagement that is thoughtful and respectful than by shouting certitudes. To write this prompts one to add: *"Duh!"*

The grander theme is that, in our pursuit of a synthesis of competing ideas, we can develop new paradigms. How does an alternative view and approach likely work?

History strongly suggests that long term success hinges upon cooperation: sharing trade, ideas, stories, and models. To further pursue the practicality of cooperation in historic detail, I recommend you read *Non Zero: The Logic of Human Destiny* by Robert Wright. The insight is that life is not a zero-sum game. We can create circumstances where we all win. This attitude of cooperation can and always has energized economic, political, and social attitudes, and biological life itself, a step at a time. Wright suggests that this has been the story of the species in the evolutionary process, and in the long run, this is likely how our world will evolve. In other words, cooperation can be viewed as flexible adaption and recognized as a strategy in the interest of all. Game theory simulation seems to suggest that nothing less will work as well in going forward. We do not have time to fully explore this perspective of Non-Zero here. So let me presume you will read Wright's book and his long diversion into game theory to be persuaded, as I am, that cooperation is the long-term, winning strategy as we break to take a look at other interesting questions.

For one last thought on persuasion, we can turn to a tool of debaters and politicians: humor. As Mark Twain said, *"nothing can withstand the assault of laughter."* A well-turned phrase may quickly persuade an audience, although it needs to be gentle if it has a chance to draw in the opposing side. But it is a mighty tool in the arsenal of the gifted.

Now, we are once again, going on a different speculative flight of thought, which is worth doing from time to time. Our next question is: When your objection, disagreement, or dissent has failed, do you give up the ghost or persist?

Do You Hang Tough in Stroke City?

"What's done is done and what's won is won," wrote Irish songwriter Tommy Makem in *"This Old Town"* with a metaphor of the Gas Yard Wall separating Catholics and Protestants in his hometown of Derry/Londonderry, Northern Ireland in the second half of the twentieth century. The question is: What do you do when a particular battle is over?

I recall our Constitutional Law Professor at NYU telling our class that when he was clerking for United States Supreme Court Justice John Marshall Harlan, the Justice asked him when he should give up the ghost and stop writing dissenting opinions every time an issue that had already been decided arose in a subsequent case before the Court. Our Professor said that, at the time, he advised the Justice to *"let it go"*, but he later concluded he had been wrong. In fact, this Professor, Norman Dorsen, was not only an enlightened teacher but a tenacious lawyer who persistently fought for and litigated some of the biggest civil liberties cases of the second half of the twentieth century. The ultimate point is that often you can revisit and revise in this life.

So, when do you decide that the war, the election, the

debate, the contest is over, history, done? As always, it depends. If it is just a bad bet, you can chuckle about it and learn not to bet on losers. On the other hand, is the fate of your family or the nation at stake?

In the case of the centuries-old and continuing struggle of the Catholics in Northern Ireland and Derry/Londonderry for civil rights and real representation in government, Tommy Makem had sang, *"what's won is won, and what's done is done"* but nevertheless, he did not have it quite right. Indeed, the conditions in Northern Ireland were rewritten and revised two decades after Makem wrote his song.

We have circled around in our conversations before, and we do so again now.

The Irish are a stubborn people. After the British passed the Union Act of 1798, a violent struggle continued, on and off, for the next two centuries. Yet it ended in a brokered peace two decades after *"This Old Town"* was written. As we spoke of earlier, the United States, the British, and the South Ireland Governments brokered what became known as *"the Easter Accord"* as the Northern Irish Protestant Orangeman and Catholic Provisional Irish Republican Army finally made the bold decision to stop ceaseless shooting and sporadic bombing, to seek compromise. The leaders of these two opposing political forces were then elected the ministers, deputy ministers, and legislators in a new government and were, accordingly, paid. Nevertheless, hardened by decades of brutal reality, they did not find a way to trust the other side to honor all the terms of the peace accord and the Northern Ireland Government was suspended. Still the truce was not done. Norms to keep peace were then, finally, implemented and the peace held. It seems that the final ingredient for achieving peace was for both sides to finally accept the advantage of ending a thousand years of conflict. Even men hardened by brutal circumstances and convinced of their cause can sometimes see a way to cooperate. A drink to them.

While I have not heard that people see the connections, I have been suggesting that we can profitably compare this Irish conflict with with similar grievances and continual rage against land taken, and rights usurped. We have looked at what I see as Daniel O'Connell's legacy, several years later leading to Henry David Thoreau's *Civil Disobedience*, and then on the next century to Mahatma Gandhi, and to M.L. King, Jr. We have also looked at less successful efforts of dissent in the Middle East, to see what might work. We might also look for instruction to the native inhabitants of North America who did not go away when their lands were taken centuries ago, leaving a hangover to this day.

Throughout we have tried to grasp reasons why evolution and revolution, dissent and protest, happen and work, or not. There is no single answer. We have now added the additional question "When do you give up the fight?" across the spectrum of human activity. When does the union give up the strike? When is the war inevitable or over? When do you divert your energy to another pursuit or winning cause?

You and I might now admit to each other that there are always competing views and varying conclusions as we focus upon the fact that *"The past is not really dead, it's not even past,"* as American novelist William Faulkner said. There will always be conflict between those who are telling differing narratives, as there is always tension between thesis and antithesis. However, I think strength can be found in taking steps toward an evolving synthesis. Reworking the story that has been examined by the ancients and continually reworked down the ages is really the story of civilization. This discussion leads us to a very big, never-ending, question of when and how we should rework a prior story wish to keep alive.

Practice, Practice, Practice

There is a joke about a man walking down 57th Street in New York City who stops a stranger and asks: *"How do you get to Carnegie Hall?"* The stranger answers, *"Practice man, practice."*

I would like to now move to an apt descriptive analogy, *"the practice of life".* We look at those who practiced before us, and it is not accidental that the term given for professions is the practice of law or the practice of medicine, and such. It suggests that we are always learning, awaiting a new use for all we learn. There is also the reverse: ignorance found in not recognizing that what we are now doing is based upon all that came before. John Maynard Keynes captures this notion in another famous quote: *"Those who think they are not practicing economic theory are captives of long dead economists."* We are in a continuum, beginning where men and women previously left off. We always start with assumptions, whether we know it or not. If our current ones no longer seem to fit our future just right, it is time to adjust or abandon them. To fail to do so is to flout Einstein's other theory, the one about insanity as continuing to do the same thing and expecting different results.

There is often a fight to write history, to claim our ideas as the important ones and control the story told. I find that prejudiced people are often purported realists that support "traditional" models of status and privilege as part of a societal system in which they benefit as their tradition elevates them, as it degrades others.

Let's take royal families as an example. As a national symbol and institution, a monarchy is particularly useful in suggesting that aristocrats, dukes, sheiks, and such, are among the lesser gods also worthy of ruling and entitled to a share of the available resources disproportionate to actual contribution to the welfare of the rest of us. And they often do so with a hypocrisy that could be hilarious if it were not so sickening. Susan B. Anthony, a New Yorker who struggled for the rights of women (and slaves) well over a century ago once said: *"I distrust those people who know so well what God wants them to do, because I notice it always coincides with their own interest."* Please note that I am choosing words carefully here because words are important. Precision of expression leads to clarity of thought, which leads us closer to the truth and the exact prescription. Moreover, the words we choose can make a compelling case or a rather bland assertion. For example, I have just come across a sentence in a New Yorker magazine article by Adam Gopnik that is self-evident in its persuasiveness, at least to me: *"How much pain, anxiety, and sheer disrupted existence are covered by the words: 'He then emigrated.'"*

What do you do with such thoughts?

"The Poet Always Carries A Notebook"

This quote from the poet Mary Oliver leads us to a very interesting question: Where can you find your stories to tell? The most important are those you learn as you observe, investigate, and seriously contemplate, like Charles Darwin looking at the life of animals and plants as he sailed around South America. And we might consider Alexis de Tocqueville, who between about 1835 and 1840 traveled and observed America. This early period of our country was the time when Ralph Waldo Emerson was beginning to formulate and articulate his philosophy for the new America. We are in as much need for such unifying foundational stories today.

I am suggesting story lines from life that are meaningful, or prompts for them, which I am confident your fertile minds can carry to a meaningful end for the narrative. Finnan and Cormac, your dad wrote about this concept of general progression in *Reflections of a Master Maine Guide*, noting that we develop a worldview tempered by our understanding of ecological processes, learning to discover patterns to changes that bring something to fruition, that "whet our scenic appetite." Your Dad notes: *"Evolution in a writer takes time and effort . . . punctuated by brief periods of dramatic change . . . to discover, explore and enjoy . . . pulling the curtain on stories . . . in reverence and awe."*

A story might first be inspired by an uncontainable concern when the author, you, sees more clearly than the rest of us. That is its power. Whether we are looking at the magnitude of life, or glories and injustices found in it, I am confident that you know that the ultimate subject we seek is the appreciation of the soul, ours or another's.

This theme can be explored with an individual representing our collective dilemma and thus offering a view of the universality of life's choices. Ideas can be found anywhere. Often our artists capture the universal among the mundane moments. Billy Joel's anthem, *"Piano Man"* sketches a waitress and a businessman sharing conversation *"as he slowly gets drunk"* and a bartender *"whose quick with a joke and to light up your smoke, but there's some place he'd rather be."* It suggests, to me, opportunities to update Arthur Miller's sad, sad portrait of Willie Loman in *Death of a Salesman,* or of the desperate Blanche Dubois in Tennessee Williams's *A Streetcar Named Desire.* It can begin with a quote from a poem or song, an incident or a scene of a moment of existence, the spark for a beautiful, deep, dark, story of the courage to hope, despair in failure, anguish in the search for connection to another human being.

Let me illustrate the point with a brief account. Joan and I were recently driving to a party, west along an avenue in Ozone Park, Queens. We passed signs on two almost adjacent storefronts. One read: *"Last Pawnshop before Brooklyn."* The other read: *"Birdsong Food."* Either seems a good jumping-off point for some yet unimagined tale.

A most basic requirement is to be taken seriously. For this you must be trustworthy. The qualification for this is to have integrity, to be real. Plays of ancient classical Greece are still performed and are moving portrayals of the human condition and its imperfections. Aristotle's *Poetics* provided a guide: to write about characters that are both realistic and able to captivate an audience. He said they should be *"good enough"* so that we can root for them, have characteristics that fit the type of person that is presented, possess human quirks that make us believe they exist, remain consistent and thus credible throughout the story, and finally take action. The details of their life, such as the food they eat and the habits they possess, get beneath the surface. They give us insight into their world even when the details themselves are trivial. Information about the protagonists is fed to the reader through the eyes and senses of the other characters. At the heart of all actions are desires. Do their words tell us what they want? Who benefits? Why do we care? Do they keep going, whatever the troubles or the cost of the venture? Does their resilience capture us?

During the bloody period of the French Revolution, the philosopher Denis Diderot proclaimed: *"To dare, to dare again, ever to dare, only therein is the safety of France assured."* Do you agree that his appeal to bold fortitude is heightened? When my children, your father and his siblings, were little, I used to recite a similar but more age-appropriate poem when we traveled in the car. They sang of Christopher Columbus with stanzas that enthusiastically ended: *"What shall you say if you sight naught but seas at dawn? You shall say at break of day sail on, and on, and on."* How it is said matters.

Reworking an old tale can create a new classic. Shakespeare reworked existing stories into masterpieces of tragedy and comedy. The most widely read novel in the world is *A Tale of Two Cities*. You might even write a modern version of Charles Dickens's wonderful political portrayal of Paris and London during the French Revolution. Would it be New York and

Beijing? Any thought can inspire a start; but then you do not copy, you just find your own way toward sharing your insight.

The world is fast becoming a data-driven world where analytics rule decisions. The huge availability of information stored *"in the cloud"* provides immense potential insight for the future. You could create an economic comparison of the twin cities of Macro and Micro as a science fiction story that is a sketch or collection of anecdotes comparable to Jonathan Swifts's *Gulliver's Travels*.

A "simple" tale often reflects a deeper message. Consider the original story of *Pinocchio*, which I found this referenced in an excellent article, *"Knock on Wood"* by Tim Parks in *the New York Review of Books*. The Adventures of Pinocchio was written by Carlo Collodi in 1883 as part of a collective effort to create Italian literature for children right after the unification of the Italian States. It was meant as a subtle warning to his fellow citizens of the time. The tale depicted the uncertain mood and conflicting attitudes of a people, unified at least in theory, and revealed their candor and lies, generosity and cruelty. In the story, set in an earlier time, the talking pine log was carved by Geppetto to be his companion *"to dance and flip,"* to help him *"find a crust of bread and a cup of wine."* The puppeteer loses control of his new creation, whose wild inhibition causes Geppetto to be jailed while Pinocchio goes home alone to find a cricket giving him traditional advice on how to behave. In a childish rage, the puppet flings a mallet and smashes the insect the wall, to Pinocchio's delight. The Disney movie of sixty years later had little in common with the earlier caustic cautionary tale of the distinction between good intentions and the discipline and ability required to carry them through.

You could update ancient spiritual themes in energizing myths in a current setting, such as contrasting a darker side of humanity like George Lucas's morality action tales in the *Star Wars* movies, which take place in *"a far off place, long, long ago."*

Next, let me repeat an earlier point that I am taking wild leaps in our conversation to prompt you to broaden your imagination. I once again boldly dive into a subject for which I have no training and little experience and take the risk for your benefit to encourage you to do the same. If one wants to create meaningful art, the task is to go beyond the surface, to hint or convince the reader what it all means, not simply tell a story. Originality, your own thoughts, is how we measure the contribution.

You could take the broad approach of historian Thomas Carlyle, assume that history is the consequence of the acts of great men, and write a comparison of leaders emphasizing the virtue found in John Kennedy's *Profiles in Courage*. You could move the scene from the United States Senate to the world stage after World War II to consider men of great fortitude seeking heroic success that rival the ancient Greeks' and with similar risk of valiant peril.

You might pick up the tale with some figures that we encountered earlier. Perhaps you can begin with Colonel Pál Maléter, the commander of an armored division in Hungary in 1958. He was sent to suppress insurgents but instead joined them in seeking independence from Soviet Russian domination. He was invited to attend a meeting arranged by the Communists to negotiate peace and was executed by them when he accepted. You could compare and contrast the playwright Václav Havel whose absurdist criticism of the Communists and whose political activities before and after the unsuccessful 1968 Czech uprising led to numerous imprisonments. The subsequent *Velvet Revolution* toppled the Communists twenty years later in 1989. Havel became the first and only president of a united Czech and Slovak Federative Republic and was elected president of the Czech Republic with an overwhelming majority of votes. He presided for over a decade and had worldwide acclaim when he died at 75 in 2011.

You could move the scene to the Middle East and the efforts of Yitzhak Rabin, who as a young army officer in Israel's war of independence in 1948, was the model hero in Leon Uris's *Exodus*. As a general, politician, Prime Minister, and two-time President, he then spent the second half of the twentieth century fighting for the survival of an independent Israel. After signing *the Oslo Peace Accord,* which sought to establish a permanent peace with the Palestinians, he was assassinated in 1995 by a right-wing fanatic. You might compare him to Anwar Sadat, a member of the young officers who overthrew Egyptian King Faruq and who, in 1970, succeeded Gamal Abdel Nasser as the leader of Egypt. In 1973 he led Egypt into the Yom Kippur War to regain the Sinai Peninsula lost in the disastrous war with Israel in 1967. The war was unsuccessful, but he soon reversed course and offered, and then went to Tel Aviv and spoke to the Knesset, the Israeli Parliament. This led to a negotiated peace with the Israelis and peace since between the countries. Sadat was shot and killed by fanatics in 1981

There are more opportunities for telling stories than time in life to pursue them all.

You might try different forms of expression to look for clues on the unique power of these various modes. Finnan, I know you are already playing several musical instruments, and Cormac, I am confident that your mother will likely have you doing so as well. Could you move from one discipline to another, to use what can be found in musical exploration of human emotion in your writing? Suppose you looked at a sonata by Wolfgang Amadeus Mozart. Could an exposition of a work by this genius help you develop a style? Could his way of being bold in a major key, or lively in a minor introduction, be reflected in your prose? Does his repetition and recapitulation enliven the movement, and could his changes in the pattern or voice be used to create your mood? What can be added that enhances or completes the work? Is there a recurring theme that develops which convinces the soul and can be translated into words? Is there imitable elegance or bluster? Are there clues to appealing to the human psyche that you can learn from the musician?

We have been tracking the emotional side to our communications. Poets say that in life and in the cemetery, *"if you say it right, it helps the heart to bear it."* Reading poetry provides insight into expression. Can it be used in the story you are telling?

And how do we say it right? Having thoughts and feelings of course, and developing habits of mind that are insightful and precise. But it is powerful to develop techniques to best express what we are saying. One example quickly comes to mind here of a common but important experience. Most of us find that when we go to mind with a problem pressing upon us we are likely to have an uneasy night. But see how Charlotte Bronte put it: *"A ruffled mind makes a restless pillow."* She focused upon two colorful adjectives to describe two nouns she was comparing, to create a memorable description that captures our imagination.

Much of this may come to you in the process of editing. One way to criticize is to damn by faint praise. When we were children we would do so by sayings such as: *"I defended you the other day. Someone said you were not fit to live in a pigsty, and I said you were."* An adult version of this is a well-known exchange between The Irish playwright George Bernard Shaw and British Prime Minister Winston Churchill. Shaw sent Churchill a note saying: *"Here are two tickets to the opening night of my play. Bring a friend if you have one."* Churchill responded: *"I'm engaged the first night but I'll come to the second performance, if there is one."*

For most of us editing makes all the difference. When we rewrite and expand upon our thoughts, we see mistakes, change our mind, and ask what we do next. This is normal and a healthy pattern of writing and living. Many writers say that they hear their characters speak to them and they follow the flow. The Pulitzer Prize-winning novelist from upstate New York Richard Russo told an audience in Lake Placid, New York that he is often mostly finished with a novel before he finds an ending. Then, when he understands what the book is all about, he goes back to see that all that everything preceding points in the right direction. *"Just go with it, and then see where it leads"* is wise advice.

Thinking deeply about these things, we move beyond the content of our first observations to new connections. Long ago, we saw that when we observed, analyzed, and gathered ideas and adopted them as our own, they became the *"furniture of the mind."* In this process, you may find yourself using the same words for differing things. Here is where a Thesaurus becomes your good friend, providing other ways to put it. Alternative words with subtle variations in meaning allow you to construct phrases that precisely describe, and convey mood as well as meaning.

Therefore, inspiration can be found anywhere and everywhere, but whatever you decide to take up, it takes patience and tenacity to work it through, circle around it in your mind, and refine the story to make a point worth making, and polish it to a point where it is worth reading.

Flourish or Perish

First, you must start. Earlier is better than later, which reminds me of a story somewhat relevant to our point here. I had a Professor of Philosophy at Iona College that told us just before the final examination that only those who had received an "A" on the midterm could write a paper, and only those who wrote a paper could get and "A" for the course. I then still had a tendency to put off assignments and catch up later, and at first I felt betrayed by having this information withheld until too late. But I later realized how important the greater lesson: it is not so much that if you try you will succeed as if you don't try, you will not succeed. I learned more from that "B" grade than I would have from an "A." If you enter the race, you might win, but if you do not you will not, ever. It still amazes me to this day how many people never enter the races that life presents us all.

A similar point from a different perspective is found in the story of an elderly speaker talking to a college business class on success. After the lecture, a student raced to the front and asked, *"But what is the secret of success?"* The old man replied, *"Jumping at your opportunity when it comes along."* The student turned away and then back, and asked: "But how do you know when your opportunity comes along?" to which the old man replied: *"You don't. You just keep jumping."*

Generally, I think a secret to success is to start early, stay focused, be willing to pay the price, and never give up. I doubt there are many people who have been successful in this world who would disagree.

There are of course many ways of winning and paths to success. You have by now probably memorized: "It all depends upon what you are trying to do." This book is an example. If this book is printed by a commercial publisher and thousands of copies bought for children, it would be a financial success. On the other hand, it might be that no one in the world reads this book except you, Finnan and Cormac, but you each read it a number of times over the years, perhaps during a summer in your University years. Essentially you would return to these conversations to ask: "I wonder what the old man thought about that one?" Both scenarios would be a success, but the latter would be the far bigger one for me.

The chronicles of this book aim to walk out of nature into

civilization, toward confident enlightenment, as we evolve from our experiences and repeated habits to greater vision, purpose, plan, and action. We build upon what we have inherited as our biological and cultural legacy. How do we get things done? *"Not by bread alone,"* says the Bible to which a brother-in-law likes to whimsically respond: *"If you don't eat, you die."* Both are right.

A Break in Our Conversation

I have referred to big ideas of the classics in our cultural heritage. We have weaved into our narrative select subjects to allow you to grasp that continuing a long pursuit can immensely add to your education, as you view it from different times and places, from as far away as ancient Greece to Europe and America, comparing different people and their thoughts and actions, from Thucydides to Churchill. Some insights are more inspirational than the original findings. Earlier I compared the suggestion of you keeping an intellectual journal to the writings by Darwin and de Tocqueville. Both of these more or less contemporaneous observers followed an interesting idea to greatness.

As far as I can tell much of what I say to you in this book are original thoughts after considering the subject for a time, such as when I suggest that the civil disobedience of Henry David Thoreau likely came from practices developed in Ireland by Daniel O'Connell a few years earlier. As we mention a subject, later resume the thread, then return to it again in a different context, it reveals itself in many forms. To me this never seems more evident than when we come back, again and again, to suppression and dissent, truth and tolerance, be it of Galileo, or Voltaire, or the revolutions in America and France, Eastern Europe in the 1980s, or the Middle East today. The subject is historical and political, economic and moral; it can be with pomp or pretense, often end in discord and sometimes success.

This stream of thinking about history as experience suggests a way of seeing the law as a series of decisions which is, incidentally, an introduction of how "case law" is taught in our American Universities, one way for you to learn. We have been chiseling away at such collected experiences, ours and others, present and past, to see what life's lessons might reveal to us. They are stories of how men and women find meaning in modern life. In the second last chapter of this book, we will next look at the question of economic prosperity, and then move on in our last chapter to the idea of spirituality.

PART V

"Tis want of sense that makes us poor."

- Anonymous

CHAPTER 9

Expanding Prosperity

Throughout our talks, my grandsons, we have noted that people evolve. In my opinion, this also means that the arrow of history points toward progress, and at no time is that more evident than when we look at economic life.

It serves our purposes to begin with this long view of the efforts we make to earn *"our daily bread."* There are marked differences in studying how a society allocates resources, and how individuals make money. Our stories will move back and forth between these important topics, between what is good for us individually, and what is good for us all collectively, as well as the tensions between these two. But first, to get at what we are trying to do, we will briefly go back to a beginning.

The Mercantile Experience is Central to Humans

People create things, grow crops, design and make products, and exchange the excess. Sellers seek customers in other lands while buyers look for different goods from elsewhere. Trade adds value, so intermediaries transport goods from places of excess to other places of demand. Merchant traders are central to the process and they prosper. Money has always been at the core of men's activities and motives.

We have long looked at the ancient Greeks because of ready access to many of their early questions fundamental to all people, how the world is and how it should be. In examining the 3,000-year intellectual journey from Troy to the 21st century, we noticed that the answers we pursue depend upon the questions we ask.

When we look more closely at the time of the saga of the Trojan War over three thousand years ago, we can see early efforts for economic survival and dominance by the Greek city states. Similar quests for resources had gone on for a long, long time before the clash at Troy to control the crossroads of trade between Asia Minor and the Mediterranean There was more than the beauty of Helen, revenge, and glory to that early Greek invasion of the Bosporus.

At that time, the Greeks of the islands wanted to take control of a lucrative trade route from the west to the east. So, the great foundational story of western civilization can also be said to be about money. You will recall that we spent a great deal of time on the importance of the fact that when the Spartans won the Peloponnesian War some seven hundred years after the Trojan War, that Sparta saw the Greek City States as one Greek people going back to that foundational story of Troy. The reasons given for that earlier invasion mattered greatly. This idea of unity as a people led Sparta to preserve defeated Athens, which in turn saved Athenian civilization and thus Socrates, Plato, Aristotle and the foundation of what is now Western thought prospered.

Yet, as we dig deeper, we find that profit, and not just the betrayal of Helen, was in the mind of Agamemnon and his warriors. So, we may get a different or more important answer if we redefine the questions. Big ideas matter. This remains true today. It turns out that a cellphone is not just another phone or a watch. But there is always a first underlying reason which is important to understand if we are going to base our decisions upon the prior experiences of history. The actual facts do mater in seeking accurate conclusions as to who wants what trade routes, or what makes people tick.

America has been a place of particular adventure and economic possibility, which has left its mark on our consciousness, and thus our efforts.

Northern Europeans sailed north to the coastal cities of North Atlantic which eventually became British, while Spanish and Portuguese expeditions concentrated on the south. The North American model of free trade and economic mobility prevailed. But it did not start out that way. I have read no book that better clarifies the early days of hectic economic movement than *The Island at the Center of the World* by Russell Shorto. He used records found in the archives of a New York State government building in Albany in recent times to tell of the Dutch of New Amsterdam, who stumbled into a tolerant economic and social culture suited to this new world which the British inherited when they took New York City in 1664. The author describes a colorful collection of misfits then considered to be the base of society, who participated in the exploding economic success of "*the City.*" It is above all a story of tolerance as the condition for the growth of a great new city, and an approach that prevailed for the new country.

Early movers were followed by waves of immigrants including Irish, Italians, and Jews to the populous cities, and German and Scandinavian farmers to the lands of Pennsylvania and the Midwest. Nothing stopped them. It was a vast country. If you did not find a house or an opportunity in one place or neighborhood, you went on to find another. Waves of immigrants continued to melt into a new way of life which echoed across the earth. Change was not just necessary in the new world, it became the way of life, a value and ideal, a vision that tomorrow could be better if you make it so. Opportunity provided motivation. And upon what is it all based?

Some General Thoughts on Economics

Ever since the American Revolution, when talking about economics in the United States, most people speak about Adam Smith's theory of free markets. It makes sense that thousands of individual decisions dictate how our collective resources will be distributed and to whom. Smith explained that the price mechanism of the free market is the most efficient way to proceed because when each of us demands a product, we are voting with our dollars as to who should continue to produce and distribute the supply of products and services that we, the people, want. The point of equilibrium, where supply meets the demand, occurs when goods and services are distributed to those who are willing to pay the most for them, which matches the number of people who will buy the best products at the cheapest prices. There are, of course, many submarkets for those who are primarily concerned about the cheapest price or the best products, but within these markets, price determines who gets what. We get to choose what we will spend our money on, which is desirable since we are the ones who know what we want. At least that is the core of how the theory works.

In economic terms, a macro view of this process focuses on factors in an evolving economy such as general decisions by government, businesses, and investors that provide the context and means of doing business. Economic decisions are structured and processed according to the way in which our society is organized. Is there a farmers' market or a computerized trading floor in which to buy and sell? Through the collective actions of government, we provide roads and infrastructure, regulations, as well as money and credit; taxes are imposed as well. Is the tax on sales at the stages of production and distribution, or on the income generated at the end of the year? What incentives and disincentives are designed to affect the availability and cost of goods and services? These public decisions have a major impact upon our economic lives and our wealth.

This is further complicated by the fact that governments at the national, state, and local levels are the largest purchasers of services and goods. Their purchases are not often governed by the discipline of the market requiring that decisions are fully responsive to competitive prices and products. Costs are allocated not to users, but to taxpayers, and government decision makers are susceptible to undue influence or corruption since there is little personal economic incentive to make the efficient decision.

The micro view is when each of us – individually and in

associated groups – looks at how and where we make money, and spends or invests it in competition with the other sellers and buyers of the components of products and services. It is our assessment as to how we choose to interact with the specific companies with whom we have a relationship as an owner, investor, lender or borrower, employee, vendor, or customer. In the aggregate, it becomes the determination of the total gross domestic product of the overall markets.

It all comes down to people making products and money by giving others what they want – or that they can be convinced they want – or are required by the government to have. In a sense, it is what is in our minds that sufficiently motivates us to act with consequent success or failure, leading people to repeat or modify their behavior in the hopes that they will either continue or reverse their results. What I want to emphasize is that every day there is a new chance to succeed.

> *"What's the first thing you say when you wake up in the morning?"* Piglet asked Winnie.
>
> Winnie replied: *'I say what's for breakfast? What do you say, Piglet?'*
>
> *'I say what wonderful and exciting things will happen today?'* said Piglet.
>
> *'It's the same thing.'* said Winnie.
>
> - Benjamin Hoff, *The Tao of Pooh*

The first thing ambitious people usually ask when they

wake up in the morning is, "What can be accomplished today?" What they often mean is "What's in it for me?" There is a personal element in each decision but there are patterns as well. Our wide approach allows us to periodically glance back for historical lessons, however tangential, to look at the reasons for the decisions and trends. In order to understand, we, like the Roman orator Cicero – ask, *"Qui bono?" Who benefits?*

How Do I Know? The Wall Street Journal Tells Me So

This is not a conversation about investing, and I have only two brief comments about your personal investing before we move on.

Being an investor in the stock market, where we know less about other people's businesses, can be different than running a business. A bad stock pick can put a big dent in a portfolio. A good alternative is to buy a collection of low fee index funds such as the Standard & Poor's 500 largest U.S. stocks and Russell mid-cap stocks over a period of time, thus diversifying your risk over industries, companies, and time. Many wise investors such as John Vogel who founded the Vanguard Mutual Fund, and Warren Buffet who founded Berkshire Hathaway suggest buying the low fee exchange traded index funds (ETFs), as superior to the alternative of making decisions on the equities of individual companies, trying to pick the best stocks, at the right times, with limited information. The overall concept is to avoid mutual funds that have income tax consequences each year as well as annual fees of a percent or more and choose low fee ETFs, and then to sit back collecting dividends and ride the averages of the stocks in broad sectors of an economy that have been mostly expanding for a century.

Unless you choose to make such investment decisions your career, this is good advice for most people.

Despite some current comments to the contrary, I support buying your first home when you are young for many personal and financial reasons, and with a final convincing observation that when you own this home or its successor for twenty years or so with the mortgage paid, you then end up owning a substantial debt free asset. You are unlikely to take any comparable alternative funds and invest them to end up this well.

While there is more to this subject, it is a story for another day.

Why Do Companies Exist Anyway?

In the *Wealth of Nations* Adam Smith emphasized that organizing the division of labor is crucial to efficient production. The division of labor is not dependent upon a capitalist economy, yet the mobility of labor in a free market best allows business to combine capital and labor for a successful enterprise.

When a successful business model is found, a corporation with sufficient resources can repeat that model in "cookie cutter" fashion to multiply or expand the profit for each store or enterprise. Profit can be enhanced when fixed costs and administrative expenses are reduced by allocating overhead over a larger group of locations and products. Thus, one good store with good advice and financial planning, can become a larger, more efficient retail chain. This is a crude way of looking at the process but it is valuable to appreciate the ability to replicate an existing model that works, rather than limiting your thinking to something totally new. Often, after there has been the first successful model, lenders and investors will take an interest and provide the funds to expand. This can be an opportunity for all concerned. Risk and reward are what motivates the free market system. A big part of success becomes the institutional memory as a company learns how to do things better as it continues operating.

While he was still a student, economist Ronald Coase asked the question: *"Why do companies exist?"* Answering that question won him a Nobel prize in economics over a half century later. Essentially, Coase went back to the fundamental factor of modern economics, the price mechanism, which Adam Smith posited in *The Wealth of Nations* in 1776. As we have seen, in a free market, prices adjust to allocate resources where they are most valued, which is determined by the demand for a product at a price the seller agrees to pay. In business, producers obtain the materials and labor at the lowest cost so they will shop around unless the company can do it for less in-house. It is often best for the company to do it within the corporation because there are *"transaction costs"* to locating as well as coordinating, transporting, and maintaining the steady flow of labor and services. Shopping around for each part of a product to assemble is too costly. So, the answer to the question is that, the success of the modern corporation is that capital can be invested to do repetitive tasks within the firm more efficiently at a lower cost. The process can be physically managed; for example, an assembly line of automobile parts. The key insight is that what the firm does reduces costs so they are cheaper than buying them externally. The core of a corporation's operations is ordinarily in-house, and those who work for the company build on their knowledge and core competency as they go along. Still, independent companies are necessary for those components not produced by the business, so outside firms and consultants are used for specialized or short-term projects that cannot be done better internally.

A firm needs a collection of employees with different talents to fulfill its many functions. The more valuable the function, the larger the pay for the job. Almost all of us will be employees for some or all of our lives, so within this framework, how can we join the team and be successful?

Getting Personal

> *"There is only one way to avoid criticism; do nothing, say nothing, be nothing."*
>
> - Aristotle

I do not know of a step-by-step manual on how to fill your personal bank account, but I do have broad recommendations for a prosperous life. They begin with training your mind to take care of the rest. Throughout our conversations, I have been trying to leave you with a mindset that crosses traditional boundaries; with a sense that everything interacts with everything else. Yet if we always entertain an overly broad view, it can leave us unable to see the choices we should make, to decide, and to act.

You should understand the big picture to know where you eventually want to be. You also need to avoid paralysis by deciding what you are going to do now, and doing it now.

Whether it is our business or our job, the study of economics trains us in ways to look for facts that identify and manage transitions, showing us where to expend our money and our effort. As we do so, we can recall Justice Oliver Wendell Holmes who reminded us, *"A moment's insight is sometimes worth a life's experience."* We need to study, but what we need more are habits learned, which serve us well whether we stay or eventually leave the company. Legendary investor Warren Buffet summed it up when he said that *"If study was all there was to it, librarians would be the richest people"*.

Mr. Buffet's basic assumption is that we look for value, asses it, buy the company or stock that we think has value, and stick with it for the long term. The stock market professionals who make money when we are continually trading have no incentive to encourage this kind of buy-and-hold investing, but for the investor or the employee, staying the course until it is really worth something is the often the better strategy.

Yet business is a series of events which are never the same twice. Renowned economist Joseph Schumpeter emphasized the fundamental point that, at the most, if things continue as they are, then they are likely to happen again. We look at the odds and we place our bets knowing that the risk means we may take losses along the way, yet we need to stay the course in order to win. You don't always win but you cannot win if you don't play the game so the question becomes: *Do I want to be in this game?*

To speak of economics is to speak of resources. As we look at this subject, we must keep in mind that the most precious resource is time. We can talk about how economies and companies are run, but you are not likely to be running a company or the economy when you start your career, and that is how it should be. You need to learn from others. Therefore, you will need a job. Let us imagine we are at this early time when you are starting out. What could an employer want? What would *you* want as an employer? Would you want someone who can do the job? Someone you enjoy working with, who reduces tensions rather than exaggerates them? Someone who not only knows what is being asked, but who lets people know not only what they are doing but why they are doing it, and when it will be done? What do you think?

I will begin with one observation: Once, when interviewing young lawyers, we had three comparable candidates. One of them had said what every interviewer wants to hear: *"I want this job and I know I can do it."* We offered her the job, and she was good at it.

Let me add that a half century of reflection urges me to state an obvious but sophisticated point: by starting early in life, you position yourself to move toward mastery of the many activities that govern your field. I think it's useful to take a wide look at this early phase of life. Especially if you are in a large organization, impressions are important. The advice varies but generally points you in the same direction.

Arrive looking like you are ready to move up, so everyone

else begins to think that you are. You will convey an attitude of confidence, friendliness, and cooperation. A broad education in the liberal arts provides the background of the many who have come before you, and serves as a historical framework and an understanding of the need for flexibility. Reactions to these experiences become sophisticated intellectual habits which people with nuanced judgment recognize. You want to project the vision that you are smart, driven, and ever-learning, and that you have your act together. You are ready for your first real job.

I will also offer you a thought aimed at ensuring success. Arrive ready to work at important things that you understood have to be completed. Be willing to complete the task, all the while, be mindful to share the credit. This is your first job, after all. Not fair, you say? Anybody could succeed if they did all that? Yes, just about.

Let's take another simple look at your job. Leave work every day knowing what you want to accomplish the next day, and show up ready to do it. That should get you through the first years ahead of most other people.

How does that work in practice? Let us imagine that you are just starting a project. Things have not been moving well, but you see a way to pick up the pace. However, it's nearing 5:00 P.M. Do you make some good notes to get a fresh start tomorrow? If you are me, you don't. Unless you have an unbreakable date, you stay until you hit a natural breaking point. Let me give you a personal anecdote to help you understand. Shortly after I opened my first law office, a memorandum of law was due for a trial. I found myself still in the conference room as the sun came up. It takes discipline to get to this point but it seems foolish to me to spend so much time trying to get something done and then walk away when you are finally achieving it. Maybe only one in ten people do this, but be that one person.

Is the secret to success doing what you are told? Hell no, that's not it! Directions are given to be followed, but you have been hired to perform specific tasks. You own that problem, whatever it is. It is yours to mold, move along, shepherd, and complete, knowing why or learning how along the way, and being aware of what you do not know. Sometimes it is not necessary to admit that you do not yet know something, but be true to what you are trying to do, and be ready with a mental high five for colleagues as you go. Most people have a tendency to think their idea is best, and if they are in charge, that may be what counts. Indeed, no one wants to be told they're wrong so it takes tact to have someone buy into your idea. But you may not be the one to decide what is the task. The idea that if they just really understood they would adopt your plan is not workable. If your approach is not acceptable, let it go if you plan to stay; if you cannot be a player on this team you need to leave, but that should not be your habit. And once you find a place that you are comfortable displaying an internal attitude of humor and kindness will be welcome but, of course, keep the courage of your convictions.

Actually, this attitude of getting whatever has to be done completed is also the approach of the good entrepreneur, which should not be surprising. An entrepreneur risks his or her own money; those who help are giving their time and talent. Both do so to be adequately rewarded. Let me repeat that. You want to do well, and you want to be rewarded for it, but the best of us do not act as if every task is an instant transaction with immediate payment. Attitude matters. But it is also necessary to know what you are doing, as that will ultimately be measured and will show up in your paycheck; work is about money. How do we measure it?

Assets minus Liabilities Equals Capital

This fundamental rule of accounting merely means that when you put up money to start a business and go forward, the amount with which you started your business, plus or minus your total net income or loss, gives you your current net worth. Familiarity with financial statements is a necessity for running or understanding any organization. Let me use another story to illustrate some of the basics.

We represented a large corporation which was owed substantial sums by a company that had filed for bankruptcy. Federal bankruptcy courts are the result of a provision in the United States Constitution. This allows the federal courts to govern debtors who seek to divert their assets from one state to another. It was also likely a reaction to the debtor prisons of England. Chapter 11 of the bankruptcy law was passed by Congress to allow a debtor to remain in possession of his or her business after filing for bankruptcy. The theory is that society is best served if a business can pay creditors some of the monies owed while allowing the business to continue providing products, services, and jobs. The availability of bankruptcy is a valuable part of our economic system, especially the part about not putting someone who owes money in jail. However, as I know you realize by now, there are many people who would take advantage of a chance to pay off their debts at ten cents on the dollar and keep their business in operation. This is why accounting can help identify those worth helping from the cheaters.

When I began questioning the principal of the business in a deposition and asked for the Cash Receipts Ledger and the Accounts Receivable Ledger, I was treated like I was speaking a foreign language. The company's accountants were no longer available and the owner just "did not understand." We were talking about the most rudimentary accounting yet he did not know what I was talking about. So, I asked whether the Company wrote down a list of checks when they came in. This posed a dilemma for the owner. If he did not write down revenues as received and keep books and records as required by law, then his business would be closed and all assets would be used to pay creditors. It turned out that he did have such a list he "just did not know its name." We could determine what monies had come in and gone out with the Cash Disbursements book. The same act played out and we moved on: although defendant debtor did not know it was called the Accounts Receivable Ledger, there was a list of monies owed the company and the accounts payable owed to creditors. By reconstructing the records, we were able to show that the assets were *"wasting"*, that is being diverted from the business, and the Court had them seized and sold, distributing what was left to the creditors.

In this information age computers keep track of financial information but, the accounting concept of tallying and classification has been the same since double entry bookkeeping was invented by an Italian monk in the Middle Ages.

Businesses keep daily journals to record each transaction as it takes place, listings cash receipts as they come in and cash disbursements as they goes out. In addition to these journals of revenue and expenditures, we need offsetting ledgers listing the asset acquired and the debts incurred. This is broken down into ledgers by class of asset such as real estate and buildings, furniture and equipment, vehicles, inventory, cash and receivables. We need to list corresponding liabilities owed vendors and other creditors. When we collect on a sale, we not only list this in the daily journal each day, we also make a debit increasing cash in that ledger but an offsetting credit deleting this amount in the inventory ledger. When we pay the vendor who sold us the material, we credit cash reducing it by that amount and debit accounts payable, similarly reducing the debt owed the vendor, thereby balancing the books. Of course, there are a variety of transactions that can occur but, in theory, the books always balance because for every debit, there is an offsetting credit to the journals and ledgers as we exchange one thing for another. The accounts are totaled to provide a profit and loss statement called a Statement of Operations and a balance sheet called a Statement of Financial Condition. These statements ordinarily list several years of transaction totals in columns that can be readily compared for a quick reference to what is going up and down, for better or worse. Comparing current assets to current liabilities on the Balance Sheet will indicate if the company will be able to pay its bills as they fall due. The desired ratio for most business is to have about twice as many current assets as current liabilities, so as not to run out of cash during a lean period.

Anyone can make up numbers and some people do. But financial statements are given credibility by an audit performed by an outside independent public accountant who test the records of management and certify that the financial statements conform to generally accepted accounting principles. It is well worth your time to take a course for a fundamental understanding of financial statements. After all, success in business is what economics is all about and, as they say, you cannot tell who is winning without a scorecard.

> *Of all sad words of tongue or pen, the saddest are these: 'It might have been'.*
>
> *- John Greenlief Whittier.*

Let me emphasize two essential points, Cormac and Finnan. Do not waste your time or your life on trivial matters, and remember that optimism is essential. There is the often used but still useful cliché of asking whether the glass is half full or half empty.

I see it as half full because optimism provides enthusiasm which leads you to continue until you find the solutions you are seeking. Confidence is catching, so others around you will believe that something can be done. It is also worth noting that the glass is refillable, so set about refilling it.

Economists have a term for this vigorous attitude. They call it the *"animal spirits"* of capitalism, meaning that those who go forward and risk, build, and innovate become the entrepreneurs who create the products, jobs, and money. Put another way, the psychological fact is that if you think you can do it, you likely can, and if you think you cannot, you definitely cannot; you get to make the choice. If you are not about avoid fools' errands, then there is no reason not to throw yourself into the task at hand.

Finnan and Cormac, as I speak to you here, I am not talking to the world at large, merely to the two of you, to emphasize one path you may choose. It is up to you, but I recommend that you are serious early in your career. Winston Churchill said, *"We shape our environment, then it shapes us."* I believe that your life will have already taught you the point I have been dwelling upon, that nothing is achieved without first thought, then decision, and finally with hard work.

I have spent a professional lifetime retelling one story which overemphasizes the point I'm making, but it is important. John Foster Dulles was the Secretary of State in the administration of President Dwight Eisenhower. Dulles was largely responsible for reshaping American foreign policy shortly after World War II. There were notable achievements as well as failures. When Dulles died, his obituary noted the fact that he had attended the Sorbonne in Paris and then Georgetown Law School. The latter was considered a deficit when applying for a job as a young attorney with the Wall Street law firms in the early 20th century. These "white shoe" law firms customarily chose from a small selection of Ivy League schools. Nevertheless, Dulles' parents had been Protestant missionaries to China, with what was probably more importance than what is obvious today, and Dulles was hired by the oldest law firm in America, where much later he became the Senior Partner. On Friday afternoon of his first week of work, Dulles was called in by the then Senior

Partner and told he needed a Memorandum of Law on his desk Monday morning. On Monday, Dulles was summoned and asked, *"Where was the Memo?"* Dulles replied that he did not have time to finish it. The Partner asked Dulles how long he had worked over the weekend. Dulles responded that he had worked until midnight on Friday, from 8:00 AM until about 11:00 PM on Saturday, and after church on Sunday until 7:00 PM. The Partner responded, *"Don't say that you did not have time to get it done. Say you wanted to go home early Sunday night."*

I am not suggesting that you spend your life this way. Indeed, when dying of cancer, Paul Tsongas, a Democratic U.S. Senator from Massachusetts said, *"No one on their deathbed says I wish I had spent more time in the office."* But the law can indeed seem a jealous mistress, and so are most other professions and things worth doing. Whatever you're trying to do will take a great deal of persistence and time, and it is necessary to pay the price, which is more easily done early in your career.

"Where there is no desire, there is no industry."

– John Locke, English political philosopher of
the late 17th century

Great risk can have great reward. And the failure to act has negative consequences. We cannot be paralyzed by indecision. First, any direction is better than none. Continuing down the same path as you have been going is a direction, and you must consciously decide that is where we want to continue to go.

Second, most existing business and investments tend to more positive than negative so a conservative approach calls for staying with what was done before; this approach is less likely to be criticized in the short term. Yet I know, my grandsons, that by now you know that this is not what I propose for you. We have come far too far for that conservative status quo mentality to be your default instinct, denying you many of the best decisions.

We do the best we can, always, which means not only being willing to accept new information but seeking it, but this is just beginning the thought process. Not only can things change, you can *make* them change. Believe in you. As Yoda, a mystical character in one of the *Star Wars* movies says, *"Do…or do not. There is no try."*

Throughout our conversations we note, again and again, that when we are talking about supply and demand of the moment, we are also talking about the psychology of individuals with their commonalities and differences, influenced by the cultural and political context in deciding what they will buy, sell, or invest, whether or not they will act, fear weighed against reward. We have seen in earlier chapters that many economists have become economic behaviorists, using surveys, studies, and focus groups to measure specific recurring events and the ways people react to them. The manner in which the user of a product reacts may be unexpected, but becomes predictable. Where would you start such an approach? Just about anywhere that is close to the subject. It is for you to determine, and you only need to select one approach to test at a time.

I will not speak directly about management style with

you, my grandsons, since my career as a lawyer with small firms did not provide much direct experience, in the style or substance of managing large groups. But I have been on a dozen not-for-profit Boards of Directors over these past two decades and will share some thoughts I have learned.

I want to say three things about managing decisions: One, I have read an article about conservation in the Adirondack Mountains which addresses "recreational hot spots," or places that are overused for outdoor activities. The headline claims that the problem will be addressed with "Leave no trace behind practices and training." In other words, leave the mountainside as you found it. Deciding to employ this simple and already prevalent practice and educating the increasing number of visitors could be quickly, cheaply, and effectively adopted and was unlikely to muster any effective public opposition because it is already commonly accepted. The decision was built on a developed culture. The program could be adopted without lengthy studies or the allocation of substantial funds. We do not need a long term committee to address every problem. We should not overlook simple opportunities to simply to get something done.

Two, talking around a problem leads to obvious – and not so obvious – solutions. There is something admirable in stating a position in a crisp, straightforward, and fair way. But, as John Stuart Mill put it, *"to know only your own side of the case is to know little of it."* If you cannot directly rebut what others claim, you do not understand the whole case or proposition. Perhaps even more important, if you do not listen to the point of view of others, there is little chance of promoting your view with them. Indeed, the failure to listen is a good way to *"snatch defeat from the jaws of victory."* Reason and the emotional side of the relationship are two sides of the same coin of group persuasion.

Three, I want to sensitize you to the often unrealized reality that, in making decisions, whoever gets to decide the question determines what problem we will address, and thus solve. *"Who sets the agenda?"*

What is to be done?

The larger point is that whoever asks the question, sets the agenda, or talks first at a meeting decides what is talked about. Those who set the table provide its direction. This applies as well to a business meeting of a few colleagues as it does to a classroom, or to the public debate of a nation.

When the situation is chaotic and everyone else is simply going day to day and doing what they did the day before, there is a vacuum and an opening for new ideas: yours. If you have already been thinking about what you were trying to do, this presents you with an opportunity to raise the issue and get it done. If you have thought about it, talked to the customers/clients/ suppliers/donors, then you are the one prepared to set a new agenda.

The organization already had a goal or mission. If you have an idea, project, or suggestions which can fit the broad goal, you can introduce them in a way that explains why your proposal should be adopted. You can prevail because you know what you are trying to do. You are now a de facto leader, at least for that moment. It's a good thing to make it a habit.

You are already writers, my grandsons. So, write a

Memorandum. Before showing the project to anyone, ask yourself the questions others will ask, write down the answers, and incorporate them into the Memo. It is a wonderful way to go from vague to razor sharp thinking and presentation.

What is the crucial point of it all, and do you get there? Does this Memo show that you have been curious to know and show what has been learned from your prior efforts? It is not likely to be appreciated if you come in and revisit a long-debated issue without acknowledging all that has come before. Have you considered examples for everything you write? Do you show healthy skepticism as well as an expression of concern by taking into account all the players, such as customers or clients, and vendors or suppliers, and other related parties? Can you explore potential common ground, even with competitors? If there are none, consider saying so. Are there no unanswered issues or parties unaccounted for? Are there unknowns that have not yet been identified? Does the reader come away with an impression of integrity and class? If so, you are ready for the criticism of others. Ask and listen, and if others are right, change your plan.

Let me praise the habit of writing Memoranda for two more reasons, Finnan and Cormac. First, it is a wonderful way to organize all of your thoughts for maximum use, clarity, and persuasion. Of course, this does not have to actually be in the form of a Memo; it can be an opinion letter to a client, a proposal, or anything that forces you to marshal all the facts, draw a conclusion, and organize your presentation in the most lucid and persuasive way, and be ready to defend it.

Second, as we used to say as young lawyers, "*life is a markup job.*" William Wordsworth described the process saying, "*As if his whole vocation were endless imitation."* But, why would you start any project, draft any contract, or address any problem that had been previously considered without the benefit of all the prior time and effort that had gone into it? They say "you do not have to reinvent the wheel;" it is too expensive to do so. Research what has been done. Then, if the task is not trivial, you need to provide your own creative solutions. To emphasize this point about the prevalence and wisdom of looking at what has come before when commencing a task, let me tell you a joke. As a lawyer enters heaven, St. Peter greets him, noting that he is 111 years of age. The attorney replies that he is 48. St. Peter replies, *"No, I am looking at your time billed and you must be 111."*

This is a bad joke, one that belittles the profession, but it does emphasize how much can be accomplished if you start with a prior answer to a similar problem; prior history has value. Let us take a moment to untangle this double billing issue a bit. Not much need be said about padding hours you charge; it is a lie, immoral, and unlawful. But let us complicate the case. What if you have just finished a long project for one client and billed the many hours it took for a very good product and result. Soon a second client happens to appear with an almost identical question. Do you bill him a couple of hours and give him the same answer that the last client paid tens of thousands of dollars to obtain? We have been looking at the question as if the time expended is the only issue, so let me relate a rather well known story of a Washington, D.C. lawyer of great reputation, influence, and judgment who received a telephone call from a client with a question of critical importance. He listened and answered only *"No you cannot"* and then billed ten thousand dollars which the client paid. We have now moved into the world of high paid consultants whose *"value added"* is judgment.

There is one more joke to polish the point. A surgeon sent a bill to a client for one thousand dollars and received a note from the client *"Please itemize"*. The doctor's reply note on the invoice: *"Your visit to my office $10, my visit to hospital $10, knowing where to cut $980."*

But to be paid you need to be doing something.

Getting a job done - a campaign

Let's talk about an example of actually getting a task done, as an entrperneur, or as an employee. Let us hypothetically assume that you have been approached to take on a campaign; it may be to launch a new product, or a public relations or political campaign, or an effort to move the local, state or federal government to do something. To get a sense of approaching such an assignment we will look at how you might organize this kind of effort.

For our purpose we will just make up a situation where the decider will be a unit of government. But this is not about good politics, it is about having the government regulators get out of the way of making money. We will say that a few small tour boat owners are part of a small new industry in Maine. They visit you because they can make money and create jobs if they can expand their territory to take tourists into small bays that lobstermen have been using for decades. In our example the lobstermen can be anticipated to push back against what they still see as an inevitable clash of uses, and will likely insist that the government retain their monopoly on permits to prevent overuse of these waters.

The government will face difficulties opening the waters to new use. First, because old time families have been making a living in an appealing ecological manner for generations, and the shacks selling lobsters on the docks have been an icon attracting tourists to this geographic market. Second, it could be a difficult problem to create a co-use system, and a lot easier to just keep the status quo. If the boat tour operators just show up at government offices and ask for a change they are likely to be politely listened to, and ignored. How could a tour boat campaign for access to local waters work?

Visiting government officials to discuss this matter can be helpful, but it will be a preliminary fact finding mission. Just going down to complain is not likely to accomplish anything. Pushing for a quick meeting or a hearing and decision without a major effort to create momentum to overcome inertia and objections is a dubious proposition. Indeed an early hearing could greatly hamper the effort since the small tour boat owners would then already have had their hearing and an adverse decision and precedent set after "the facts" had been considered. So acting prematurely and then going back to try to correct the mistakes is not the way to begin. There is a need to organize. The form this takes can seem mundane, but little will be achieved until this is accomplished.

It is likely that only a few tour boat operators fully recognize the need and opportunity in the beginning, and these are likely to be some of the bigger companies. They need gain the support of the rest, or most of them, for both their time, influence, and money are needed. These boat people could form an informal coalition but this is likely to lack sufficient continuous attention. Forming a not-for-profit corporation as a trade association is the next step, and retaining a Director, full or part time as needed, to get the organization operational. Depending upon the budget, the small project staff might be part time, or outside help. To help create a viable trade association other benefits of belonging will be useful, even if unrelated to the narrow initial purpose. Advertising, pooling common purchases for insurance or rigging, or whatever advantages can be found, will solidify the effort, Annual meetings and seminars can provide glue to keep the association together.

Now that there is an organization there is the initial purpose to be addressed.

Inevitably there has already been discussion, letters, notes, and memos about the problem, solutions, and the difficulties of achieving them. A Positon Paper is needed stating the case up front, clear and concise, covering all the points you decide to make. What is the objective to be achieved and why? List all the benefits to all concerned, as well as the best response to removing all the objections, one by one.

Do you offer compromises up front? That strategic decision requires reflection. Is early compromise possible? Can you decide that public opinion is the main venue of argument, and that you want your best and most reasonable case up front? In this overall presentation you may be able to enhance the appeal through the benefits of additional business this activity and advertising will bring the entire community including those lobster shacks on the docks. Particularly in the early shoulder season, when business is otherwise slow, this additional activity is welcome and it may be that the boat tours can be limited to early Fall, with site protection thereafter, every year.

This *"white paper"* should make clear that there really is no alternative to adopting the proposal, wrapping up by explaining the common ground where all can benefit, or if necessary that the advantages clearly outweigh the disadvantages. Then read it out loud, noting subtle or startling changes in language to provide the most convincing explanation, with the phrase that captures the essence of the argument completing the first draft. This motto, this battle cry, will be modified many times as it passes by all the interested parties, allies and then opponents.

In virtually all cases the crucial ingredient is the strategic approach undertaken in the beginning. It is time for an Einstein thought experiment: who do you need to talk to and to convince, what is the best way to frame the question, and how do you make it impossible to say no, at least in the long run? We take it step by step. Our group would like to enlist early allies, support of at least a part of the community, and especially elected government officials, with the representatives of most use to your group being the federal, state, or local government level that has jurisdiction to make the decision. Having some introductory calls supporting your initial meeting with the relevant government officials will get you attention. But first we need to know the exact process for making and changing government decisions. Our *"verbal walk through"* of the problem will suggest the need for research.

In this case is there even a public regulation governing the use of these coastal waters and coves? Or has the government just been issuing lobstermen exclusive site permits on a grandfathered or first come first serve basis? Is there any formal policy objection to just coming into the coves where the harvesting takes place? Is it time to make the case, to test the waters, if not literally by running boats into the coves, then to go talk to those interested parties and let them know that we see no jurisdictional objection to our use of these waters. Or if there is a contrary public pronouncement, is it just someone who decided without authority? We are a nation of laws not men, and government officials are just people who cannot just act *"ultra vires"*, that is without authority, arbitrarily deciding to allow some things and not others.

If there is a regulation which actually governs the use of the waters, and not just lobster sites, and what does it say? It may be unlikely to actually say that the waters of the coves and bays cannot be traveled, so there may not be any actual prohibition. If the language of the regulation does seem to squarely fit the entire body of water and prohibit interference beyond the actual lobster harvest sites, what statute passed by the legislature allows this regulation to be adopted? Does the underlying law really say that the regulation can be so broad as to prohibit lawful conduct that does not interfere? There is often *"a legislative history"* where the sponsors state the purpose of the law. Was it a narrower reason then the regulators are now trying to apply? Was there any hearing that demonstrated that this strict language was necessary to achieve the purpose of regulating fisheries? Is there precedent for and against such an approach in this or any other state? Are there scientific studies or an expert who can demonstrate that co-use is possible, or even on balance desirable, from an economic point of view at least. What are demonstrable economic advantages to the community in permitting a dual use?

We now have a message, and our audiences: the media and the public for support, the legislature which has to take into consideration the possible economic gains, especially if cooperation is feasible, the regulators who do not want to be perceived as unfair and biased or acting beyond their authority, and of course the lobstermen with whom we want to cooperate in sharing the waters. For example, our season may only extend into early Fall Season, and could be curtailed thereafter. Compromise may be possible if we are proceeding from both reasonableness and strength.

Moreover, even if a decision is made under *"color of law"*, that is relying on a regulation or statute, if it unduly and unnecessarily favors one group over another the action of the government may constitute a denial of *"equal protection under the law"* to our group, which is impermissible under our Constitution. So, for this and many other reasons we may also have resort to the courts if nothing else has worked. Being clear that we will reluctantly commence litigation, if it proves necessary, can motive many a government to act.

We started our campaign knowing what we are trying to do, analyzed the steps we could take before we started, organized the resources necessary, and executed the plan to build momentum as we proceeded. But wait a minute, could we have just gone and agreed with the other side before we began? Well, your Dad notes that the Interior Department, the Forest Service and the Parks Department, all now recognize that the best beginning strategy is to initially go to all the stakeholders for their input before making a public policy decision, rather than just decide and then put it out for review and let the decision be criticized after the fact. If you could effectively do the same it certainly could be best to explore the possibility. But it is not often that one commercial interest concedes a portion of the pot, even if not clearly detrimental, until it has to do so. And while it is praiseworthy to cooperate when possible, here we need our instructive example, my grandsons, so we have assumed the contrary, the need for the campaign.

"Just do it." ™

The Nike slogan has a point. When you are working or building a practice, there is great advantage in just getting a campaign, a project, or a case, done.

Unless you are doing everything by yourself, which is largely impossible, you will need to negotiate. We have our needs and wants but as you go forward you will find that squeezing the most out of every person and every deal is never the best way to proceed. Your first observation should be to determine with whom you must work or cooperate, and what they want and will do. Their objective is their best interests, not yours. You need understand what makes them tick and align your interests with theirs.

The traditional definition of "*market price*" is "what a willing seller is willing to sell for, and what a willing buyer is willing to pay." Let me tell a story that may or may not be true about an Arab horse trader. As the story goes, the horse trader went to market early one morning and sat down next to a merchant who had two fine stallions tied to his stall. They sat there all day talking about crops, local events, their villages, and families. Finally, as it got close to day's end, the trader said that he had no interest in buying a horse, but if he did, he wondered how much one would be. The merchant responded that he loved both horses and had no interest in selling either of them, but if he did, the price would be one thousand. The trader was shocked by such a high price and said that if he were going to buy a horse, it would be for a fraction of the price. After a period of time, they came to an agreement and the horse was sold. Another man sitting beside them said he would buy a horse for the same price. The merchant replied, *"No, for you, we start all over."*

If you are in a hurry and just want to pay fair market price, it may be that a horse trader is not for you. But the sooner you start, the better. But before you start, and from time to time, you should step back for a moment and take in the wide view of the market; look at the big picture of what you are trying to do. Recognize that what most people are interested in is the bottom line. How do you give them what they want, and get what you want?

Negotiating

It is never, "Why don't they?" it is, "Why don't we?" *"The fault dear Brutus is not in our stars, it is in ourselves."*- Cassius in William Shakespeare's *Julius Caesar*. When faced with opportunity, an abundance of caution or debt can make a coward. But there is also a story about Julius Caesar having massive debt as a young man. He borrowed much, much more than "the farm." His creditors could either destroy him or back him; they backed him and he succeeded. He was the ultimate salesman.

The ultimate salesperson has an almost unearthly lack of care and sense; he or she is convinced every deal is a sure thing. Yet in all negotiations, both buyers and seller face a common predicament and stress, the egos of the negotiators, their self-esteem, and how they think they are perceived can be decisive in whether or not a deal is made. So, like always, there is the rational and an emotional component to the effort.

One story is illustrative. A woman was sent by her Company to negotiate with some tough-minded labor leaders. As she sat down, the union head said, "*The Company must be not think much of us if they sent a girl.*" The attitude of the other side could either become a pattern that could be inflamed or defused. The woman could have asserted herself, yet instead, she said, "*All the men were busy.*" Both sides successfully concluded the negotiations and, as the story goes, in future negotiations, the labor leaders always asked for "*the girl.*" The woman in this story remembered what she was trying to do, the goal of the Company.

There is a second lesson to be learned as well. We do not always know how much leverage each side holds in negotiations, but whatever the power of the parties, there will be negotiations in the future, and you are creating connections and conditions now that will bear fruit the next time. This is why it is important to spend time clarifying your understanding before you start; you may have to live with the consequences for a long time. Ten hours up front may save one thousand hours trying to repair a broken contract.

You are capable of writing a clear agreement of the understanding, to provide for contingencies because you have performed an intellectual "Einstein walk-through thought experiment" before you started. You have isolated the known ambiguity and prepared for it. You know where you can modify your position, where you prefer not to bend, and where you cannot. There is no need to highlight your vulnerabilities; rather you should fold these needed steps of performance seamlessly into the natural process for performing the terms. If any of these nevertheless do come up and become an issue see if there is a creative way around the problem. Maybe the concern of the other side is guaranteed delivery and your main concern is assured payment. Escrowing funds can resolve the concern. If there is no deal to be had with terms you can live with, there is no deal; walk away.

It helps to understand if there is a backstory playing out in your moment with the other side. I spent a short period working for a corporation whose main function was buying out other corporations. They understood their main objective was to make a deal, not get the rock bottom price, which they did not need. So, they opened negotiations by saying, *"let's be fair"* and if they got close, they would say something like, *"If it's worth $60 million, it's worth $62 million, we have a deal."* Price was never the most important thing. They knew what they were trying to do.

There is a fourth lesson to consider in approaching negotiations. Long-term recurring trade is the prize of any business. Once you have a customer or client, you may extend the advantage and find other things you can do for them; this product expansion is the path to growth. Here is an example of unforeseen advantage to be gleaned from beginning a negotiation with a cooperative approach. A partner in the law firm where I began had a large food corporation as a very important client. There was an internal famous story that years before we had sued that corporation, but that our partner's fair, even handed, cross examination of the defendant, recognizing the other side's perspective in the argument and suggesting common norms and grounds so impressed the President of the other side that he retained our firm as General Counsel, the next day.

The approach taken can be so important. You start with a strategy and rehearse before you show up for meetings and negotiations. You may want to come prepared with some insider news or a joke to loosen up the room. But everybody knows they are there because there is something they want, so do not stray too far from the topic. What are the options for both sides, what can you give up, and what won't you give up? Do not presume the other side sees things as you do. It is not *"come let us reason together."* For example, there is a little-known but well rewarded practice in negotiating real estate leases in New York City that an out of town client of mine once experienced. My client had retained special counsel to negotiate a new lease for large office space in Manhattan. This special counsel spent the first two days of negotiations insisting that the lessor must have a right to occupy the space three hours earlier than was customary. Of course, this would entail substantial expense for the landlord. Finally, the special counsel conceded that his client would concede the time of day occupancy would begin, a demand his client really did not want in the first place, in exchange for a series of other demands with wanted monetary consequences.

There is the other side to this issue of getting what you feel you need.

When counselling clients, I would often point out that acting first might have its risks but, particularly when dealing with the government, being refused and then acting afterward was far worse. In some circumstances, what you need may be of little value to the other side, but they may demand a large ransom. Perhaps, when it is a one-time need, you should not negotiate at all. There is a useful saying that, "*It is better to act first and apologize afterward, than to ask and be denied.*"

Some deals you just do not want on anything near the terms offered. I once heard our local counsel characterize the other side's unbalanced offer as reminiscent of a Donald Duck cartoon showing Donald dividing jelly beans. The caption said: "*One for Huey, one for Uncle Donald, one for Dewey, one for Uncle Donald, on for Louie, one for Uncle Donald.*" For whatever reason, it can become apparent that a deal cannot be made, possibly because of hubris, the arrogance of the other side. Sometimes it's the personalities or the way demands are made that can poison the relationship. Early in my career, we had a corporate client whose Factory Controller demanded a large raise in early January. This was a sensitive time for the Corporation which was just beginning to gather the records and statements of its diversified plants to be consolidated with the home office numbers for the annual audit. The Corporation agreed to the large raise exactly as demanded. When this Controller arrived at his office on the first Monday in May, he found it locked and his desk and personal belongings had been moved into the hallway; he had been fired. Beware of prior harsh demands when the leverage is gone.

This general idea of arrogance, hubris, plays out across the scenes of life. To deepen an appreciation of this recklessness I urge you, my grandsons, to read *The March of Folly* by Barbara Tuchman who chronicled four of the great losses in human history, all of which she suggests were caused by hubris. In each situation the people "knew" their side was right which recklessness led to calamity. There were the Trojans who unquestioningly accepted the Greek gift of a large wooden horse which they brought within their gates. There was the Medieval Papacy refusing to recognize the call for the reformation of the Church. There was George III rejecting the pleas of the American colonies. And there was the United States insisting on moving into Vietnam as the French left and had warned us not to become involved, leading to twenty years of escalating hostility and then defeat. Convincing yourself that you are right is not the same as being right.

As we spoke of previously, money is not the only thing that moves people to act, but it is usually the first thing, the *"sine quo non,"* the *"not without which"* people will sign on, or stay on. Their primary concern is likely to be them, not you. In individual transactions what makes our partner, supplier, competitor, and customer tick? What do they want besides money? How do they make their decisions, lead their lives, and consider their relationships? Their individual habits, approaches, and styles are a personal culture. Quite often the ideal negotiation is to identify and focus on what will meet the needs of others rather than simply the dollars, quantity, and quality of the goods and services requested in their transaction. Students of negotiations with Eastern cultures such as Japan or China learn that contracts are more about taking time to develop relationships than getting the precise wording on one agreement. It is less about identifying specific tasks then doing what everyone believes to be in their long-term interests and building trust. Some may prefer to do business with you because you may be more likely to protect them even when they are not looking, and honor the cooperative spirit of the ongoing venture. This process is obviously not designed to work on a single transaction on a competitive daily trading floor. It would also be naïve to assume that anyone is necessarily doing this for you. Long-term partnerships are founded on such trust, but in the shorter term, we might be guided by the frequently quoted words of President Ronald Reagan, *"Trust but verify."*

"All other things being equal"

For a more than a century, isolating one factor and assuming all others will remain constant has been an accepted tool for testing hypotheses in the field of economics. If we assume everything else will stay the same, it allows us to focus on one variable and study how its change may affect the other factors. We can therefore examine the dynamics of the problem we are looking at. But we need to remember that this approach blindly assumes that the rest of the factors are as we have assumed, which is often not the situation. So, after we finish a study assuming that *"all other things are equal,"* we should think about each of the factors which may not necessarily be equal. Such skepticism can make anyone a potentially great thinker if you can find other clues.

You just need to find the other information that you trust as likely to be accurate. It might be a Federal Reserve Board policy about raising and lowering interest rates, or increasing or decreasing the supply of money. It might be freight car shipments, or the inventory of parts available that your company needs to increase production. Data is becoming a major world currency. We might begin by watching what knowledgeable people have been doing. For example, if you are in the business of making or installing solar panels, global data about the efficiency of current models of competing renewable energy or fossil fuels and their supply and demand could be pertinent to your venture.

The point is that you need information; contacts can become part of access to it, so we cultivate both. As we go along and meet and cultivate relationships we can be conscious of avoiding the opposite as well. A friend has a wonderful sign on her desk that reads: *"You do not have to enter every argument to which you are invited."* Rather than being set off by some annoying emotional trigger, it can be helpful when a dispute seems to arise if you focus on the people to note there are different points of view. Just acknowledging that there is validity to others' opinions helps. A kind word in a heated moment may be remembered for a longtime.

I noticed during many meetings that our client and government officials would be moving toward conflict and we would interject that when reasonable men disagree, it is sometimes necessary to call in an arbitrator, which in our system is a judge. But first, as reasonable men and women, we wanted the opportunity to review the matter and present facts and our reasons to convince them that our view was correct. The intent is to suggest that our mutual assumption, rightly understood, was that common ground was possible. It was. Of course, having a convincing story and information to then back it up proved useful. Common advantages can be well thought out and phrased in your mind beforehand. The right words at the right time cannot be overestimated.

> *"There is a time and tide in the affairs of men leads on to fortune"*
>
> - William Shakespeare

If you look, there are opportunities everywhere, if you keep looking. I frequently used to give talks to trade associations about looming legal threats to the industry. I often used the Chinese word for *"crisis,"* which uses the symbols for both danger and opportunity and noting how often both circumstances can exist simultaneously. That same situation occurs when someone loses his or her job; almost always a difficult time. Yet in these situations when someone becomes unemployed, has few choices, they often find the courage to start a business, which becomes a success. Of course, the trick is having something to sell, which requires giving people something they want. How can you start? How can you go about it? One way is to have a great original idea or know someone who does and needs help. But it's more likely that you will do something you learned in your last job or venture that you can now do yourself which is how most businesses begin.

Someone you know may help you get started. When I was a young lawyer working for a law firm, one of our clients made *"closures,"* the tops for bottles, jars, cans, and such. It was a relatively niche market and this client was one of the biggest and quite profitable. The backstory for this company was illustrative of how you can get started in business. There was a fifty-something engineering executive at a major oil company who had lost his job. This often leads people to take drastic measures since, despite federal laws banning age discrimination, it was not easy to find another job at this late stage of his career. Our protagonist, and he is a hero to me for having the fortitude to go forward, asked advice from a public accountant he knew who gave the engineer a spare office to use while suggesting that he go around to visit others, asking what they needed. The unemployed engineer had friends and acquaintances at his old company's purchasing department. It turned out that they had difficulty finding enough of the closures they needed for small oil cans. A look at the telephone book led to a visit to a small tool and die shop in Brooklyn run by an immigrant whose abilities running a tool and die shop exceeded his ability to speak English. So, you had a classic situation of *"the inside man"* and *"the outside man"* joining together to run a company. This led to a partnership for the venture, as metal was purchased from a vendor on terms to pay at the end of the week. The new customer/purchaser – former co-employees – agreed to pay cash on delivery, and within a week of round the clock work, the new venture had its first order completed, which was paid for at once, allowing for timely payment to the metal supplier. Once you have done it once you can do it again, so more of the same soon led to a successful business which eventually became one of the leaders in this small industry.

Keeping one's options open is standard practice for a lawyer, but may not be the best choice at all times. Decisiveness is required. It is necessary to commit to the deal, to be all in. Our business clients readily take it a step further, abhorring indecisiveness, and saying that any decision is better than no decision since it gets you moving somewhere. *"Run it up the flagpole and see who salutes"* or *"throw the spaghetti at the wall and see if it sticks"* are two colloquialisms that accurately point to another analogy: *"We cannot see the light at the end of the tunnel when we start our walk."* If you are right, you reap the reward; if you're wrong, you move on to something else. This adventurism of entrepreneurs seems counter-intuitive to many people because they want a plan for certain success. Yet they never seem to find it because they fail to try.

But let's return to our first idea: leaving employment to go into business for yourself. This is how I started. Here is another wonderful example: A good friend from childhood quit college after our first year, as a surprising number of very successful entrepreneurs have done, but which I do not recommend. He went to work for a few years for a company that fed other company's employees and then opened his own cafeteria company. Starting with sandwiches for retail customers, he found one small company in the financial district where he began serving lunches in their corporate back office. He found another client, then another, and another. A half dozen years later, he became a client of our law office and I represented his company for the next twenty-five years while he bought one small competitor after another, simultaneously opening larger and better in-house restaurants in large corporations, colleges, museums, and other public places. I retired and he kept going for almost another two decades, eventually selling his family and employee-owned business for a great deal of money. He had talent but it was obvious to me that real success was the result of the guts and years of persistence he put in that allowed him to overcome thousands of obstacles for half a century. I never met anyone who more deserved their success than he did.

> *"Were you ever out alone, when the moon was awful clear... with only the howl of the timber wolves and you camped there in the cold... a half dead thing in a stark dead world, clean mad for the muck called gold."*
>
> *- Robert Service*

We have not been speaking of evolution at the moment, but are there lessons we might learn from the evolutionary process. Being smart and strong is a great advantage yet Darwin noted that, *"It is not the strongest of the species that survives, nor the most intelligent that survives. It is the one that is the most adaptable to change."* We adapt or die, figuratively if not literally. Practices develops habits of adaptation and the character to succeed. It is a long process but we begin with believing in what you do as a powerful initial motivator to provide the persistence, stubbornness, and refusal to give up.

Aiming for minimum achievement is a good way to refrain from achieving anything but forgiving yourself for inevitable failures is necessary and desirable since we will all fail many times, and it is upon failure that success is built. Let me tell you a few more lawyer tales to sensitize you to a natural reaction to those who would "eat your lunch."

I will begin with a simple one. As I was going about my first real estate closing as a young lawyer, the older attorney for the other side suggested his client should take possession of the title now and we could trust him to take care of some closing details – which we can translate to pay some money – at a later time. Probably because I had grown up on the sidewalks of New York City I could not avoid offending him with a laugh. What was puzzling was that this seasoned fellow was still using this line so some people he'd dealt with in the past must have accepted this offer, which is contrary to the nature of what lawyers do in the first place, protect their client.

Soon after in the early practice of law, I represented a buying cooperative where a group of retailers across the country pooled their resources to purchase common merchandise sold in a joint catalog in their separate geographic markets. A corporation much larger than the others was joining the cooperative. It was suggested at a planning meeting that a large company, and thus an important one, should be able to receive their catalogs first and make payments periodically thereafter. It sounded tempting to have such a sizeable addition to the group with the resulting efficiencies of size and savings to everyone. But the other cooperative members were horrified to be responsible for carrying the debt for someone else, and they declined. Sure enough, a month or so later it was this insistence on payment in advance that saved the other members of the co-op from the same fate that befell the larger corporation: bankruptcy.

There is never a scarcity of offers or gambits by those who see you as a mark; they like to suggest what they would do for you tomorrow, or would concede at trial, if you would just provide your corresponding favor today. It has always seemed that once you insist upon corresponding collateral now, or put it in the trial record, their offer shrinks or disappears. I was once part of a trial that illustrates the importance of getting it in writing, in advance.

> *"If you pick up a starving dog and make him prosperous he will not bite you. This is the principal difference between a dog and a man."*
>
> - Mark Twain

On one occasion a new client came to me with a litigation problem. He was a famous perfume maker who had started a new company with a much younger partner. After a few years, his perfume corporation was successful and needed financing to expand. He and his then partner had equal equity in the corporation. The partner's father was willing to "lend" the corporation some money and take a small percentage of the corporate shares as payment for his risk. By the time my client arrived in our office, he had signed a contract which provided that he now owned less than fifty percent of the outstanding shares, and had been fired. He had a minority interest, lost control of the company, and had little hope that he would ever collect dividends or payment for his minority stock since all the profits could be paid to his partner and his partner's father as salary or consulting fees, or kept internally to expand the business until my client died. At the time he signed over control of his company my new client had not previously had his own legal representation. The transfer documents were prepared by the corporate attorney hired by his partner.

We brought a lawsuit alleging fraud in the inducement, conflict of interest, and unconscionable conduct in having the company attorney represent the partner against him. It was a good story to tell and we told it; the judge took some time to decide but concluded that the agreement to sell the swing shares was made by a responsible adult who chose not to have independent counsel when he signed a binding contract, and he was bound by the contract he had signed and we lost.

There are three important lessons to take away from this story:

First, if you do not maintain control or have a contract protecting your interest before you enter into a deal while you have leverage, you may face the same fate.

Second, as we talked about earlier, my grandsons, you have no business entering into any such an arrangement until you have done "an Einstein thought experiment" and mentally walked through every step from the first planning session to the eventual sale of company stock, or whatever else your exit strategy may be. In other words, the exit is part of the entry strategy since few people prove to be more generous than they have to be when it comes to counting money at the end.

By now you are understanding my point about being prepared in advance, so I will shift to another scenario;

sometimes you come upon a situation that you cannot avoid and where you cannot continue as you have been. You may prefer not to give up and lose everything you've put into the venture. Then there is the third point I would like to make: look for other leverage, a point where you can maximize the strength you retain while you still retain it.

Finding an Alternate Survival Strategy

The following story about a close friend and client is inspiring to me. One evening as we began wading through my friend's considerable corporate difficulties, he told me a story about his family company's prior experience. His grandfather, father, and uncle had previously been owners of a large construction business which had been responsible for a huge project in New York City that had been built with government funds. One Friday evening, the family gathered in a shed on the construction site to discuss the fact that they could not meet payroll the following Friday and would soon be out of business. However, the time for completing construction was critical to the public agency; it was a highly visible and important project for the government. Delay would spell disaster for all involved. Even with performance bonds to pick up the task, there would be cost overruns and huge delays. My client's family recognized that the government had a bigger problem than they did. On Monday morning, they went to the government offices and told them what was happening. By Tuesday, the government had found the means to buy the company's heavy equipment for a large amount of immediate cash, and to rent it back to the company to allow them to finish the project. The necessary cash flow was there and the project was completed on time. Everyone did well, and to this day, that company remains one of the largest construction firms in New York City.

The essential problem for my friend at the time of our later discussion was that he could not meet payroll for his construction job. He had a performance bond that had been required by the public owner for protection. This bond had been written by an insurance carrier that stood to lose large sums of money if it had to gear up a new crew to complete an unfinished project. We had commitments from our client company's key personnel to see construction completed. Then we met with the insurance company and negotiated a deal. In return for efficient completion of the project using the insurance company's money, they would release our client from all personal liability. There was still another similar problem to be overcome. My client had bank loans and had given his personal guarantees that our client company could not pay. The bank was convinced to take those sums we could quickly raise in exchange for release of the client's personal guarantees. The bank *"workout team"* agreed since they would collect far less during a long, drawn out alternative when the bank would become one of many creditors chasing down dwindling assets. Both insurance company and bank were willing to trade the dubious chance to collect on any personal guarantees for timely help in limiting any loss on the job.

I do not want to suggest that you ever cheat your creditors. I do not think this is "smart" and I abhor the idea. What I suggest is that when you find yourself in a difficult situation, find a way that best serves everyone.

Let me give you one clear example of what I condemn: I knew a young woman who was a good friend of the family for a long time. She had been babysitter for your father, your uncle, and your aunt. One day, she came into my law office with a problem. She had recently began working for a real estate broker in the next town. The broker had been the subject of newspaper headlines concerning questionable business practices. The woman (our client) had earned her commission, which the broker refused to pay. After a brief letter of demand, we commenced a lawsuit. In response, the broker offered to pay two thirds of the amount due my client, leaving her with a dilemma: should she accept the payment now or go through with the lawsuit, knowing that if she won, she would receive the same amount after paying us our one-third contingency legal fee. Of course, a larger corporation may well have gone forward and countered for other incidental damages forcing the reluctant debtor to spend money and effort for his willful delay in paying a debt. My client really could not afford the time, risk, or emotional commitment of going to trial, so I advised her to settle, which she did. The law's delay is often not a trivial matter.

As Abraham Lincoln famously said, litigation is to be as avoided like death and taxes. If you can. What lawyers know is that more than ninety percent of lawsuits will be settled before a verdict is issued by a judge or jury, almost always somewhere in the litigation process before trial. The judge will call both sides into his or her chambers and push for a settlement that no one finds fully acceptable. It is called compromise, and the parties will take it. So, why go through all of this pre-litigation when you can position yourself as favorably as possible early and then make clear your willingness to compromise as reasonable people. And if you recognize that you are not dealing with reasonable people up front, do not do business with them. But there will be disputes that cannot be settled.

We represented a number of corporations that sued much larger companies, often for unpaid debts but also for alleged violations of law. In earlier days it was often a trade regulation case such as alleged violation of the federal and state antitrust laws, that there are rules of the game and cutthroat competition can violate them. It was common at attorney seminars to hear legal counsel for both sides refer to "*defense by expense*" and "*attrition by addition*" (of the costs to prosecute the claim). Beyond the distraction, worry, time, and money involved in litigation, there is often incredible delay. In 1971 while I was a new attorney at a small firm, I once commenced a large antitrust case in federal court in San Francisco. Our local counsel was of a similar size of about a half dozen lawyers. I left the firm a few years later to start my own firm. All trials and appeals in this case were finally resolved in 1989. Our side won, yet I expect that the man who hired us was long dead.

The potential delay of the law was made famous in the novel *Bleak House*. The litigation that spans a century in Chancery Court in London was over a family inheritance with conflicting wills. In the story, Charles Dickens explains that "... *Jarndyce v. Jarndyce drones on.... Innumerable children have been born into the cause; innumerable young people have married into it. ...Fair wards of the Court faded into mothers and grandmothers; a long procession of Chancellors have come in and gone out"*. The conclusion: *"The whole estate is found to have been absorbed in costs."*

To come back to another of my cases and cautionary tales, a friend and client was a small lumber broker trading large quantities of board feet, bought and sold nationwide by telephone. Prices change throughout the day and payment is made by letters of credit delivered upon receipt of the goods. My client, who was located in the State of Washington found that even with a written confirmation of the sale to a large discount lumber yard in New York City, the letter of credit would not be paid because the buyer inspected the railroad car, declared the goods inferior, and refused to pay. My client could have hired his own inspector, tried to sell the goods for what he could, sued the lumber yard, and hoped to win the trial a few years later and break even, minus my legal fees. But he could not afford the money or the risk. The railroad sold the goods at auction and the same lumber yard bought the special order for cents on the dollar, leaving my client responsible for the cost of purchase and transportation fees.

Unfortunately, in the practice of law in New York City, the market and courts were full of businessman who found it greatly improved their profit margins to flat out refuse to pay their debts. Some of these chiselers have gone on to achieve high political positions. The best advice I can give is to shun such men and women in your business and social dealings, and when you confront them, challenge them whenever you can in business, in person, and at the ballot box.

There are scores more stories of mine, my colleagues, and my clients that illustrate my point. So, what is the lesson for you?

As we have noted before, Nietzsche observed that *"the doctor alone learns."* Let us diagnose and prescribe. The lesson here is a broad one. The general, diplomat, politician, administrator, and businessperson looks for leverage to find an advantage, and uses any temporary edge while it exists. Our search is for strengths and weaknesses, yours as well as theirs, to protect from the assertion of a point of view not bargained for, or to compel if an agreement is not honored. This may be unlikely unless you have positioned yourself to do so. Written agreements are often not enough. I had a much-admired uncle who was a banker who would regularly tell us that no deal was better than the person with whom you made it. Anyone can promise the money and the moon if they do not intend to deliver them. Contracts and documents are nice and necessary, yet there remains the question: how will they be enforced if someone breaks the deal? And what if everyone honors the agreement but it is structured so they win and you lose?

After law school and several years as an attorney with the federal government, I spent a short time at a large corporation called a "conglomerate". Finnan, I know you know this word as a composite rock, but it was also the term given to a corporation which bought a collection of companies that had little to do with each other. In the very early 1970s, these were considered "go-go" companies with very high prices/earnings ratios. The way it worked was that such corporations were seen by the financial market as growth companies because of the seemingly ever rising price of their stock, which, in turn, was based on presumed ever increasing earnings. If you bought corporate shares of one of these conglomerate companies with earnings of $1 a share for $40, the price you paid was 40 times your earnings. Entrepreneurs quickly found the way to enhance the share price was to acquire company after company at lower price/earnings multiples than their 40 to 1. If they acquired a company for 20 time earnings and added this to earnings of the conglomerate, the market gave all of the combined earnings a 40 to 1 value. So mere arithmetic increased the stock price of the combined company increasing the value of the company bringing the stock market price of the conglomerate to new heights. Since all the conglomerate had to do was buy out some company – just about any company – at a lower P/E for the magic of arithmetic to work this increasing valuation. This worked beautifully for a while. But it stopped when the conglomerate runs out of companies to use to confuse with this overvaluation. It was legal but it was and still is an equity market Ponzi scheme. The excess value reflected in the stock price is not real value added, the stock will tumble and the last buyer will take large losses. It should be noted that for everyone taking those large losses, someone nimbler and more unscrupulous had been taking profits. Like musical chairs, the last ones holding shares becomes the big losers.

There is another variation on this same theme. If you join someone else's game that seems too good to be true, you will lose. This story came ten years later in the early 1980's. This scheme precipitated what became known as The Savings and Loan Crisis. As the 1970s progressed, inflation was high and smaller local banks had created a big problem for themselves when they lent depositors money for long term mortgages of up to thirty years at rates of four to six percent. Then they had to pay eight to ten percent or more for short-term deposits. In other words, they had to pay out more than they were taking in, which is not a recipe for success or survival. These local banks became easy targets for enterprising financiers who saw an opportunity and began selling very risky junk bonds to the local savings banks companies paying high interest to local banks. They had pledged the assets of the companies they acquired as collateral to the banks. But after taking over an acquired corporation who issued the junk bonds, those in control could pay a high interest to the local banks for only a short period while the take-over artists enriched themselves with high fees as they sold off and closed manufacturing plants, distribution centers, stores, or any other assets the acquired company had. They were cannibalizing these corporations. Eventually, the acquired companies defaulted on their loans, going bankrupt while the lending banks lost the money they lent. It was lawful on its face, it was avaricious and every dollar an avaricious predator took was paid for by the many in local communities, both where the banks were located and where the acquired companies had closed. These were devastated by the staggering loss of money and jobs. Lender beware.

It was a time of predators offering deals too good to be true. There are a number of clues I want to leave you with, my grandsons. First, there is little reason to trust those who cannot rely on the weight of the facts but insist on their truth loudly. As a wise client once said, *"The louder the voice, the weaker the argument."* A very early question in business dealings is what is being proposed, exactly, and by whom? How confident can we be? As we have noted elsewhere, as the ancient Roman senator and orator, Cicero asked, *"Who benefits?"* In life, as in a trial, the truth may best be gauged by focusing on the motivation of the person speaking.

To carry the thought one more step I will mention that in our first day of training on my first job as a public accountant, we were presented with a decision to advise a theoretical client. His largest customer offered to provide all his business if our client would invest in sufficient new equipment and devote most of the factory to fulfilling these orders. It is, of course, efficient to eliminate most marketing expenses and very profitable if you have a captive market to sell. Should you advise your client to do it? What will you do when faced with the leverage this customer will then have over your client? The potential loss of this large customer threatens the company's continuance. The lesson we were being taught was that it wasn't really a question about accounting. It was strategic; it is dangerous to place your existence in the hands of a customer, relying upon their goodwill. In fact, many a factory was "captured" by a large retailer who vertically integrated by buying out suppliers who had previously agreed to supply most of its merchandise to that one customer.

The next story, which I have not seen in print and which I cannot say is true, but it is instructive nonetheless. J.P. Morgan was an immensely powerful banker in the early 1900s. He once tried to stop a stock market crash all by himself, a feat that would be unimaginable today. Supposedly, he went to see Henry Ford in the 1920s and said that he wanted to buy into the Ford Motor Company. Ford responded that it was a family company, to which Morgan suggested that without his support, financing would be difficult for the company in the future. It was a threat but Ford declined the offer and then found that he could not obtain substantial financing from any bank, making it difficult to continue to do business. But Ford was not about to give up. He advised every Ford automobile franchise dealer in America that if they did not put up the cash in advance for the entire year's inventory for the cars in their lots he would pull their franchise license and give it to someone who would. He did just that. Some view this survival of the fittest the only law of business. You need know when you are dealing with them.

The rule of law is essential to economic trade, but our society needs more than that, it requires trust. Who would give their goods or time if they were not confident they would be paid? We trust; if someone fails to honor their contract, we sue but why are you dealing with scoundrels in the first place? When the system is manipulated, the perpetrators are not "smart," they are self-serving and crooked, and we should avoid them and call them out for what they are. This may not be possible in some situations so a firm exit strategy is essential before we begin.

Let me conclude with the observation that we recognize the potential dark side of these transactions so we will not fall prey to them. When it is necessary to enter the arena with the dubious, you must be prepared to act and react at once. Yet it is a small mind that cannot hold two contradictory thoughts at once. As grandsons of a lawyer, you look at the other side of every situation as well. In the long run cooperation is the grease that makes our civilization run, and it is the best long term strategy, so let me give you another instructive viewpoint. We have a very good friend, a young woman who has had an inspiring career running a not-for-profit corporation surviving among the coyotes and predators of which we speak. Yet she tells young leaders at forums that the most important thing in your career is developing relationships of trust. The insight is clear because when you see that trust is missing, its value becomes so obvious. In summary, whenever you have a choice, work with those you trust.

> *"Oh the sea is full of a number of fish, if a fellow is patient he might get his wish."*

> \- McElligot's Pool, Dr. Seuss

What are the Odds?

Weighing decisions and acting upon them is central to every aspect of our lives, yet in economic matters we focus more directly on the risks and rewards of each transaction and venture because that is their purpose. It is not a question of certitude. Alternatives, trade-offs, choices, and their costs and consequences are our focus. To limit the risk and maximize the reward is an enduring habit of the astute trader, producer, investor, creditor, and consumer since everyone, by definition in economic matters, are in it to make money, avoid losing money, and spend as little as possible to get as much value as they can.

To be able to diagnose various situations, we acquire a set of ideas and language including the context of the problem, the opportunities, available alternatives, possible developments and consequences, possibility, and loss. Part of this is learning about the tools and language of the trade. With a good set of economic tools and good judgment in using them, you could eventually find yourself on the Federal Reserve Board. But for now, we're just getting a feel for the questions and some mental pegs on which to hang concepts. We're developing some tentative conclusions as *"furniture of the mind."*

We are not precise here; we cannot be and that is not our purpose. We are speaking about attitude and approach and there is always the caveat, "on the other hand." It is worth emphasizing that people have a tendency toward excessive confidence when there has been prior success. We have looked at Daniel Kahnemann, in his book *Thinking Fast and Slow*, stress this propensity for *"irrational exuberance"* as Federal Reserve Chairman Alan Greenspan put it. This, in turn, is a sophisticated echo of a forever popular book on Wall Street, *Popular Delusions and the Madness of the Crowd* written in 1841. The essential point over the centuries has been that when things are getting too good or too bad to be true, it probably is too good or too bad to be true.

As we have discussed, Kahnemann won the Nobel prize for Economics studying human behavior in the marketplace warning that once people accept a pattern of behavior as an operating theory, they usually close their eyes to the possibility that it might be wrong the next time around. He emphasizes this "over reliance," this inertia that has people hang on to their conclusions and their losses for far too long. For example, in the stock and commodities markets, because of the psychological fact called "risk aversion", investors do not want to lose and so stay in the market after their reason for entry has passed. On the contrary, they often sell out a good idea quickly to assure they were right and take some profit, rather than to maximize their gain. It may be a good decision to continue to hold a losing investment if it's a solid company in a fluctuating market like oil or copper and you know that the demand for the product will return. But if there has been a permanent dislocation in the market such as when digital cameras replace photographic paper, we have to overcome our reluctance to face and cut our losses. Once an idea is accepted, it should be subject to your periodic review, revision, or reversal.

This blind side in not re-examining our earlier decisions is so predominant that it is almost always useful to bring in someone new to assess a venture and the way we do things. Your grandmother Joan was a successful nursing consultant for decades because she was independent and removed from the experience at a particular facility, so she could always offer fresh insight. When first out of college, I worked for a large public accounting firm for four years and had the same experience noting how improvements to work procedures and internal controls could work when first we walked into a large corporation that had been doing the same things year after year. In practicing law, you would see a client's long-standing problem anew. One of our repeating pieces of advice and counsel was "you cannot do it that way." This did not mean you could not do it another way. Of course, which "it" we were talking about was important.

Facts and Economics

> *"The enemy of conventional wisdom is not ideas,*
> *but the march of events."*

- Economist John Kenneth Galbraith

Let's briefly refocus some particulars of the subject of Economics. It has long been called the "dismal science" because it is murky and when we look to uncover the cause and effect of all the interconnections between thousands and thousands of transactions, events, and decisions, it becomes murkier still. Reading tea leaves is not a plausible way to proceed, but economists have their own version by finding statistics that seem to foretell what will happen next, whether it's the changing Gross Domestic Product (GDP) of a country, or the trends of an industry foretelling the future. Economists are always looking for signals of the consequences of a variety of economic decisions.

The Baltic Dry Shipping Index was a long-honored leading economic indicator as it measured the price of transporting major commodities, raw materials, and products such as steel and building materials in Europe. It told what was happening in the European economy because the supply of cargo ships was fixed and people do not book a cargo ship until they have a demand for the goods. The ability to forecast economic activity in these industries in Europe rested on the price of leasing a cargo ship in the Baltic. Before the goods are delivered, people could know that the price of a product such as coal or steel might be increasing, since there would be concomitant pressure for its price to move up if more products were being shipped. If demand is up, prices were likely to follow.

Astute students of the economy seek ever more obscure, preferably under recognized data to give them an early clue to changes, and thus an advantage in making money whether buying or selling relevant commodities or corporate stock. For example, businessman in the United States often see the price of copper as a leading economic indicator of the near term future of market activity since it is used in a number of different sectors such as construction, manufacturing machine and supply parts, and consumer goods. As plans for a slowdown result in a drop in demand, the price of copper also drops. This price decline foreshadows a drop in productions, sales, and the price of the stock of these companies' and further impacts an entire industries' stock market prices.

Gathering such knowledge matters because the actual facts matter. It can be profitable to match data to predict outcomes such as decreasing or increasing demand. Political and cultural movements impact longer term decisions; data may even tell us far more in the shorter term. For example, when there was a large ramp up in production for military uniforms before WWI, it signaled military preparations in Europe were underway. In this instance, the preparations for war signaled that war was coming far before it was officially declared.

When there is a major change in mood, a change in price inevitably follows. I started this book asking you to look up a word, and I will do so as we near the end. Try *"paroxysm"* and you will get a feel for the potential volatility of markets in a downward direction. Or the phrase we have been repeating of the former Chairman of the Federal Reserve, Alan Greenspan, describing a booming technology stock market rise of the 1990s being caused by *"irrational exuberance"* and you get the feel that the market might be in a bubble preparing to pop. Greenspan was premature; the market did not top out for another four years and your grandparents did quite well in the interim, which in turn, helped our early retirement.

A Sword for the Future

We have seen that economists and businesspeople speak metaphorically about *"reading the tea leaves"* or foretelling the future by identifying events that indicate and measure activity in the economic chain. Many businesses are now using newly available Meta data, possible because of ever more powerful computers, to measure persistent occurrences on a large scale and the actions that follow recurring events. According to the former Chairman of the Board of the Alphabet Corporation, formerly known as Google, incredibly important jobs will be those that are able to relentlessly find and interpret information among a mass of chaotic data that is available through the internet. Such jobs are already appearing with names like *"data analytics."* At this moment, four of the highest paying jobs for new college graduates use information technology to analyze large amounts of data in the developing field of artificial intelligence. It seems that if you put a large set of this data into a computer and change the variables slightly, you get a consistent curve in the outcome to guide your decisions. Modern tea leaves indeed.

For example, the ability to reduce inventory and still have the needed product available when you want it in real time has been developing for a half century which became particularly evident as companies like Walmart and then Amazon used information technology for "just in time" purchase orders and sales distribution to recreate a new consumer economy.

Let's look at a current example of how evaluating information in real time works so well. There is a Space Storage Company that owns over 1,000 facilities and manages another 500 for other owners. People store furniture and other things for short periods of time. The price of leasing a unit is a straightforward matter of supply and demand; when there are few units available in a geographic market, the price can go up. When more units become available, owners need to lower the price to capture more business than the competitor. But when do they lower the price, and by how much? The current number of customers who need storage space is critical to decision making. Yet a local manager sitting behind a desk in some town does not know how many vacant units are out there, nor how much he can charge and still get the business. Space Storage Company uses a technology platform to maximize revenue as its computers analyze many data entry points online and from sales and inquiries throughout their chain to gauge available units and the responses of customers to differing prices being offered across markets. They can then adjust the prices in real time in order to capture as many customers at the highest price possible. The process is critical to getting the best price and not losing sales.

Much of this *"data mining"* requires formal training in mathematics, computer technology, and economic research.

It will also require those with different talents, broad exposure to the humanities to understand the big picture, and thus a broad view of where it is all going, and where it could be going. The general process circles back to earlier discussions about finding the facts of our collective experience and sorting the information so effects are more transparent. As we have been saying, actual facts matter, yet we go around and around in life, including our economic life, we refine and reframe what we learn, and contrast risk and reward.

Good judgment is needed. We can be too quick to jump, but in these times, the greater danger is likely to be in being too slow to consider new information and reacting to it. In the past, prestigious secondary schools used to emphasize the Latin phrase *"carpe diem"*, meaning *"seize the day."* Among the fog and uncertainty of any moment, there must be a refusal to buckle to the pressure of others, not to lose heart and flee the threat of the field or market. In order to avoid being an economic loser, you have to have the backbone critical to running a business, investing, or completing a project. Persistence usually carries the day and eventually the struggle. Having information that suggests the future provides fortitude, without which business cannot flourish.

Rational Economic Man as a Theory

We have spoken of self-interest as the motivating factor of most human activity. To many this is self-evident. But any idea which becomes unthinking ideology is likely to be taken too far.

While lobbying in Washington D.C. in the early 1980s, a

number of large corporations had economists and attorneys espouse a school of economic thought that pays great attention to a concept called *"rational economic man."* The idea is that just about everyone will do what is in their own economic interest, so you can predict the future with statistical formulas and such. More recent research shows a number of fallacies in using this concept as the sole guiding measure. First, because most people have imperfect information, that is unavailable or inaccurate data, they cannot be expected to make a certain choice. Also, as we noted, in the stock market investors like Warren Buffet have made fortunes by ignoring the mood of the moment and relying upon long term reliable data and are willing to bet against expectations reflected in current market prices. Also, because there is a psychological aspect to every decision, there often is *"irrational exuberance"* or over-emphasized fear that overcomes the price circumstances would otherwise warrant. This concept of "rational economic man" was carried to great excess in the Administration of Ronald Reagan from 1980 to 1988, when regulators and policy makers suggested we should measure the ultimate economic good as merely a *"supply side"* problem, or the total production of goods. To me, it was reminiscent of old Soviet Communist five-year economic plans where setting production goals for tonnage of things like steel could be met with one giant ball of metal, useless for anything but weighing. The acceptance of the theory as fact by regulators was being used to overturn antitrust and intellectual property precedent. This, in turn led to assertions that producers should be allowed to fix retail prices of things like watches, cameras, and electronics which the manufacturer sold through distributors to retail stores.

The argument was that the manufacturer would not insist on selling at high manufacturer retail prices unless it increased total output. In our practice of law, we used to lobby Congress against this position, pointing out that profits for the maker of the goods in excess of what would otherwise be paid ignored efficiencies in the distribution chain. Ignoring efficiencies in distribution was not and is not the aim of the free market. I bring up the point to emphasize that any time you hear someone urge a course of action based on an rigid dogma or system, economic or otherwise, be very cautious before you bet your own, or the public's, money. And we *are* talking about making money.

The larger point for you, my grandsons, is to be wary when an economic proposition begins to sound like the dogma of a church. In a way, when we talk about what should be done in our economy, it may begin to have a moral ring to it.

Warren Buffett has said that in the short-term, equity markets are voting machines, but in the long-term they are weighing machines for valuing a company. His point is that on any given day, the equity markets are something of a popularity contest. And we have already visited the concept of Ponzi-type schemes that sound too good to be true. Stocks with stories with a lot of *"sizzle"* may shoot up the charts posting dizzying returns, while those seen as *"ugly ducklings"* are cast down. Yet, to continue the metaphor, over time, beauty fades. Investors evaluate companies based on what they return to their shareholders in earnings and dividends, as well as what they expect will happen in the future. Markets may be emotional in the moment, but must be rational over time. So Mr. Buffet has spent his life making Berkshire

Hathaway and the subsidiary corporations it has bought and managed one of the most valuable companies in the world by ignoring the flavor of the moment and concentrating on long term value. Most people prefer to do business with the honorable, and so do Buffet's investors who are loyal to his company. In the long run, rationality and honesty can win out. At least, that is, if most of us insist on it.

Morality and Economics

Our entire civilization moves on the exchange of money.

We asked earlier if the individual pursuit of money and developing an economy are the same thing. In one sense, Adam Smith said yes in the foundational economic classic, *The Wealth of Nations.* The pursuit of individual prosperity leads to prosperity of the nation, which is the nature and effect of the free market economy.

The theory of capitalism is that an *"invisible hand"* will guide us toward the most efficient and therefore, best allocation of resources. But there can be fundamental problems. One is when competitors get together to fix prices, or monopolize a market, or use control over local regional or national governments to tilt the system in their favor. There are also wrinkles such as what you eat and where you sleep if you do not have any money and no way of making an adequate amount. It is also troubling when people spend all their money on products that are destructive to themselves and others, such as heroin. Adam Smith pursued this other broad issue of wealth and self-interest in *The Moral Sentiment.* You should read this as well. It is a good foundation for a university course but as we finish our conversation, I wanted to give you this thought to hang onto: the purpose of capital investment in the free market system is to be productive, by effectively providing products and jobs for our society. Making money should be the reward for that productive effort. When we do not help ourselves and those around us, we ignore the underlying glue, the trust and cooperation that holds us together.

Take one broad historical macroeconomic warning, which Joseph Schumpeter explored in his classic work, *Capitalism, Socialism and Democracy*. When the people in a society begin to criticize an economic system, they may not stop at the credentials of kings, popes, or titans of industry. A *"populist attack"* may be made upon the whole system when people see manipulation by one group taking vast amounts of private property for themselves. This great economist was writing well over a half century ago at a time when Communism was a great threat to the Western civilization, yet we see similar issues arise from economic inequality today. Such a populist reaction may veer off in a different direction at any time. An entire *"material-oriented society"* is put at risk if it does not reflect that society is made of all the people. If pushed too far, there will be blowback. Overstating the contribution to our economy of "job-creators," who then take most of the reward, may be seen as the hubris of those who arrogantly pretend to be a chosen people. This is far too nuanced an issue to be accurately examined here but, as we have been saying throughout, everything is related and you can begin to see and state the advantage of being able to state the other side of these issues, whether we are speaking in terms of economic regulation, governance, politics, morality, or the psychological fabric of our society's laws. The rules of the game should be fair. *"Stacked decks"* lead to frustration, dissent, conflict, and revolution. Dissolution of our society is neither good for us collectively or individually.

There are many, many examples of perceived overbearing and political pushback throughout history. We have looked at some. Now let's glance back at one of our foundational historic episodes, Britain's relationship with its American colonies in the 18th century. I was recently sitting in a coffee house on Vendue Street in Charleston, South Carolina when I looked up to see a prophetic headline of the *South Carolina Gazette* of July 1757 hanging on the wall: *"His Majesty's Declaration of War Against the French King."* It was not the people but a king sitting in far-off London who had never and would never see America who decided that those living in "his colonies" would fight and die on the North American continent. This echo could still be heard in another declaration twenty years later, this time by the colonists meeting in Philadelphia and addressing their grievances to the successor of that English king. And again, several decades later our first President, George Washington, warned his countrymen against such "foreign entanglements." Why cede to others the right to decide when we spill our blood or spend our treasure?

Yet we do not get to decide such big questions individually. Our elected representatives make them for us, so our elections are so important, and our vote is a moral issue.

Political Discussion is Largely about Economics

"It's the economy stupid," was the famous maxim of the 1992 presidential election campaign of soon to be President Bill Clinton. Most elections are.

By definition, businesses are designed and operate to make money, firstly for their owners. So far, so good. But this has led to some extreme and candid moments of people claiming that *"greed is good."* Of course, this can have an element of truth to it. Economic incentive for the individual has made the United States and Western Civilization the most prosperous in the history of the world. Free markets have evolved and fostered freedom of choice, and also freedom of ideas and representative government. Yet it gets complicated; when political decisions become economic ones the question of morality is not far behind.

Many free market proponents point out that contrasting economic ventures run by governments are inefficient because they are not required to have revenue exceed the costs of the most efficient producer of a service or product. Those who get to decide operating decisions for government-subsidized businesses lack discipline and have no *"skin in the game"*, since they can rely on charging more or receiving more public money to cover inefficiencies due to ignorance, disinterest, or corruption. Without the incentive to make revenues that will more than offset expenses, such businesses cannot survive competition for long. As Charles Dickens had Mr. Pickwick say, *"Revenue 20 pounds, expenditures 19 pounds six pence – recipe happiness. Revenue 20 pounds, expenditures 20 pounds six pence, recipe disaster."* You have to be able to pay all your expenditures to continue to operate.

For this reason, most commercial ventures are best run privately, yet the exceptions demonstrated by historical experience can be found when the goal is not to generate revenue, but a common purpose such as municipal services, schools, libraries, museums, hospitals, roads, and jails. Here the profit motive is likely to interfere with the purpose of the organization. If your purpose is to make money, the care of those served is not the primary mission, and in a fee for service model, there is no reason to be more efficient than when the operation is run by a not-for-profit agency or the government. Actually, the profit-oriented corporation has the added distraction of having to serve the owners first, and thus ignoring those it serves, making it susceptible to ignoring or abusing those it serves while seeking higher profits through public corruption.

It is necessary to take a broad macroeconomic view when we are talking about measuring revenues and offsetting expenses before we ever get to the real net profits of a business. We should not forget all costs that businesses generate in operating should be counted if we are to measure who gets what and who pays for it. These costs include roads and utilities to the plant as well as the fire, police, and municipal services when subsidized by the government. Costs of making a product have another corollary that has been often ignored until recent times: the external costs of a product to our water, air, and land pollution are borne by the whole of society and are eventually paid for by taxes on the rest of us.

> *"The law locks up the man or woman who steals the goose from off the common, but leaves the greater villain loose, who steals the common from the goose. The poor and wretched don't escape if they conspire to break the law, this must be so but they endure those who conspire to make the law."*
>
> *- 17ʰ century rhyme*

Next, we can consider how decisions are made to distribute the net proceeds of businesses.

We have often looked to history for lessons, but current headlines suggest much the same. A recent *New York Times* article by Economic Nobel Prize winner and Yale Professor Robert Schiller notes that the extreme gap in income and wealth that has taken place over the last thirty plus years has become *"a nightmare."* Another economist called this increasing economic inequality, *"a grotesque expansion"* as sides organize politically to protect or protest their current circumstances. To more easily grasp the economic question, we will ignore for the moment the successful political ploy of diverting peoples' attention with emotional and moral appeals based upon social issues irrelevant to economic issues, such as who gets to marry whom, whether there are restrictions on arming ourselves, and who must have a baby. Experience shows that we need deal with these aspects of human nature, but underneath we should recognize that the results of an economy are largely governed by its structure.

Those who can grab political control then set the current rules of the game. My take on it, my grandsons, can be understood by going back to a law review article written in the early 1950s by Arthur Goldberg, then General Counsel to the AFL-CIO, and later a United States Supreme Court Justice. He pointed to the concept of *"countervailing power."* He was making the case for the labor movement of the first half of the twentieth century being a force to counterbalance the large corporations in order to achieve rising wages and worker's rights both through collective bargaining, protest, and lobbying for legislation through the years, from child labor laws, to overtime pay, safety regulations, and minimum wage laws. We have been exploring these subjects throughout. But now we will focus on the means to balance these interests, a countervailing power that need be built into the political/ economic system for transparency, accountability, and the necessary checks and balances on overreaching by any of the groups in the game of life.

This same concept of having opposing leverage has long applied to Adam Smith's underlying concept that competitors provide the necessary balance and discipline on pricing, acting as the means to efficiently allocate resources in a market economy to those who best perform each function. Just as this principle of competition is thwarted if there are monopolists who can charge whatever they want because there are no checks and balances on the reasonableness of their prices or conduct there is this same need for a countervailing power to balance excesses when fundamental to the governmental system under which we live. The genius of our Constitution is that it is designed so government action is balanced for the people in each of our three branches. There are overlaps of course, but Congress makes the laws, the Executive branch enforces them, and the Courts decide what the laws mean and if anyone has broken them.

There comes a time when some large corporation loses money, cannot pay its bills, and files for bankruptcy. At this point, it is not management's money. It is the shareholders and creditors who are at risk. Yet corporate charters and by-laws are created to ensure self-perpetuation of management. Even if the majority of shares of a company voted against a Board member, he or she is still re-elected unless there is an opposing slate that receives more votes. In other words, if 100,000 votes are cast against an incumbent Board which does not have a competing slate of Directors, then one vote can keep the Board in power. Such exaggerated control provides some understanding as to why Boards are willing to vote for huge pay packages for the management who put them there, and why the top one percent make such multiples of the pay of the average worker in the same company, and count their wealth in hundreds of millions of dollars. It certainly suggests that the check on excess of this gross economic inequality in our system is missing, which is not likely to solve itself while one group retains so much of the power.

A common accepted truth is that *"business is business"*. It is undoubtedly true that it is necessary to concentrate on doing business in order to succeed. Yet we do not accept it as truth that we can rob banks, widows, or anyone else to be successful. As John Sturt Mill taught us, your individual rights end where mine begin. Even if the law may not presently have sanctions, I suggest that thriving by planning on defaulting on your creditors, or driving a town to social bankruptcy by selling off a plant's assets and jobs obtained by a bank financed leveraged buyout are morally reprehensible. Let's take a closer look at the subject of morality in business. My response to those who currently scream that "anything goes if you are smart and can get away with it" is that those who espouse it deserve jail time for their efforts and if the law does not provide for this result the fault is in the law.

This principle, with a need for checks and balances, for transparency and accountability, applies to management of large corporations owned by the public. A societal criticism of business is that it leverages as much of someone else's money as possible, and keeps as much of the profit as possible. When Chief Executive Officers are being paid ever-increasing million dollar salaries by friendly Boards of Directors while company employees see little increases in pay for thirty to forty years, we should recognize that the balance of control and needed checks and balances have been lost. The leverage of checks and balances is thwarted if professional managers take over large corporations without accountability to the shareholders. It is thwarted if our corporations buy elections and politicians so the laws and regulations do not provide a fair playing field.

If history has taught us anything it is that money and power will be used to keep those holding them entrenched. This is exacerbated when there are means to funnel huge amounts of funds into political campaigns. It does not pass the laugh test to say that everyone has an equally effective right to speak and have their opinion heard while vast sums are spent to buy public decisions every day. If there is to be "liberty and justice for all," the question is not whether governments should act, only how it can best design checks and balances against over-reaching by those who lead our government and our financial institutions.

What Might We Infer From This Exchange?

I have provided my thoughts and experiences and some mental pegs to hang some of these upon as you consider how we prosper. We now move on to our last chapter, my grandsons, and to more thoughts on moral sentiment.

CHAPTER 10

A story for all the ages - the deity as a metaphor...

"And which of the gods was it that sent them on to quarrel?"

- *The Illiad*

Man's evolution has been survival first, while the idea of progress has been to limit, that is not repeat, our mistakes.

We contemplate the thoughts of humans' from before the Ancient Greeks to the present to understand what the future of Western civilization can be. We wandered widely in our search as Homer's *The Iliad* and *The Odyssey* provided first archetypes, often about war but also heroic ideals, where realists met idealists and discovered they are often the same people.

These meandering tales have led us by twist and turn through our own journey, as we circled back to the final question: what is life all about?

In our earlier talks we spoke of Thomas Jefferson expressing the ideal objective of government – that is us collectively - to allow the aspiration of people for "*life, liberty and the pursuit of happiness.*" Today international organizations take surveys of citizens of the world to measure pride, pleasure, and purpose in order to measure happiness. It is time for us to hear reflected echoes one last time, as we pursue the goal of purpose. We will roam from a straight course as notions of light and dark, good and evil, bounce off the underlying theme of life itself. We will foreshadow our final chapter by asking the question Lao Tzu put forth in *Huahujing:* "*With all the talking, what has been said?*"

It has been my hope that this book has made you both think and smile, and that I have encouraged you to lead a full life. I hope that all that has come before in our conversations has lead you to this question: what is life about?

How do we know? I know of no more elegant conclusion to our conversation then this central relevance of so many peoples, religion, and search for spirituality, which provides one final opportunity to examine the development of a big idea, one which stretches beyond the memory of a people and what they were attempting to accomplish. Let us explore.

<u>Where do we begin?</u>

The language of the gods can be life altering.

The Jesuit, St. Ignatius Loyola, asked, "*What does it profit a man if he gain the whole world but suffer the loss of his immortal soul.*" But what if our expectation is that our individual existence ends with this world? Well, we live life with the additional Biblical maxim of the Prophet Isiah from the Old Testament: *"Here on earth God's work must be our own."* So, with these dueling ideologies, we will pursue the question further. Our exploration of spirituality rests upon the assumption that we both can and want to improve our authentic selves. So how might we put this? We might start with a Buddhist saying: *"You are all perfect exactly as you are. And all of you could use a little improvement."* We might consider that it's not that we become different, but that as we move forward as a species, and as individuals, some of what we do needs to be different.

What period in history might we choose to draw a meaningful line to map changes in religious attitudes? For Western civilization, we might start after the beginning of modern scientific thought. One could do worse than the year 1759, *The Year Britain Became Master of the World*, according to the subtitle of a book by Frank Mc Lynn. It was the middle period of *"the 18ᵗʰ Century Enlightenment"* with newfound insistence on freedom of thought; political movements were accelerating toward full-fledged individual independence, moving toward greater tolerance and democracy as our modern world was born.

Mc Glynn explains:

"By 1759, belief in the supernatural was encountered less and less by the intellectual classes of Europe but it is difficult to be certain about the extent of the skepticism since a curious two way process was observable. On the one hand there were …. the believers, who hid their lack of

Christian faith so as not to lose valuable benefices or livings. On the other hand intellectual sophisticates probably affected a greater degree of disbelief in the supernatural than they really felt... even some unbelievers skeptical of their own skepticism."

Many, if not most, were probably still believers. This is still likely the case.

"It cannot be doubted that each of us sees only a part of the picture... Human knowledge grows from the relationships we create between each other and the world. And it is still, never complete."

– When Breath Becomes Air, Paul Kalamth

Spirituality

"Come dream a dream with me, come dream a dream with me, come dream a dream with me that I might know your mind."

- Hymn

The world did not start with a manual, although some think that the Old Testament, begun some three thousand years ago, provides one; it professes to. What general themes can we pursue in our own search? Since we began our conversations, I have been telling you that everything of which we speak is related. We break up the subject of life into categories, classifications, subjects of convenience to understand this one life we have to live. Yet our life has multiple relationships or *"dependencies in our web of connections,"* which arise from the multiple mutual events of our existence. Upon what events and relationships shall we focus our attention? What is the dream? How do we decide what to do? For our last task, we will look back to see how people have collectively cultivated the soul.

I think there has to be a foundational core to being, a rock bottom integrity to one's self, and, as Polonius advises his son in Shakespeare's *Hamlet*, *"and it will follow as the night the day that thou shall be false to no man."*

"To dip my toe into a bit of truth."

- Andrew Wyeth

And what information answers the question of the soul? Today there is a complicating reality in this pursuit. You live in the information age, and *"facts"* are easy to come by; all sorts of pieces of information are readily available for study. You can be *"informed"* of just about anything, given so much information that you don't have time to truly examine it. We have access without understanding. When you have a question you can "Google it", but then what do you do with it? Trying to decide what to do can become paralyzing. Data is not useful if you cannot use it. What is becoming rare is a way to fit together into rational explanations these facts, those phenomena, this thought, or that event that informs you about the world in which you live.

Having the ability to process information in context so

as to best understand the issues and get at the core of the question is essential to begin moving in the right direction. This is not simply separating the wheat from the chaff. Rather it is selecting information that provides a pattern of possible meaning, as a thesis to test, to see if it actually reflects the world as it is, and to see if the model is subsequently followed by antithesis and a synthesis, all of which leads to new insight. It all begins with a broad view informed by experience, ours or someone else's, which addresses the current moment.

"Every trail has its end, every calamity has its lesson."

– *The Last of the Mohicans*, James Fennimore Cooper

We need to be able to manage. This need to be able to cast a wide net does not mean one cannot major in mathematics or economics, literature or art, medicine or law, at a university. It *does* mean that one has familiarity with the enduring debates of mankind over the centuries, as our thinking and our emotions have evolved, all of which can enhance our search for the credible.

"I can see clearly now ...

It's gonna be a bright, bright, bright, bright sunshiny day."

- Jimmy Cliff

The French philosopher, Rene Descartes famously said, *"I*

think therefore I am." I start by knowing I exist. This is not so helpful by itself. For a moment, we might turn to a meditative state. In a dark room at the day's end, or under a cloud around midnight, you can get a quiet sense of nothingness. The perception of time moves slowly; ghosts begin to stir. It is peculiar, a calming moment of motion at rest, between past and future. As usual, poetry can provide some sense of how this feels.

I recently came across a poem I had memorized during my time in college, by the Romantic poet of the early 19th century, George Gordon, Lord Byron. Like many students of that age, what captured my imagination was a preoccupation with the limits that time imposes on us. I find this to be true today, perhaps evidence that we – or at least I – refuse to grow up. Almost two hundred years ago Byron wrote:

> *"So, well go on more a roving, so late until the night, though the heart be still as loving, and the moon be still as bright. For the sword outwears its sheath, and the soul outwears its breast, and the heart must pause to breath, and love itself must rest. Though the night be made for loving, and the day returns too soon, yet well go no more a-roving, by the light of the moon."*

Why does the mood and the moon in the poem capture the imagination? What are we yearning for here? I think when past and future combine in our immediate memory, there is a transcendent awareness of self that suggests that our time matters. *"I am alive here- this I"* wrote Harold Munro in *Living.*

It is not often recognized that moral questions are woven into almost every political and economic decision. We have studied contrasts between what tradition teaches is the correct way, and the objection of dissenters to the status quo. As we reflect upon the continuity of earlier lessons, it seems that the time in which we live is central to the process of deciding. The questions of life become, who should do what, when, and why? Success is often deferred. It may be necessary for the time to be ripe, and when the time comes, early adopters are likely to be the young. The great German physicist Max Planck said that it is not so much that good science prevails as that old scientists die. As we have seen, ultimately protesters need the consent of a majority to sustain a new collective goal, yet the majority of people are often disinterested or non-believers until the day is won. And, as we have noted before, often it may seem at that time that an idea's time has come, but it will not happen until there are those who are willing to take action.

So, we remain in the flow, time goes on and relationships come and go as we strive to achieve our goals in life. It is a marathon, not a sprint. Many historians might be surprised to hear it, but they are in the business of portraying a quest for spirituality, as men and women look to re-examine parts of the past for something that gives new meaning to today; new possibilities, insights, and inspiration as to what we can become. In these assessments we may become aware that a belief system may be corrupted over time, so that a formerly useful model is now useful only as a means of escape rather than instructions for a life lived fully, or used to deny its fulfillment to others. Does it matter? Yes. Life is not a linear path, so we cannot schedule the spontaneity necessary to find and build an enriching life. Rather we go 'round and 'round *"till we find ourselves in the just the right place"* according to a Unitarian hymn, taken from an old Quaker tune.

"While life and voice shall last"

– The Yale "Whiffenpoof" drinking song

What a remarkable fact it is that we exist. How extraordinary it is to be us. From a collection of genes comes an individual who actually does something, works for something, and strives to achieve something. So, to me, the basic task of our human nature, as night follows day, is to find what fundamental purpose for which we will use this extraordinary life.

"Obedience to the holiest of laws, be alive until you are not."

- *The Singular and the Cheerful Life,*
Mary Oliver

St. Augustine, the Bishop of Hippo, Africa, wrote in his *Confessions* during the decline of the Roman Empire seventeen hundred years ago: *"Where is it, this present? Gone in the instant of becoming."* For me, the first question then becomes: In the dark quiet of the night, are we just reacting to the calm of the moment, or in the interaction with stillness do we perceive a mystery of life itself? Does time matter because it ends, and is therefore precious? Is the quiet present an awareness of our existence as we contemplate how to make the most of it?

There follows a second fundamental fact: the power to reproduce, to replicate ourselves, differentiated by changes in the genes of two different sexual people which give us our children. We follow our nature to help both our biological and metaphorical children travel further down the path we have explored. To me these two essentials, life and descendants, merge as celebration of the most spiritual question: the continuation of life itself.

To contemplate these paths eventually leads to the inevitable questions: *"Why do good? Why be good?"*

To again foreshadow a primary point of our conversation, my grandsons, it seems self-evident that when we build external expressions of ourselves, they should not be wasted contradicting what we are about. For example: building bombs to extinguish the precious lives of others. It is upon such basics that the foundation of our morality rests. History tells us this is not self-evident to all, and certainly it does not tell the whole story.

A goal of our exploration is to get a good look at whatever governs life itself. One obvious tendency is to lean toward the survival of us, our progeny, and our society. Civilization tends to view this continuation as morality. As always, my grandsons, we must define the terms we use, so how do we define "morality?" I think it advantageous to consider this fundamental issue of life as one of spirituality because it suggests a poetic approach which moves us to look at alternative scriptures while we examine the exhilaration and frustration that oscillates between intimacy and isolation. To what end? We examine values, mores, and assumptions in symbols, images, and echoes of the mind that men and women accept in our common conversation about what it means to be in our common predicament of being human. As we have said when speaking about the Law, we begin with *"the felt experience of the times."*

Creativity:

> *"The only things I find rewarding are variety and the enjoyment of diversity."*
>
> -Michel de Montaigne.

> *"The possibility of having a dream come true makes life interesting."*
>
> - *The Alchemist*, Paul Coelho

Could novelty be the point of it all? Might we emphasize an under-appreciated aspect of our psychological nature, this appeal of and the tension between the new and familiar? We have previously looked at the comparative emotional conflict between risk and reward, romance and adventure, as the spice of life. We have focused a great deal on learning from our experiences as well as the experiences of others, looking back to collective wisdom through the millennia, which we call tradition, that which repeats and refines the alternatives we face.

Early in our conversations we spoke about the search

for the secret of beauty by the classical Greeks and of their fascination with the legendary face of Helen of Troy, *"the face that launched a thousand ships"* and began the legendary epic adventure of the Trojan War. We also spoke of another view of the romantic concept highlighted by G.K. Chesterton in *Orthodoxy* where a group seeks adventure by sailing off to discover what was beyond the seas, only to sail into a storm and awake the next morning safely beached on sand, which turned out to be on the other side of the same island. It is the combination of the risk of journey in sailing off to sea, and the safety of the familiar when arriving home, that provides the romance, that *"stirs men's blood."* - Marc Anthony in Shakespeare's *Julius Caesar*.

Recent evolutionary biological studies have found that emotionally pleasing aesthetics, the attraction of the beautiful, has enough of the new to excite, yet enough of the familiar to provide assurances of safety. An evolutionary explanation is that our biological ancestors were excited to see a new animal or plant as intriguingly novel, yet still possessed sufficient familiarity to assure that they would not be eaten or poisoned.

Other studies explore biological sexual preferences, the attraction of the other, as most appealing when possessing safe enhancements signifying a healthy body such as large antlers, colorful feathers, or athletic dance rituals of seduction. The familiar is played against the attractions of the many evolutionary benefits of diversification, which can lead our descendants to prosper and multiply. When we say *"beauty"* we intuit a natural propensity for the purpose of successive lives for ourselves, our offspring, and their successors. Responding to seduction, we hear echoes of Genesis: *"God made woman, and it was good."*

There is a universal paradox in that continuity, when the past contrasts with the reality that everything we do must be now, this is what matters to us now, and it is new since things must change as we learn more. *"The day returns but nevermore, returns the traveler to the shore."* wrote William Wadsworth Longfellow. At least it is no longer the same ever changing shore, my grandsons.

When we discussed your early days at university, we looked at your imagined experiences to recognize the importance of relationships with others. This led to a second question: how can we relate to the other people in our world? The consequent questions include how our world reacts to the risks and rewards of traditional or idiosyncratic behavior, yours or anyone else's. *"For time is like a fashionable host that lightly shakes his parting guest by the hand, and with arms outstretched as he would fly, grasps in the comer, welcome ever smiles."* *"Ulysses Advises Achilles,"* from *Troilus and Cressida* by William Shakespeare.

As we reinterpret life, moral issues litter our paths. While we decide what to do, to help or to hinder, we must reject changing the facts of what happened to justify our opinions and actions; in so doing, we avoid becoming liars. *"Fake"* and *"authentic"* are not simply words. Why does it matter? Because truth matters. Why? Because when we disconnect from the truth, we start with the wrong information, we are misled and we become lost, and we end up at the wrong place at the wrong time or with the wrong conclusions. That poison can easily kill you, your soul, or someone else.

All this idealism is fine and dandy but what does it have to do with *"the real world?"*

One of the wonderful ways men and women have enhanced their common lives is through community, and the common way people have historically adopted and institutionalized this sense of togetherness has often been through religion. There can be tension between recognizing the mystery of our connectedness and those who would exploit the other. Let us again consider a pair of opposing quotes to begin imagining where it all might lead:

> *"Both in space and time we seem to be brought somewhat near to that great fact – the mystery of mysteries – the first appearance of new beings on this earth."*
>
> - *Voyage of the Beagle*, Charles Darwin

> *"Brave men are all vertebrates. They have their softness on the surface and their toughness in the middle. But these modern cowards are all crustaceans; their hardness is all on the cover, and their softness is inside."*
>
> - G.K. Chesterton

It should be obvious that this, our last chapter, has a jerky, murky path, but the whole point of our long discussion is not to avoid uncertainty but rather to move forward through the thicket with optimistic courage.

Let's look at a few habits we have been developing. First

deciding what we are trying to do. Taking a look at religion presents a formidable task in deciding where to begin. But we have already begun and we have also been developing another technique of looking at a collection of quotes as we start the process; this gives us a tone to prompt us to proceed in this endeavor. We might also begin the subject of religion with enough unassuming tolerance to take into account the advice of Albert Einstein who said, *"Whoever undertakes to set himself up as the judge in the fields of truth and knowledge is shipwrecked by the laughter of the Gods."*

We might further reflect that men can greatly change their circumstances, but they do not create the world's basic truths, nor the fortuitous events or acts of others for good and evil. Upon this at least, most religious believers and non-believers can agree.

There is also that other universal truth, that like all creatures, men and women are hard-wired to scramble for their own survival. Absent some variation of that goal, such as a compulsion to preserve and advance our children, or broaden the definition of "our collective self" to our family, neighbors, tribe, nation, fellow people, or all living creatures, we are not likely to incline toward sharing prosperity, and so we start with the "what's in it for me?" approach to life. This is not inevitable, but it is the default position of human nature as far as I can tell.

"Apres mois, le deluge."

- King Louis XIV of France

The quote above translates to *"After me, the deluge."* The Sun King ruled France, then the most populous and wealthiest European country, for about three quarters of a century, until 1715. He controlled the nobility and centralized the nation, seeking that all pay homage to Louis XIV. It can be reassuring to know one's exact place in the world when your social rank dictated what you could do in society. This was more convenient the higher you went up the social and legal ladder, yet it dictated that salvation in this life and the next depended on submission to the authority of the king. Vices were tolerated, but disloyalty to the King was a great sin and a crime. As Louis XIV predicted, the structure of this excessive and authoritarian rule eventually led to the French Revolution which radically upset the civil order of France, causing aftershocks that influence the world to this day.

Why bring that up now? Because the whole underlying premise offered by Louis XIV and the privileged few who supported him was that he ruled by the divine right of the God, and he was anointed to know what was best for everyone, especially himself. Autocrats have been making similar claims, saying, *"I know best, trust me,"* both before and since, and we see it to this day in America and elsewhere. Those who deny the claims of the would-be autocrats are said to be *"heretics,"* *"false prophets,"* and *"purveyors of fake news."* George Orwell warned of such times: *"During times of universal deceit, telling the truth becomes a revolutionary act".*

Truth is reality which we know by observation, demonstration, intuition, and calculation. It corresponds with the way the world is. It is not a series of unverified assertions, repeated in a loud voice. One wise counsellor told me: *"The louder the voice, the weaker the argument.*"Never has this been truer than it is today. We are talking about reasoning with relevant facts. We can use intuition and fresh viewpoints and criteria such as the simple likelihood that something occurs to find a possibility. But then we test our assumptions. The point that I continue to make here, my grandsons, is that we need to review and validate our claims whoever we are, and whatever they may be. We seek to confirm the world as it is, even as we try to make it what it can be.

Religion:

There are many reasons religions have dominated history. They help explain life, they *"give shelter from the storm"* as Bob Dylan put it, they provide common values and rules for interacting, and they guide, or control, us. The other side of the issue found in these last three words should prick the ears of democratic republicans.

A most basic universal principle of human conduct, a golden rule, tells us *"to treat others as we would have them treat us."*

We can view how his guiding principle has been interpreted in the context of the three most prominent religions of Western civilization. The Old Testament allowed a limit to the rule of the Chosen People who observed the God-given law of Moses; offending Jews or neighboring tribes could be slain or enslaved, detailed explicitly in Leviticus. Jesus added, *"Love thy neighbor as thyself,"* recognizing the psychological truth that we cannot appreciate others until we first accept ourselves, and lastly added *"for the love of God."* As

I understand it, Muhamad provided *"desire for your neighbor what you desire for yourself."* And as I noted earlier, the Old Testament Jewish prophet, Isaiah proclaimed: *"...that here on earth God's work must be our own."*

From the Ancients of Egypt and Jerusalem and the other civilizations of the Middle East, from the East and the West, from medieval Europe to traditional kingdoms of today, there are echoes of *"the divine right of kings to rule."* Says who? In classical Rome it was *"The safety of the State is the highest law."* Maybe, but we need to define *"the State"*. Today it is not the king, not the tribe, not the political party, not our economic class, but as the Enlightenment led us toward the more powerful concept of the collective us, what we Americans like to call *"We the people."* So, we say goodbye to the concept of a god speaking to only one chosen people, or a divinely ordained royal family, or those who get to designate the priests or officials to rule the rest of us for generations. The concept of who is entitled to the protection of the golden rule has expanded through history, and this issue of who is considered *"us"* remains a central question of morality today.

Part of my concern with how religions are organized is that formal dogma emphasizes rigid rules that become more important than the underlying purposes. The risqué comedian W.C. Fields was once asked why he was reading the Bible. He replied that he was *"looking for the loopholes."* Funny. Sacrilegious. Also an undercurrent to the formalistic way many people look at and guide religion, robbing, or at least lessening, the ultimate idea that it is not the rules but actions and consequences that matter.

And life can give a warped sense of it all. As Kurt Vonnegut had a character say in *Timequake*: *"If there is a God, He sure hates people."*

Let's briefly examine this concept of attitude.

I often use an Irish phrase *"generosity of spirit"* (gladly giving and not feeling the less of others for giving to them) as an ideal way to live your life. Many religions speak of a similar concept of compassion, empathy, or sympathy for others. I prefer to look at it as developing our spontaneous instinct for a way of living rather than first identifying victims in need. There are people who need help and we should help them (individually where we can, and together through government), but there is a nuanced psychological difference in searching out victims rather than accepting that we all need assistance at some time in our lives, which should make us ready to naturally respond. I have not fully thought through the consequences of the difference but rather than *"take pity,"* which I think contributes to impoverishing the soul on both sides, the approach I prefer is about helping others think well of themselves and encouraging them to be their best. The polar opposite is to belittle or dismiss others with a lack of respect, a sure sign that a moral compass is off when this is translated into a culture that belittles or condemns the other by division, exclusion, criticism, or ethnic jokes. We then breed hatred and conflict, and begin to build bombs.

"Stand up and give birth to your betters."

– Maya Angelou

The poet Mary Oliver pointed to a world of mysteries

too marvelous to be fully understood. Nevertheless, as in all other matters you will make up your own mind. What I am encouraging, Finnan and Cormac, is that as you find your spiritual life, not simply adopting a life offered up for you, seek to learn from all traditions as you decide for yourself. We might start with the suggestion of the author Pat Conroy in his autobiographical book, *The Water is Wide*, *"…to embrace life openly, to reflect upon its mysteries, to rejoice in its surprises, to reject its cruelties."* With a strong love of life, we are likely to quickly recognize the Biblical proverb that indeed *"not by bread alone does man live."*

Where do we begin?

> *"We lack not songs, nor instruments of joy, nor echoes sweet, nor waters clear as heaven, nor laurel wreaths against the sultry sky."*

> - William Blake

No introspective life can avoid facing the claim, which has differed but persisted throughout the recorded histories of the past 5,000 years, that there has been some powerful God watching to measure and hold people accountable for their deeds. People have had different religious codes and stories, but similarly provided values, rules of life and order, an explanation of and a feeling for a place in the cosmos, hope and comfort for a better day to come, and a powerful explanatory mechanism of life, providing a center for cultural and social life as well. The historical value of these claims to the peoples of their times cannot be denied. There is also the question about religion as a means of controlling the people. We have moved on to the essence of us ruling us. The idea of an all-knowing deity who created us and keeps score of our personal lives had its uses. But it was poetic and political inspiration or necessity, not fact. What is fact?

Acceptance of the claims of religion by Western civilization became far different after the Enlightenment. And now socio-biological research and neurological and cognitive studies of recent years have provided dramatic insight into a religious sense as a natural, biological phenomena, in part the consequence of the process of raising children. My grandsons, I know that you recognize by now that this lens of evolution has been a major theme of our conversations, and once again a way to explore the subject, this time spirituality in the lives of men and women.

As has become our custom, my grandsons, let me repeat myself for emphasis. Tradition has great value yet we can outlive the usefulness of an old custom. Undeniably, the power of religion has a hold on us. The desire to transcend a short or petty life is real to us. Yet the focus has shifted from heaven to here on earth. Others may not agree, yet we cannot be timid in making our own search and following our own conscience. This was said close to two hundred years ago as Ralph Waldo Emerson spoke to his countrymen about accepting self-reliance over traditional religion in a lecture to a graduating seminary class at Harvard University. *"Let's not demean our friends and those who we care about in speaking to them only in careless bromides, but test their tolerance in having us speak to them of the exploration of human nature and the world as we see it."*

Emerson and Henry David Thoreau emphasized a developing new American way of looking at the influences of other people, cultures, and concepts to *"transcend"* the limits of our personal, family, and tribal experiences for spiritual lives, following such threads where they led.

When I was entering NYU a half century ago, the Dean of the Law School sent each incoming student a book, *The Predicament of Democratic Man,* which stressed that in a democracy, we choose our leaders and are therefore responsible for their actions. It is us who have the credit or blame for what our nation does, and the responsibility to undo its injustices.

Much earlier we noted that your experience presents you with facts, patterns, options, decisions, and conclusions about the more mundane as well as the grander moments. In considering *Thinking Fast and Slow* we focused on the underlying assumptions of our decisions and beliefs. Much of the human decision process is unconscious or made with what trial lawyers call *"facts not in evidence."* Deliberate choices to act are often based on unexamined hypothesis. So, we examine them.

If *"the soul,"* the personality, us, is more than a collection of biological inheritance, prior experiences, memories, prior decisions, acts, habits, proclivities, and an articulation of belief, does it die with us? This can have consequences such as heaven and hell. It seems clear to me that claiming a duality of a soul separate from the body that survives death is beyond scientific laws so far discovered; it flatly contradicts all known science. It also appears unlikely. How can we know and think without a brain to process the information? Would my body-less soul not find and take over another brain it encountered as its non-material consciousness floated out there? And exactly where does this eternal soul reside after earth and the universe cease to exist? Those who propose such a triumph of religious belief over observable fact and known science carry the burden of proof. It seems to me that this burden of proof is not met by asserting that one simply *"has to have faith"*, meaning *"my faith,"* which is merely saying that my ancestors were right because they told me so, and you have to believe them too.

Today, for some, prayer is still seen as talking to God. For others it is a more meditative talking to oneself. In this sense, poetry can place an emotional appeal within the context of framing the ideal as a spiritual alternative, rather than a revelation from the gods. *"Not in the clamor of the crowded street, not in the shout and plaudits of the throng, but in ourselves are triumph and defeat."* *The Poets,* Henry Wadsworth Longfellow.

Appeals to a person's emotional unity with others can constitute tribalism, or substitute readily apparent religions. Some modern psychological variations of collective transcendent human purpose have been political movements such as Soviet Communism and Nazi Fascism taking on the emotional appeal of solidarity of the group while the actual practices are clearly evil. "Is it true?" then becomes the stark question to any collective cause including any "ism" or religion. In *Breaking the Spell,* Daniel Dennett uses a quote that focuses on the ultimate point: *"Philosophy has questions that may never have answers. Religion has answers that may never be questioned."* Questions and answers both deserve exploration.

> *"I am ashamed to think how easily we capitulate to badges and rank, to large societies and dead institutions."*

> \- Ralph Waldo Emerson

Finnan and Cormac, since the beginning we have been tracking some subjects by first looking at the surrounding terrain to establish initial footing. One reason we do this is to find available points for stability, mental pegs to hold thoughts we encounter, as we begin the unfolding of events, a preliminary picture in our mind of how the day may go. One example of a mental peg we might use to weigh the context of war is a statement attributable to the General in the movie *Patton*: *"Looking to die for your country is a lot of crap. The idea is to make the other poor son of a bitch die for his."* This is a gross over-simplification, but it makes a stark point about the reality of war. We should be honest with ourselves. We are well served to look beyond platitudes to reason and consequence as we attach meaning – both rational and emotional – to actions and events. We may not want to reduce ourselves to a transactional world, but we also don't want to be willing to die for someone else's platitudes or purposes.

When we examine this issue of spirituality further we quickly arrive at the question, why we should do things for others at all? Can we be altruistic even without the sanction of authorities, or the promise of a future reward in heaven?

We have now moved into the realm of morality. The answer *to "doing good"* was explained in religious terms in the past. Today I am suggesting that we *"do the right thing"* because it best fulfills our short life on earth by transcending a transactional model of life that is petty and rife with narrow self-interest. It has roots in biology and survival, yet it satisfies us today to help our children, relatives, peers, neighbors, and country and it extends to the world's people and the planet. We are all in this life together. And no one can take their riches with them anyway.

How do you measure the value of a life? First by its survival, and then its quality. Protection, production, and pursuit of perfection have to be part of this measurement. What jump started the homo sapiens long road to success in the first place? It has been suggested that in ancient times a shift in chemistry may have provided increased incentive and the advantage of cooperation in a feedback loop of the early organization of life as it evolved to feel secure in affiliations and then from the biological urges of family. Such relationships are the core of life.

We have touched upon the theme before, but the discussion has its circular aspects and it is worth revisiting. Some of the important events in our world occur at the edge. At the fringe of a scene, artists find the display of subtle uplifting light. In our personal psychological world, when we notice someone at the edge of a group and bring them in, a metaphorical light reflects psychological and social rewards and makes us a friend. A bond can be formed by both sides. Poetry can also prompt harmony as we perceive and organize thoughts and emotions that reflect this metaphorical light that prompts serenity or action, and a sense of living more fully. Developing relationships and expanding them is key. Much earlier, I said I would add to my particular definition of poetry. Now seems the time. I am paraphrasing here but it makes the point well. The conversation of a poet is not really about your demands, but more likely points you to a junction of paths where you sense new life and dream of promises to yourself and others, while our new selves are formed.

Metaphors are just metaphors, as comparisons are just comparisons, and all of this may sound like unexplained mysticism. Yet we also discussed much earlier, my grandsons, how comparisons and metaphors permit us to focus not only upon facts, but to assemble them in ways that provide new meaning for us. Bob Dylan recently won the Nobel Prize for Literature for the metric tone and meaning of his words which have been compared to bards and storytellers of history. Their job was to add meaningful imagination to their world, leading to richer emotion, ideas that led to ideals, and a new way of understanding things in relation to others, including how we see ourselves, how we think others see us, how we perceive them, and how we want to be perceived. This impacts how we lead our lives. We are the poorer if we choose to ignore the emotional potential. When you open your mind, these notions come in and shape it. A purpose of using poetry is to pursue spirituality and attach meaning.

I will continue, Cormac and Finnan, searching in our conversations for any more insight or explanation we might find.

> *"You have today no future fears, this day will last a thousand years. If you want it to."-* Moody Blues, *Dawn is a feeling*

Hope serves as a psychological defense mechanism to carry us through the blows of a struggling life. It is also a way to inspire us to realize goals and dreams that outlast us.

Everything comes to fruition as we contemplate the life we have been living. What have we learned? One, in many ways, the self is made up. Two, we did not begin us, someone or something else did. To my mind, there cannot be an atheist with certitude, since we are here and we do not know how we got here. All known cultures have a creation myth and while this does not mean that any of the myths created by men or women to explain their existence are true, we should also remember that through their long history, men and women have longed for greater purpose. "Why are we here?" OK, there may be a cause you can isolate, the Big Bang and its chemical consequences, but what caused that cause? So, how should we lead our lives?" Maya Angelou provides a good answer: *"Do the best you can until you know better – then when you know better, do better."*

So, we can accept that there is life to be led beyond the analytical; between the psychological and the mysterious people can be moved to realize both inspiration and the patience necessary to pursue long term answers. Going back to the past suggests what may have worked in the past. It might be a very good hint of what will happen in the future. But, by definition, the past does not always provide an answer in the present. Claims fade in the retelling and the possibility of prior accidental correlation spurs us to compare the story to see what will prove true for us in the future. That is, even if our assumption has seemed correct so far, will it continue to prove useful or adaptive as we go forward? And what mental processes can we use in speaking of such meaningful subjects as religion and morality?

People have their human sensibilities and intellect, which can move them to a higher level of learning and living, to recognize that cooperation may be the most successful long term strategy. A broad sense of boundless curiosity and fundamental fairness can be a central part of that collective human experience as the more noble force, and thus the aim. Life is not an argument against itself where *"red fang and claw"* describe the essence of it all.

We have seen that when we actually look at moral development we usually start with the ancients and continue through modern cognitive behavioral growth studies. The first provides traditional lessons and aphorisms we often fall back upon. We have dwelled on the Ancient Greeks far more than the Romans, because they faced the eternal questions first, and I believe answered them far better. The poet Virgil wrote the classic Latin epic poem *The Aeneid* to tell of the founding of Rome by Aeneas, whom the poem describes as the ancestor of the great Romans. He was said to be one of the few who fled the destruction of Troy by the Greeks, taking his father and son on the journey by ship to Italy. Virgil stresses the ideal of respectful duty as he focuses on the ideals of *"the glory"* that was the imperial Roman Empire, rather than *"the grandeur"* that was democratic Greece, at least for those who were citizens of ancient Greece. Latin was the language of the educated throughout the earlier centuries of the modern era of European education. It thus marked a large part of our heritage. One of the more important of these Latin writings was by the Roman Orator Cicero who counseled that a thankful heart is the parent of all other virtues. Moral lessons continued through the Ages. Recently Martin Luther King, Jr. boldly told us that we should measure humans by the content of their character rather than the color of their complexion. It is an overwhelming understatement to say that such moral examples have not always been the guiding principles of ancient Rome, nor the past practice of America, but they are the nature of the pursuit.

To return to the primary issue, to me there are basic laws of conduct and morality. For example, there is a fundamentally accepted human law that none of us can claim the right to kill other people. There is a natural abhorrence to the act. Yet almost all cultures and religions, Quakers and such excluded, recognize the existential right of self-defense, and concomitant extension for killing other human beings for "*just wars.*" I use the words "*existential right*" because I do not have to think long and hard about it. The most fundamental right is the right to exist. If someone comes to kill me or my loved ones, I will most definitely kill them first if I am able. Disputes quickly arise about the definition of the acts, the surrounding circumstances, and soon enough about whether "*the other*" was or was not "*worthy*" of the same protection. So, it always comes down to context and circumstance in deciding moral questions.

As far as we can tell, men have always accepted that the moral objective is that we do unto others as we would have them do unto us. That comes with the caveat many times "*the others*" may be limited to our group, or the possible exception "unless I need or want what you have," which is why we have always needed laws and group enforcement of said laws by our collective government. The trick of our times is to expand the definition of other to include us all, and to deny that there is an exception in the case of avarice. You cannot take my land by defining me as less and still be considered moral.

> *"Yet if hope has flown away, in a night or in a day,*
> *in a vision or in none, is it therefore the less gone?*
> *All that we see or seem is but a dream."*

- *A Dream Within a Dream*, Edgar Allan Poe

I find a quote from computer pioneer Alan Kay hopeful. Kay stated that the best way to predict the future is to invent it. And it is of some considerable hope that people do seem to be hard-wired to be virtuous, even in conflicted situations. The sense of it can be refined, but it seems to come naturally. We might illustrate the point by looking at one virtue such as loyalty, and its opposite vice, betrayal. Or another virtue, dignity, and the sin in denying it to others by disrespect, exploitation, or murder. As we considered much earlier, these are so fundamental that even very young children recognize them. Those that act differently than our internal moral compasses are judged and labeled by our civilizations as wrong, sinful, sociopaths, or worse.

> *"God employs several translators... the bell that*
> *rings calls not upon the preacher only, but upon*
> *the congregation to come..."*

- John Donne

Echoes of our spiritual traditions are heard in earlier merging cultures, only partially formed. To do this in a meaningful way should lead us beyond the arbitrary line drawn to designate the Christian era of the past two thousand years from what came before.

We might, for example, notice the remarkable era around the fifth century B.C.E. The Jews during Babylonian captivity in about 540 B.C.E are estimated to have been some eight hundred or so years beyond the time of the Old Testament of Moses. Cyrus the Great led a Persian army in this sixth century B.C.E to conquer the Babylonians. He then decided to free the tribes subjugated by the Babylonians, including the Jews then held in captivity. It is pointed out that the more modern Jewish religious story which we later hear reflected in the New Testament began to emerge as the newly unrestrained chosen people built a new Temple in Jerusalem. A half millennium later came the New Testament, and in another 600 or so years, the Koran.

The same historical development of great secular social change is found in the successive civilizations of this time and place. Classical Greece was emerging in the mid-fifth century B.C.E. The Greek City States united in 490 B.C.E. to defeat the invading Persian Army in the first Peloponnesian War, and they did so again in the next ten years. These victories were followed by a Golden Age of Greece for much of the next two centuries. As we have observed, my grandsons, this Classical Greek period was so critical to the insights and values of our Western civilization. This foundational period of western thought continued until the mid-third century B.C.E. when, after the Greek army of Alexander the Great conquered Persia, the rest of the Middle East, and fringes of India merged with Greek culture into the hybrid Hellenistic Age. This world faded into the power of a new harsh Empire that was *"the glory that was Rome."* Merging geographic lines, values, and intellectual boundaries of Athens, Rome, and Jerusalem over the next millennia combined to underlie Western civilization as it became mostly Christian.

It seems instructive that at about these same early stages of the transformative period of early Western civilization, an ascetic sage in India, Gautama Buddha, became a great spiritual leader as he searched for solace from the pains of living. He did this by accepting a way of enlightenment through detachment from earthly concerns in what has become known as Buddhism. Buddhism remains dominant in much of Asia and is influential throughout the world today. At this same turn from the fifth century B.C.E. to the fourth, Confucius was teaching warring Chinese states that morality, justice, and social order were to be found in respect for tradition by honoring the way of the elders and ancestors. Much has been learned from these Eastern alternate concepts of balancing life. The philosophical concepts of the Buddha and Confucius and the variants of these teachings overshadow Eastern civilization and influence the West up until our time.

Why did such spiritual traditions arise at about this same

time in history? And why are such spiritual awakenings worth our time today? What were the psychological underpinning to man's reaction to the circumstances of the time?

The Singer not the Song was the title of a movie about a Mexican bandit and a priest, where the bandit is captivated by the strength of character of the priest in a small village of farmers. Is it the man or the religion? The movie does not answer the question but a look at the poster does. The romantic notion is about the power of an individual to influence his or her world. So, is it the man or the story? Indeed, are all movements the shadow of a man or men ?

Some say so. Thomas Carlyle, an English historian, writes of history as the consequences of its leaders. The question leads us to the facts behind the religious giants of our civilization. Confucius' life is so vague that his actual existence as a person has been questioned. Indeed, facts surrounding Moses and the religious foundation of the Old Testament, Jesus, the New Testament, Ulysses, Helen, Homer and the Trojan War, and Sun Tzu and the strategic military masterpiece *The Art of War* are all elusive enough to suggest that the religious movements they inspired might be more compilations of developing dogma by a people through the ages. Nevertheless, even if they were evolving stories, the power of the story is a fact of critical importance to their civilizations and ours, true because of the insight and values they provided and which have been relied upon since. Again, the story we tell ourselves about ourselves becomes us.

These stories of people bind them together and guide their lives. We cannot overemphasize that the minds of people mirror the narratives they accept. Our view of the world matters. Each new version has its consequences so we should not readily abandon what is tried and true about us, yet we must be open to new ideas. It is the unavoidable job of life to balance the new against the old, risk against opportunity, and doing nothing is a choice with consequences, as much as changing is. As we have seen before in our discussions of these tales, when Athens decided to invade the smaller city states that refused to join their alliance and pay tribute, at that point, a new relationship developed that was life altering for both sides. For the satellite cities being an ally of Athens could be more dangerous than being an enemy; but those who chose to rebel were destroyed. These events, this harsh treatment of satellite cities, precipitated the Peloponnesian War and Athens' defeat by Sparta. Yet again, there were serious decisions to be made. Warlike Sparta was convinced to adopt a story that saw the Greeks as one people, and with adoption of that version spared Athens and thereby advanced civilization.

One last tale of the power of a narrative rounds out this sketch. In his last exile, on the island of St. Helena, Napoleon wrote his *Memorial*. He explained how his triumphs had "saved" the French Revolution and given France the law of The Code of Napoleon providing equality for all. This version took many liberties with the truth but gave us the story of "liberal France" that exists to this day.

The stories we adopt matter.

Do our stories reflect our nature?

You can look through many lenses to see how dominant forces seem to rule our lives. For example, consider a small moment in a movie with some significant insight. The actor Orson Wells played Harry Lyme, a bootlegger of the newly discovered antibiotic penicillin in *The Third Man*. This 1949 film noir took place on the bombed out streets of Vienna just after World War II. There is a bleak scene on top of a Ferris Wheel where Wells tosses off a line, saying: *"For thirty years Italy had war, terror, and murder under the Borgias, and in that time produced… Michelangelo, Leonardo da Vinci, and the Renaissance. In Switzerland they had five hundred years of peace and democracy and produced… the cuckoo clock."*

Maybe there is something in human nature that has always needed a wolf at the door, barbarians at the gate, the villagers coming with pitchforks, or fires or floods to heighten the necessary intensity of spirit. And maybe there is the need for a countervailing force to provide balance and prevent a chaotic end to it all.

Were there cross fertilization of ideas from the fifth century B.C.E. in the Middle and Far East, not so far away from each other, that were natural reactions to periods of blood and mayhem in Greece, the Middle East, Italy, the warring states of China, and India to which men psychologically reacted? Did life appear so desperate to the Buddha when he left his protected childhood in the palace on the fringes of the Indian continent that he saw there must be another way? Just as the institutionalized violence of Roman rule needed the alternative of Jesus' lesson that each man is one another's keeper, a lesson of such importance that it dramatically divided our dating of history? Was enough truly enough for

Gandhi and Mandela to recognize a similar message of civil resistance and non-violence in more modern times? Martin Luther King, Jr noted that *"an eye for an eye"* found in the ancient Code of Hammurabi leads to *"a valley of the blind."* Can it be some psychological principle of toleration and cooperation that some men train themselves to tap as a sense of nobility to which others naturally respond?

This seems an important question when we look at the acceptance of three propositions for how men should live. The creation story of the Western Judeo/Christina/Muslim culture, which is the Biblical story of Adam and Eve in Genesis, tells us that humans are born with original sin inherited from the first ancestors who disobeyed a commandment of God in the Garden of Eden. Does man need an external check upon himself, substitute parents, as he grows up to control his passions? If we let this idea of original sin directly imply that man's basic nature is sinful and that it needs be beaten back, requiring a harsh stifling of human exuberance, it suggests an authoritarian approach to life with what I see as a clear danger. The Enlightenment period of the late 17th century was an intellectual rejection of earlier harsh and autocratic demands of acceptance of traditions that had come before. The great English political philosopher John Locke, like Aristotle before him, thought that man was born with a *tabula rosa*, that is a blank slate to be written upon, with men's experience crucial to whom he would become. Soon after Locke, Jean Jacques Rousseau in France, like Plato before him, suggested that man is inherently good or at least can be educated to be good. Does toleration and education trump autocratic demands by those who would control us? Or can we live within the social contract within the limited restraint of a government set by the governed?

As we have spoken about earlier, recent studies have shown that even small babies have an innate sense of fairness within the natural requirements of their environment and existence. Sociobiology may help us determine answers to these historical questions suggesting the more apt metaphor is not original sin to be purged, but that biology confirms a developing childhood away from an initial and natural self-centered beginning of life.

In modern times, child behaviorists such as Jean Piaget have closely studied how a child is born helpless, dependent upon his or her parents for everything. The naturally self-centered children learn to follow what their parents show them, learning to balance what they immediately want with their parents' emphasis on acts and rules that are good for them in the longer term. Children are born to look up to this higher, parental authority. For many, this continues throughout life.

Cormac, we were on a delicious Christmas season vacation with our entire immediate family on the Big Island of Hawaii, a rare moment of so much time to be together in your young lives. As usual, we were sitting on the beach in the shade of some trees. Your mother and father had gone off for a swim while your Grandmother Joan continued playing in the sand with you and Finnan. You were not yet three, and you looked up and noticed the absence of your parents and began a never-ending demand that we "Go away". We understood that it was not our absence but rather the result of it, the return presence of your parents was your priority. Actually, your insight into cause and effect was a sophisticated one. It was also a delight seeing you exhibit bold claims of independence emphasizing "no," "mine," as well as "go away," with the enjoyment of a newfound control of your surrounding circumstances. Your parents were most important. That is life, and it is important to us that we recognize differentiation in the time and relationships of the moment. There will always be such differences, they are natural, and let it be so. We will grow.

There was an earlier story from when you were even younger and you and a playmate were waking up from a nap at pre-school. You both took off your pants and ran around announcing that "you were showing off your butts," another bold declaration of independence. It was the natural you, what you were meant to be doing at this time of your life.

As we grow, we learn to cultivate our relationships with a growing number of people recognizing common interests and advantages. Eventually many of us achieve a state where we are willing to put the interests of others ahead of our own, be they spouses, children, family, tribe, nation, or globe. But at no point in our development is self-interest an inferior position to cooperation or collective action. Quite the opposite, as I understand it, the fundamental psychological principle Jesus taught is to *"love thy neighbor as thyself."* To me this means as a first spiritual principle that we all need to be encouraged to live life well for ourselves if we are to act well for and with others. In a broad sense of understanding, this includes the war hero who dies young for the larger service of the people, as well as secular and religious saints who spend a large part of their lives in service to their brothers and sisters. My experience suggests that the more joyful they are, the more successful is living life, both for themselves, and for others. Enthusiasm, or if you prefer, motivation or inspiration, mean a great deal.

If we take this broad view one step further to discuss inspiration, some have come to call the process from the perspective of spirituality a *"cumulative fluid moral intelligence,"* which considers human nature as a continual context in which we live. This entails what we have been doing, an examination of where human beings have been in order to see, as best we can, where we can go, indeed where we want to be, which is what we have always been trying to do, my grandsons.

To take another look at the broad task we have undertaken, we can look at a far-fetched novel by Daniel Quinn that was popular when my children, your parents, were in college, entitled *Ishmael.* The main character is an extraordinarily intelligent and gifted ape with the ability to communicate with people by direct thought transmission. Ishmael tells the anecdote of a time traveling anthropologist who goes back a half million years to interview a jellyfish, then the most advanced form of life on earth. The jellyfish explains that the purpose of life is clear: jellyfish must evolve. This story has an ironic appeal to college students first considering weighty questions about life itself. Here the juxtaposition of the jellyfish for man suggests that more humility might be appropriate to humanity.

"Humility is the proper estimate of oneself."

\- Unknown

A certain skepticism is called for in self-examination. Today corporate organizations frequently ask candidates to do a SWOT analysis to consider their own strengths, weaknesses, opportunities, and threats. One goal of this book is to encourage you to consider these points early in your own life. Balancing the first two opposing personal characteristics should become a habitual part of your life, as you are also sensitized to be aware of the second two external situations of reward and risk while remembering what you are trying to do is to achieve a meaningful life.

This reference to SWOT analysis offers a clue to the frequently asked question about one's own strengths and weaknesses. One should:

1. be aware of where you can make a contribution by both focusing on the task at hand, and by looking for alternative ideas and how to use them,
2. have the ability to encourage others to help expand those ideas and enhance their implementation so everyone succeeds in maximizing the opportunities, while avoiding or responding to threats, and
3. see the risk that if you spend all your time on alternatives, you may not get done what you were hired to do.

Finnan and Cormac, we could view the paragraph above as an "economic" approach to doing business, with a "spiritual" aspect of cooperating with others in a common venture, finding common ground as an example of an essential lesson of our talks, as the ingredients all come together in one broad subject.

> *"He poured out the coins of the money changers, as he overturned their tables."*

- John 2:13, the New Testament

We noted in earlier chapters that it seems self-evident that life would be shallow and frustrating if it were merely transactional, if our values and relationships meant no more than "I give this and I get that," with all of life a marketplace for money changers. I do not have to believe in all the theological assumptions to recognize the lesson that there is a place for commerce but that it can kill the soul when it enters the realm of the spiritual. Transactional relationships are not founded on common values and commitment, and can even go beyond that to all against all. Unless we get my way we split. It can be the trophy spouse who earns a higher breakup fee for every year of endurance. I am not urging that these relationships be prohibited for those who can do no more, or choose not to, but I think it a poor life for those who want and can have more.

It can be a nuanced concept but our mental approach has its consequences.

Let's take one example of the recognized common virtue of loyalty. It would be sad and boring if I would only help you because I am assured you will pay me back equally. To make the point vivid, I recall a cartoon in *The New Yorker* magazine which depicts a very successful man in his large office, a cigarette holder in his mouth, speaking to an old lady dressed in a black shawl sitting in a chair beside the edge of his desk. The man is saying: *"I know Mom, I know, but what have you done for me lately?"* The humor is enhanced by reality and thus this joke is funnier if you have spent time in the competitive commercial world of places like New York City and Los Angeles.

A virtue such as loyalty can be a subtle thing. The closer and larger the nature of the relationship, the harder the test. Times change; we grow; more is expected of us. Loyalty is not automatic and can be misplaced. In William Shakespeare's *Henry IV, Part 2*, in the last scene, Prince Hal has become King of England and confronts Fat Jack Falstaff, his former drunk witted companion. He says: *"I do not know thee old man. Fall to thy prayers... reply not to me with a fool born jest. Presume not that I am the thing I was. For God does know what the world shall perceive, that I have turned away from my former self... and as we hear you do reform yourselves, we will according to your strengths and qualities, give you advancement."*

And what of another form of loyalty, duty? An early 19th century American Naval Officer, Stephen Decatur gave a famous definition of patriotism: *"My country, may she always be right, but right or wrong, my country."* He was speaking about affairs with foreign nations at the time, but it has since been widely accepted as the definition of patriotism, the rightful duty of loyalty to country.

The truth is that patriotism and wars cannot depend on the subtlety of every question of every citizen at every moment if a country is to survive and prosper as a united people. But as we have been suggesting in our discussions of

Daniel O'Connell in Ireland, Henry David Thoreau in 19th century America, the 20th century movements of Gandhi for Indian independence, or the civil rights struggles of America, civil disobedience can become a greater duty than loyalty to the commands of government. And there is always the underlying question: are we talking about our country or just the current leaders who presently insist upon their point of view? An interesting take on this question is found in a book, *The Price of Loyalty* by Paul O'Neil, Secretary of the Treasury in the Administration of the Second President George Bush. The author and former cabinet member answers the question with the title of his book: when the reasons of the State actors have little to do with the interests of its citizens, then the price can be too high and should not be paid.

In these days of current politics one echo remains a haunting reminder. When looking back on the horrors of Hitler and Mussolini's National Socialism for his France, General Charles de Gaulle noted that *"Patriotism is when love of your people comes first. Nationalism is when hate of people other than your own comes first."*

> *"Politics is not for the innocent child you see, but the Mighty Finn's going to set you free."*
>
> - Bob Dylan

In this book we have been visiting some heroes and villains to consider as you go through life. We have already noticed that most of us are not perfect, and that sometimes heroes and villains are the same people.

The book *Valiant Ambition* explores the duality of one such saint and sinner of patriotism and loyalty found in one man, a great American Revolutionary War hero who is also its arch villain. He is our prime example of virtue and valor, former loyalty turned to contempt of the traitor in a way that rivals the great fallen angel of the Judeo–Christian tradition, Lucifer himself. No one reflects this dual figure of American political saint and sinner so well as Benedict Arnold. Military hero and a self-starting leader of the American Revolution, Arnold was descended from a distinguished line of Americans who arrived fifteen years after the Pilgrims in Massachusetts. Arnold was the great-grandson of one of the Governors of Rhode Island.

We have spoken about the north/south waterway intersecting the northern and southern Colonies before, and Arnold understood its current significance. He was one of a few who saw the critical opportunity for the American Revolutionary Army in the poorly defended British cannons at Fort Ticonderoga on Lake Champlain in upstate New York in 1775. The cannons were seized by Arnold and the more famously credited Ethan Allen and the Green Mountain Boys of Vermont. They were later delivered by Colonel Henry Knox to George Washington, in the midst of a siege of the British in Boston at the beginning of the Revolutionary War. Washington kept these crucial cannons throughout the Revolution and used them in the final battle of the war at Yorktown, Virginia.

Experienced at sea, Arnold also was the *"the first father of the American navy."* He had a fleet of small boats built in Whitehall, in Upstate New York, which he used at Valcour

Island on Lake Champlain in the fall of 1776 to stop the advance of the British Navy and Army on its way from Montreal, Canada to New York City. The British plan was to split the American Colonies in two; a first step to ending the American war. Then, a year later, Arnold's strategic brilliance and battlefield bravery was a major contribution to the British defeat at the Battle of Saratoga in 1777. This victory led to the subsequent entry of France into the war on the American side, and eventually America's ultimate victory in the war at the Battle of Yorktown, six years later.

It was a series of feats *"like no other"*, to quote the Ancient Greeks. Arnold had spent his personal fortune building the small armed boats for the Valcour Island naval battle and arming his army in the north. Yet his receipts had sunk on the Royal Savage at Valcour Island and the Continental Congress failed to reimburse him, leaving him without his fortune. Moreover, petty political bickering among other American officers, and the failure of the Commander General Horatio Gates to recognize Arnold's bravery at Saratoga in a Report to the Continental Congress, as well as subsequent indignities during a long recuperation from a leg wound suffered at Saratoga, left him bitter. Then he met a young lady in Philadelphia whose parents were loyalists and his loyalties changed. So, despite General George Washington's continued backing, Arnold turned traitor and almost succeeded in turning over to the British the American fort at West Point, a strategic place at a narrows on the Hudson River, which deliverance could have changed the outcome of the war. Had he remained loyal, Benedict Arnold would have been one of

America's greatest heroes rather than a hated turncoat who died in England.

There is another point to this story, mentioned earlier in our conversations but I see it of heightened importance worth re-emphasizing.

New York waterways were crucial to three successive wars: the French and Indian War of 1757-1763, the Revolutionary War of 1775-1783, and the War of 1812. It is impossible to understand the importance of these events concerning Lake Champlain and the Hudson River in New York State without referring to a large map of northeastern America including eastern Canada to the north. It was extremely difficult to move men, cannons, and supplies through this vast forest and mountain terrain of early America. Yet a pathway of water could be used to sail from the Atlantic Ocean up the St. Lawrence River, west past Quebec City, and just before Montreal, follow the River Richelieu south across the border between Canada and America. With a few portages readily manageable for a navy, it could enter Lake Champlain, sail to the border of Lake George, and then on down the Hudson River to New York City and the Atlantic Ocean once again. This strategically separated New York and the six New England colonies from the other six American Colonies in the Mid-Atlantic and South, to divide and conquer.

So, this act of betrayal which rose to monstrous proportions, leaves open an opportunity for a psychological or, if you prefer, spiritual study of how a mind can turn in so short a period of time. Of course, Lucifer who dares to challenge the highest authority, God, is a looming metaphor for such a study. The ultimate point I am suggesting is that moral questions pop up in most places and our views of them can change when we realize the implications of our answers.

The story of Benedict Arnold is a great morality play. Like our earlier imagined drama of Thomas Jefferson and John Adams entering heaven in 1826, such high-stakes tales with moral dimensions are often found in the dry pages of constitutional law decisions of the United States Supreme Court. We have gone to this source before and will do so one last time for American wisdom reflected in *"the felt experience of the time."*

When going to school became a great moral question about freedom of religion and freedom of speech

Two United States Supreme Court cases illuminated the tension of balancing competing rights while drawing the line in deciding what is acceptable as moral conduct. The issues of the First Amendment rights of freedom of religious conviction and freedom of speech and its inevitable corollary, the right not to speak, were starkly similar in these two cases.

In 1940 the Court heard the first case of a sister and brother who were expelled from school by a local Pennsylvania School Board. They had been told by their parents that to salute the American flag would violate their faith as Jehovah's Witnesses. Of course saluting the flag is meant to announce loyalty to country as much as if it were verbally spoken. This case was in the dark days just before World War II. Justice Felix Frankfurter wrote in the decision that national unity is the basis of national security, and that religious toleration does not relieve citizens from a general law not aimed at a specific religion. The students must salute the flag or be expelled.

Yet, only three years later, the world had seen the degradation of humanity in Nazi totalitarian insistence on outright obedience to orders of the State. In an extremely similar case against a West Virginia School District, with two new Justices on the nine-person Court, the Court issued an outright reversal by a six to three vote. Justice Robert Jackson held in words that can still serve as a warning echo to us today, that even in this time of war, the freedom to differ is not limited to those things that do not matter much, and that those who begin coercive elimination of dissent soon find themselves eliminating dissenters. The Court ruled that we must trust citizens to make their own choices about what they want to believe. It reversed the prior precedent. The students had a constitutional right to attend school and not salute the flag.

When we look at where to draw the line in weighing the facts of these cases, we must fully appreciate that actual facts do matter. Most Americans I know will readily point out that free speech does not include the right to yell fire in a crowded theatre. But there are two other relevant issues to focus upon here. First, yelling fire is not just an expression of opinion but an act that threatens to panic people into a dangerous stampede. Second, this metaphor comes from a World War I protest case where the Court was not actually considering yelling about a burning building but was a case of a war protester who burned his draft card. So, the actual facts were a far different case than first presented. The decision did deal with fire, but the act found a crime by the Court was burning a draft card in protest of the war, not about creating panic in a theatre.

<u>Hard facts, hard cases, and muddy history call for clear lines for freedom of choice.</u>

If we jump to conclusions we can also readily gloss over our earlier contradictory American history. It was the Puritans in New England who insisted upon a legal requirement for all to practice the State-sanctioned religion. This concept of mandatory Christianity continued on down through the Southern Colonies. Mandatory religion was debated during the adoption of the United States Constitution before being rejected and the Bill of Rights was passed.

The proposition is clear. All thinking men and women seek links to *"the divine"*, but that does not mean that you will conclude spirituality will be found in a god.

If you are thinking, not simply accepting what you are told, the search must be personal and we must learn to tolerate others' right to search for their beliefs, as they tolerate our search. So, I do not see how I can have freedom of religion if I cannot have freedom from religious acts in public places. That means we draw the line against requiring a profession of any particular religion in public places so that none of us can foster our religion, or absence of it, on the rest of us. I do not want to extend this subject too far but let me gently suggest that if we are to have publicly sanctioned prayer in schools or other public places each morning, rather than the Lord's Prayer, I would prefer that everyone paraphrase Ralph

378

Waldo Emerson's words from On Nature: *"We seek a new original relation to the universe where we are each free to face god or nature face to face as we find it."*

We have moved through our discussions with stories, my grandsons, and they most certainly can help as we consider how they play out in life. We have seen that all ancient peoples we know of have had stories of the creation of their people and the world, most including powerful gods and other parables and tales to explain existence. Because leaders tend to want to remain in power and they often seek more, these stories often entwined their authority with the will of the gods. The notion of divine kingship became embedded with the offer of providing greater stability and prosperity in this life and the next. Huge Egyptian pyramids now in the barren sands still mark the strength of such claims.

We noticed that the medieval kings of Europe made similar allegations of a divine right to the throne, often with the strong support of the Church, which expected reciprocity. Indeed, on a recent river boat trip from Budapest to Amsterdam, your Grandmother Joan and I were struck by the three grandest buildings in the river city or town on most mornings. They were castle, cathedral, and Bishop's residence. This certainly was convenient for those in authority.

But it is cynical to fail to recognize that sacred stories have served the very real purpose of guiding us through life. We have discussed that, in Western civilization, the primary foundation has been "the good book" or more accurately, the three books, or, if we are to include the Book of Mormon, the four books. For most it has been the Old Testament of the chosen people, given to Israel well over a millennium after the pyramids were built. This Old Testament was adopted by the new Christians over a thousand years later to which they added a New Testament about the teachings of Jesus whose followers discerned he was the divine Messiah. Then, six centuries later, Mohammed adopted both of these two holy books and added the Koran with the teachings of Mohammed which became the way for Muslims. Thus, three great religious books of modern western civilization became foundations for personal and spiritual conduct to this day. All the books could be true, some combination thereof, or none at all. It depends upon which mosque, church, or synagogue you are in when you ask. Indeed a great many people, including me, accept the historical facts of the people of the Middle East of those times, just not that there was a divine intervention in the actions of the period. A great many of us believe this was the self-evident need for the adoption of the First Amendment to the United States Constitution. That the right to practice one's religion must necessarily encompass the right to practice one's belief that possibly none of the others are correct.

Let's do some simple thinking here. To so many, by definition, the point of religion is to do good. Religion can bring comfort and peace. When there is disaster in a community it is often the churches who are the first on the ground in the community to help all who need it, and are a major force for a better life, building trust in the community. By this measure when it does the opposite such as killing in the name of religion it is self-evidently bad. If this sounds absurdly simplistic I can only say that our history as humans has shown us that far too often people have resorted to the worst of these evils in the name of doing good. Some still do.

Christopher Hitchens, a writer and professed atheist, placed a contemporary feel on this point when asked in a radio interview if he would not feel safer walking down a dark street on a Sunday night if a group of men he was passing were just leaving a Congregation of worship. He replied not if he was Catholic passing a Protestant Church in Northern Ireland, or the reverse; and not if he was a Muslim passing a synagogue in Israel or Palestine, or the reverse. But Hitchens is only partially right, his vision too narrow and his aim too short. We can dampen down the differences. As we have found throughout the facets of life, the world is made of situations where there is one fact, but on the other hand there is a dissimilar or contradicting fact. Out of a dialectic of thesis and antithesis comes a synthesis where the tension between two competing ideas comes a new, holistic, one. Not tidy, but at least a step on the long arc of progress. Things can change.

But violence remains a predisposition for too many sects.

One need only think of the violence between Hindus and Muslims in India after its independence in 1946, or the Balkans after the breakup of Yugoslavia in the late 1980s, or the chaotic violence in the Middle East in the present day to fully capture the inhumanity of man toward man in the name of God and religion. Much of it has to do with underlying political control and economic advantage. This should be recognized and conceded, but religion is far too often the excuse for acquisition of power, theft, and murder.

We can capture the long-term depth of the problem in recognizing that in those turbulent days in the Balkans in the late 1980s, Serbians sang songs to their children about Christian babies being murdered by the Muslims at the

Battle of Kosovo in 1389. The Bosnians also sang songs to their children about Muslim babies being murdered by the Christian Serbs at that same battle. Much of both armies were wiped out in 1389, but is it really relevant to how people act six hundred years later? Murder in the Balkans was likely as much about political control and its spoils. There is evil in this world. The question is how is religion contributing to rather than alleviating harm.

"Let my people go."

-Moses, *Genesis*

We can take a deeper look at how prophecies play out as some newer prophets react to evil in a secular world. Rather than taking an approach that oppressors must be destroyed, they focused on the victims who would overcome their oppression. When they focused on the hurt rather than the oppressor, they found a way of overcoming the condition rather than perpetuating it. Rather than a path from the rhetoric of stamping out evil, with the resistance leading to violence with acts that lead to increased human suffering, some recent secular prophets have found the clarity to aim instead for the alleviation of the condition.

Focusing on the unfairness of the condition, with demonstrations spotlighting the evil being perpetrated, meant that the dominant people who pretended to be good found it increasingly difficult to look at continual suffering. Gandhi, King, and Mandela strove to create ways to communicate to "the others." They could observe what they and their oppressors' children all had in common. To the extent that there could be a broader appeal to the common condition, universal humanity, a conclusion became more evident. So, their best possible action was a response that focused on the deeds, not the persons, in a way that might remind us of Jesus telling us to hate the sin, not the sinner. So much depends on the narrative we choose to tell.

We might shift to a different scene. When given a specific short-term task of ascertaining the truth during a trial, a jury is said to decide by putting together a life story of that event that might have happened as if in their daily lives. There are gaps in the two competing stories being told at trial. The jurors fill in these gaps with a common sense of what happens based upon their own experiences, customs, and the opinions they have formed. It may not be easy. There is a problem with this approach in that there are usually strongly held beliefs so that the jurors, as the persons charged with deciding, can often reject information contrary to their personally held beliefs in deciding whether these other claims are credible or were misunderstood. In other words, they start out tending to believe what they already want to believe and fill in the gaps with assumptions that fit their beliefs.

If you want to overcome prejudices, you need build trust. When you would convince or lead you must be able to overcome countervailing suspicions. A determined persistence to point out a fair-minded decision is inevitably required. But people can be influenced, and it can be subtle. We can tap into other life experiences to suggest what we have seen. I heard an example of a nuanced approach to persuasion as a young lawyer while I was involved in an antitrust case in Dallas,

Texas. The lead local counsel for our side was summing up the case for the jury. In discussing the reliability of vague testimony of a witness for the opposition, he told the jury a story of two linemen who were called into the Home Office because of a complaint about using foul language on a job site. One lineman explained to the Supervisor that the other had dropped a live wire on him and he had merely responded: *"Smitty, you must be more careful in the future, or words to that effect."* A smile of recognition of the human condition can turn away objection and convince.

I am mixing times, subjects, people, images, sounds, and themes as they echo what is now your country, culture, and century. It will be up to your generation to make them good ones, make them what you find true and useful. You do not need to take a poll to formulate your fundamental beliefs. What I strongly suggest is that people develop human intellectual and emotional sensibilities that can evolve to a higher level, to recognize that the strategy for our common fate on this planet is cooperation, and this strategy is available for your use.

Religion in politics?

There is no doubt in my mind that the lessons of history are clear. We need keep an absolute "wall" between Church and State, as Jefferson cautioned. Any blur in the line between religious institutions and government is likely to seriously harm both. But, of course, this does not mean there is not a morality to decisions of our government based upon its effects upon we, the people, and our institutions.

Our history tells us that we have come a long way, and the American experiment is now a world experiment which has proven it can be successful. Yet recent history continually reminds us how fragile a democratic republic can be, a strong argument for the moral nature of politics when the casual and the avaricious can so readily endanger the liberty and prosperity of us all.

As has been our custom, my grandsons, I will take a moment for personal reflection. When I was about twenty and attending Iona College, I was attracted to the Conservative political movement in New York, particularly the Libertarian philosophy. As I saw it, the philosophy stated: Let me be free to create my own life, unfettered by the decisions of someone else, often far away, who does not know and may not even care about my needs and wants. It had echoes of John Stuart Mill, which still has its allure. I would travel around the New York Metropolitan Area to hear speeches sponsored by William F. Buckley, himself less than a decade out of the university and founder of *the National Review,* the goal of which was to change what he saw as the erroneous liberal political culture of the time. I once heard Senator Barry Goldwater of Arizona speak, the evening he introduced his then new book, *The Conscience of a Conservative.* However, I soon came to the conclusion that the reality is that we need government to address our collective needs for stability and liberty, prosperity and justice, and that too many missed half the equation, or used this conservative song merely to take as much as they could and give back as little as possible. I decided I was a Democrat and voted for John F. Kennedy for President. It is not startling that so many young people pick a political persuasion based on who is running for President. Regardless of our initial selection, it does not excuse us from a continual examination of our own conscience.

For an illustration of why this is so let us take a look at the current political moment.

Humanity is not a zero sum game.

1. *"Acting,*
2. *on conscience and principle*
3. *is the manner in which we express*
4. *our moral selves."*

This is the core of a speech recently given on the floor of the United States Senate by Republican Jeff Flake of Arizona. His speech to the Senate marks an important time in our history, and it holds together much of what I am saying to you. He continues:

"We can all be forgiven for failing in that measure from time to time... But too often, we rush not to salvage principle but to forgive and excuse our failures so that we might accommodate them and go right on failing – until the accommodation itself becomes our principle. In that way and over time we can justify almost any behavior and sacrifice almost any principle.

"When a leader identifies real hurt and insecurity in our country and instead of addressing it goes to look for somebody to blame, there is perhaps nothing more devastating to a pluralistic society... We have been at our most prosperous when we have been at our most principled."

I will go on a bit more with this timely speech, speculating that Senator Flake will not mind.

"There is an undeniable potency to a populist appeal – but mischaracterizing or misunderstanding our problems and giving in to the impulse to scapegoat and belittle threatens to turn us into a fearful and back-ward looking people… We must respect each other again in an atmosphere of shared fact and shared values, comity and good faith. We must argue our positions fervently, and never be afraid to compromise. We must assume the best of our fellow man, and always look for the good. Until that day comes, we must not be afraid to stand up and speak out as if our county depends upon it. Because it does."

The United States has so much to offer us. There is far more to unite us than divide us. That should be our goal. And my grandsons, even in these times where truth and lies are considered exchangeable, I think most of us will come to agree with that motto of West Point, our first American military academy, and particularly the most relevant last phrase. It says:

"We neither lie, steal, nor cheat, not tolerate those who do."

EPILOGUE

"No one but you can build the bridge on which you, and only you, must cross the river of life."

-Frederick Nietzsche

This has not been meant as a survey, but rather a narrative to sink into your soul as you feel loved when you wake in the morning. It is you, beginning.

You will recall that if you run swiftly but in the wrong direction, you will quickly get further and further from your destination. Like sailing, if you know where you want to go, you are likely to get there. I hope you also remember that you cannot keep your destination a secret to get anywhere with anyone. We proclaim and then convince. What comes next is not a sequel, it is your story, for you to write your own chapters.

"Unless someone like you cares a whole awful lot, it's just not getting better. It's not."

-Dr. Seuss

Where does all the time go? We have moved interchangeably between economics, politics, and spirituality as if they were the same thing, because in one sense, they are life, liberty, and the pursuit of happiness, at least as I define them. Let me sum up our case:

American Revolutionary War hero Thomas Paine said: *"I have only one religion, and that is to do good."* Former Democratic United States Senator from Massachusetts and Presidential Candidate Paul Tsongas is reported to have said as he was dying of cancer, *"No one on their death-bed says 'I wish I had spent more time in the Office'."* Will Rogers, folk comedian of the 1930s once said that *"One must wait until evening to see how splendid the day has been."*

Much of this conversation has been a celebration, much of it about mysteries. Life would prove dull without them, and so we welcome ambiguity with which we can make so much of life. The creative impulse has not been satisfactorily explained as far as I know but as we have said, there seems little doubt that creativity is bound up in innovation, or said another way *"the new."*

In a search for a big idea I have been suggesting that you look at evolution as the engine of all life, including our organization of civilization. The excitement of the new might be an historical explanation for understanding our progress within this framework.

Creativity is probable in peace or war but, while disturbing to me, war seems to have stimulated far more of civilization, and we need ways to challenge that energy that prove constructive. There are certainly far more choices by the time we have made it this far.

There is no doubt that much of the risk taking and consequent advantages in life result from having few other choices; the trek of the immigrants to America is one dramatic example. Even so, the question becomes: can we evolve beyond impulse for battle to a time for building through cooperation? Many think we cannot, but I believe we can. The human spirit can evoke fresh layers of meaning from so many scenes and rhythms, in short, the poetry of life.

The guiding principle of what I have been saying is that the pursuit stems from optimism, confidence in oneself, in others, and in the future. For if you think you cannot do it, you likely cannot, either alone or together.

How would pursuit of ancient ideals play out in everyday life?

You start with what you know, which I suggest in this case is human nature. When you enter a room, you may notice someone that thinks they are the center of it all. You may be thinking, "Wait a minute, I'm supposed to be the center of it all." You should by now, be recognizing that you have gone too far and need to deal with it. The purpose you may choose to address is that actually you have both gone too far. Your Aunt Deirdre used a quote in college to make this point: "*Well enough of me talking about me. What do you think about me?*" Maybe there is something besides both of you in all of this. Moral values, principles for getting people to do what they should do in a positive manner, is a way to fill gaps in our understanding of how the world works, why we are here, what we are to do as solace for our disappointments, and courage for our accomplishments.

Religion is of great importance for many; as the poet Mary Oliver put it, it is: "*the possibility of eternity.*" But regardless of how we decide the question, we must take responsibility for this life while here on earth.

We celebrate the beginning and hope of life in birth; since death is the natural consequence of this life, it would seem unnatural not to celebrate the accomplishments at the end of the cycle of this biological rhythm. I certainly hope you will celebrate my life this way. Not mourn, but celebrate; have a party, and enjoy it. I would also hope you would have an annual celebration between your birthdays of February 7 and April 7, taking time around the first Solstice of the year to talk about things as they are. It would be a way to fulfill what I have been trying to do. When you do so, as I hope, will you refer to this book and think of us? For this book is about you and the continuation of life.

All things must end. Or do they?

Eventually all journeys end. The word "*apoptosis*" is used to describe the pre-arranged disposition of cells that trigger the process of death, inevitably, to make way for new life. Time past creates time present, making way for time future. Now that you are grown, should we speak in more sophisticated terms? If you want, but for me, let me end as we began.

Let us revert back to the beginning of our talks and imagine we are all back in the Adirondack Mountains. We start a short cross-country ski from where we began, behind the barn on our Boulderwood home, as we come to the foxhole we found early in this tale. The afternoon light reflects the *alpenglow*, pink mountain top snow. We began by recognizing that you might not fully understand or agree with many ideas threaded through our talks. But I have hoped that you would understand some *"insights of the hour."* The idea has been to look at them as seeds, some of which will grow to inspire you to action, becoming dreams achieved. Along the way, we have dug into the meaning of this world, and the world will soon answer us once again, with Spring, the new beginning. Cormac and Finnan, the world is a better place because you are in it.

I intended to end this conversation to coincide with your leaving a university where you will go on to accept, reject, and synthesize some notions we have explored. Perhaps at the end of the next century, you will be having a similar conversation with your own grandchildren, having kept the dialogue going over the years.

I hope you revisit our talks with a feeling of *"regret at leaving, and happiness to be flying home."*

- The poet Gallway Kinnell

Your grandfather

Printed in the United States
By Bookmasters